Millie Samuelson
Journalism
Please Return

Samuelson

# STUDIO SECRETS FOR THE GRAPHIC ARTIST

Kodachrome
Kodachrome
REXEL CUMBERLAND Derwent Studio
MADE IN GT. BRITAIN
Deep Cadmium 6
rotring T20
Made in Germany
rotring rapidograph ISO
UNIQUE
MADE IN ENGLAND

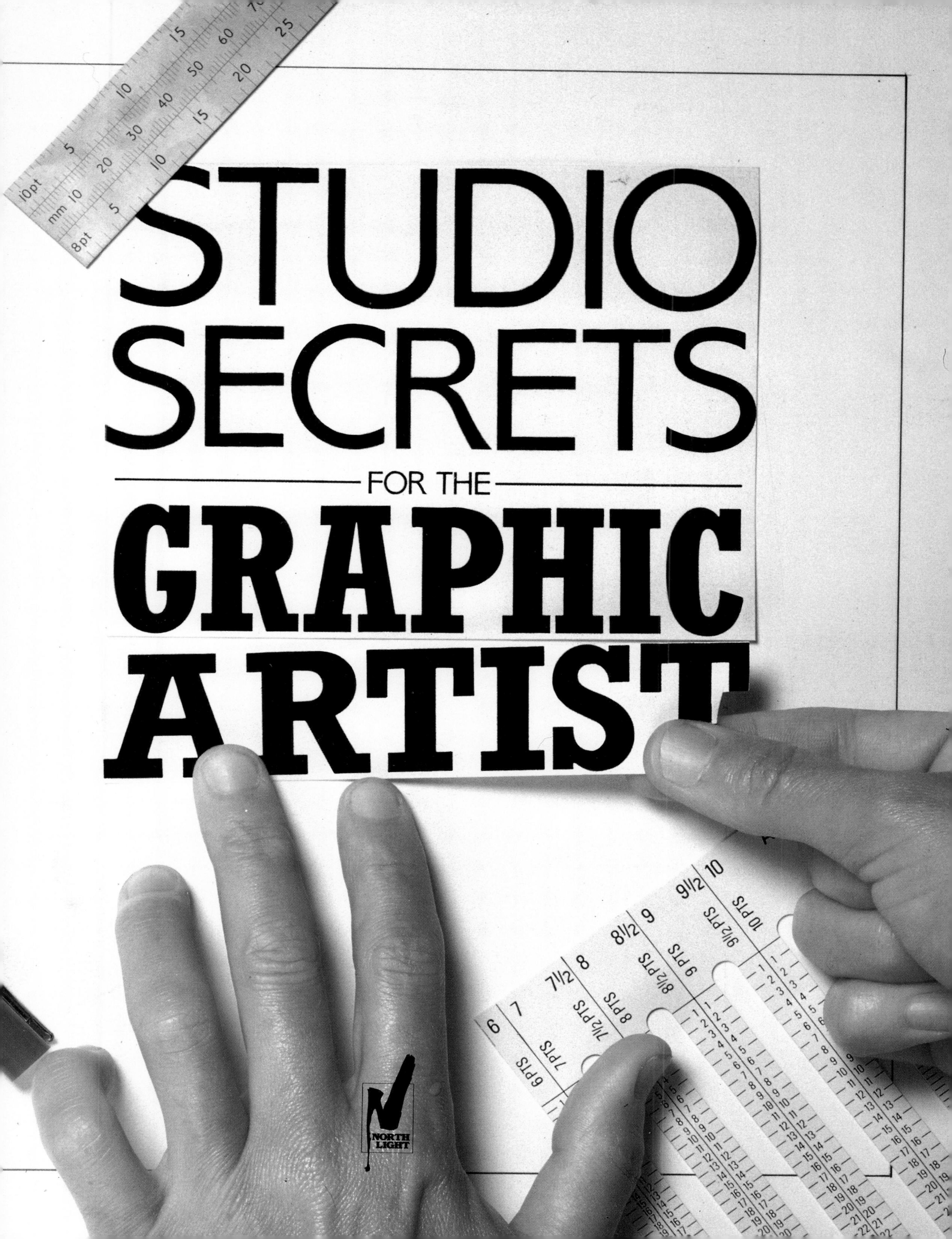

# STUDIO SECRETS

FOR THE

# GRAPHIC ARTIST

NORTH LIGHT

A Quarto Book


First published in North America by
North Light, an imprint of Writer's Digest Books
9933 Alliance Road
Cincinnati, Ohio 45242

ISBN 0-89134-144-7



This book was designed and produced by
Quarto Publishing Ltd
The Old Brewery, 6 Blundell Street, London N7 9BH

**Senior Editor** Lorraine Dickey
**Art Editor** Anne Sharples

**Editors** Eleanor Van Zant, Sophie Hale, Deirdre McGarry

**Designer** Pete Laws

**Photographers** John Heseltine, John Wyand

**Paste-up** Steve McGee, Michael Leaman

**Art Director** Alastair Campbell
**Editorial Director** Carolyn King

Special thanks to Hazel Edington, Polly Powell

Typeset by Ampersand Typesetting Ltd and QV Typesetting Ltd

Manufactured in Hong Kong by Regent Publishing Services Limited
Printed by Lee Fung Asco Printers Ltd, Hong Kong

# CONTENTS

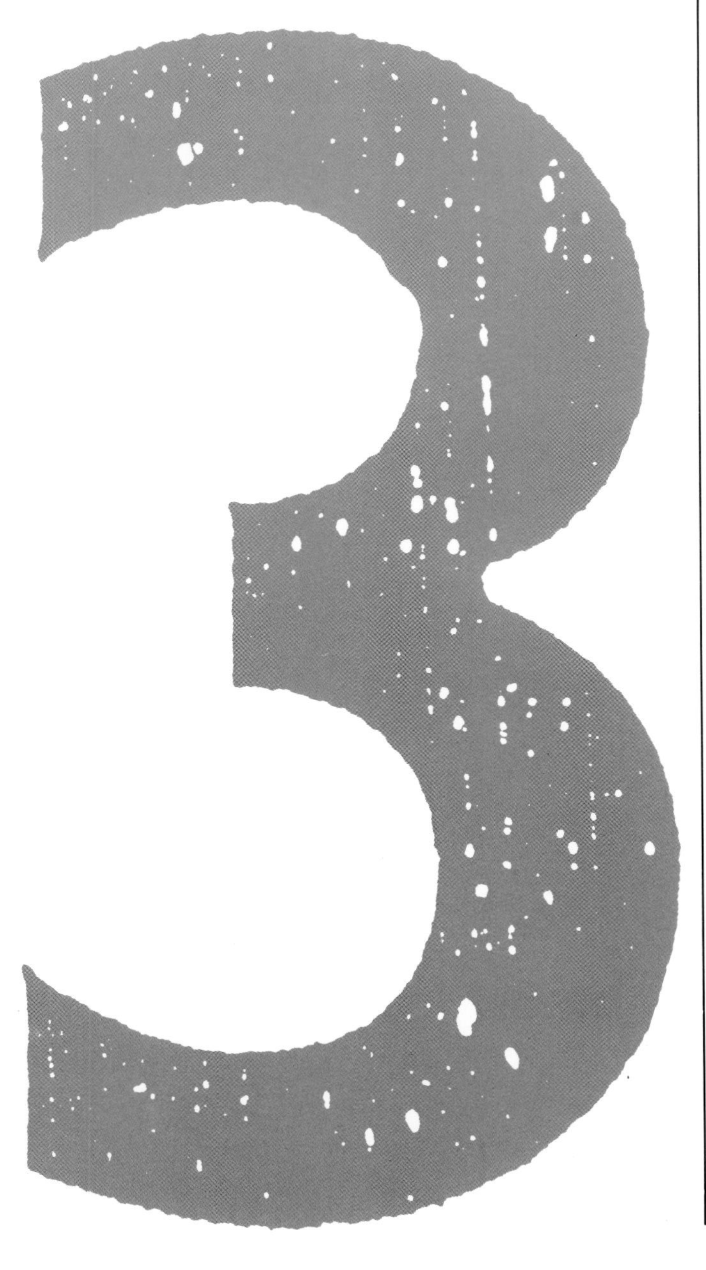

# INTRODUCTION

Like any profession, graphic design has its own vocabulary of "jargon" words and its own shorthand methods of notation, all impenetrable to an outsider. There are many short cuts in technique and procedure and an ever-increasing range of design-oriented new materials and equipment that can make any job easier and more successful. For students entering the profession or for practicing graphic artists learning new tricks, there's a lot to keep up with. You may need to know in principle what a laser scanner can do, but in a day-to-day context, you'll find that a simple can of lighter fluid is an indispensable graphic aid. This book is designed to demystify the jargon, explaining basic skills and the use of specific materials, equipment and technical processes. Selected projects show every stage of the graphic artist's work, from taking a brief to presenting finished artwork.

Graphic art is an exciting area – the presentation of a product can be largely responsible for its success or failure. The sudden success of a new magazine or advertising campaign shows how influential the graphic image can be, but many jobs are deliberately limited in range and intention – so it's no good entertaining fantasies of hi-tech styling when the job in hand is a simple black-and-white newspaper ad.

The first idea a graphic artist must absorb is that however confident and innovative the individual approach may be, design is basically a service, your responsibilities are to the client, the product and the market – to conveying information effectively in a way that suits all three. At the most basic level, it's wise to remember that it's the client who pays the bill. This doesn't mean, however, that the customer is always right; good design, in a sense, comes from an efficient and sympathetic "committee" process. The client knows the product, whom it is for, how it has been presented in the past, and where a possible new market lies. The artist is being asked to assemble a given number of elements and contribute the overall style and visual details that make the product attractive, accessible and functional within its intended market. This means offering a creative individual approach; it does not mean imposing your bright ideas on an unwilling audience.

**Taking a brief**

An important stage of any artist's work is the initial briefing from the client. This introductory section necessarily touches on the business aspects – time and money – rather than the creative side. Many graphic artists have learned the hard way that being businesslike is just as important as being able to wield a Magic Marker or use a PMT machine.

Whatever you are asked to do – whether it's a poster, a catalogue or point-of-sale material – it's up to you to find out what is involved and whether you can handle the work before committing yourself to the project. Being able to handle it doesn't just mean having the technical skills and a lively approach – it also requires you to work to a specific budget and schedule, and to feel confident that you can organize typesetting, photography, illustration work and printing as necessary.

Take some information during the intial contact on the phone, so that you go to a briefing meeting familiar with the subject of the brief. Some clients know very precisely what they want and are asking you to do a fairly mechanical assembly job; others will be expecting from you that extra input which they can't supply themselves. It is advisable to take along a few work samples; these could help you to convey the points you wish to make.

During the meeting, make as many notes as you want – it's embarrassing to have to phone the client later if you have forgotten a crucial detail, and bluffing it out risks the kind of glaring inaccuracy that will not enhance your reputation. Write down brand names and unfamiliar product titles, and be sure exactly who is directly commissioning you – is it an in-house designer or art director, the president or marketing manager? Keep a careful check on the deadline for the whole job, intermediate meetings and presentation dates for roughs and visuals. Be alert to strong preferences which may be aired during the discussion – on color, style of imagery, headlining of type, and so on.

Remember that you don't have to agree to take on the job at the first briefing, nor does the client have to accept you. You may wish to settle the terms right away, or defer agreement until you have a chance to look into the time and expense involved. You may be asked to present samples or first roughs before a definite decision is made. It is your business to estimate a realistic fee in the first place and carry out the work efficiently within that set limit. Once established, the fee should not be altered unless the job description changes substantially. Include provision for a rejection fee, in case you can't agree the design approach after roughs have been submitted. When the terms are agreed, whether at the first or second meeting, ask for a contract letter setting out the schedule and payment (and payment stages if appropriate). Have the job description set down in writing; you can do this yourself and give the client a job sheet for approval.

If you are working as a freelance graphic artist, check which side is supplying artwork, photography and so on. If you are expected

· QDOS ·

| | | |
|---|---|---|
| CLIENT: QUEBEC CATERERS | JOB DESCRIPTION: BROCHURE | JOB NUMBER: Q/107 |
| DATE RECEIVED: 29/7/86 | DATE REQUIRED BY CLIENT: EARLY NOVEMBER | DATE COMPLETED: 28/10/86 |
| | DATE REQUIRED | DATE COMPLETED: 2/8/86 |
| VISUAL: FULL PAGE LAYOUTS, 2 or 3 JACKET ROUGHS | 3/8/86 | DATE COMPLETED: 12/9/86 |
| ARTWORK: Commission to freelance | DATE REQUIRED: 12/9/86 | |

**BRIEF**

Redesign company brochure

8 pages (inc jkt) with fold-in flaps at back to take loose-leaf literature. Front jacket photo to commission – plus portrait photo of company director. Visuals to make use of existing photographs from previous brochure as well. 2 year shelf-life intended (must not date too quickly!)

**PRINT DETAILS**

- SIZE: A5: 148mm x 210mm
- EXTENT: 8 PAGES (INC JACKET)
- QUANTITY: 1000 (+ run on)
- COLOURS: 4 COL THROUGHOUT
- STOCK: JKT 250 GSM, PAPER 158
- DELIVERY DATE: END OCTOBER

**CREATIVE COSTS**

| MEETINGS | HOURS | | |
|---|---|---|---|
| 29/7 | 2 | £60 | 00 |
| 1/9 | 1 | £30 | 00 |
| **VISUALS** | **HOURS** | | |
| 2/8 | 7 | 210 | 00 |
| 9/8 | 4 | 120 | 00 |
| 2/9 | 2 | 60 | 00 |
| **ARTWORK** | **HOURS** | | |
| 10/9 | 8 | 120 | 00 |
| TOTAL HOURS | | | |

**EXTERNAL COSTS**

| | | Retail cost | Invoice cost | |
|---|---|---|---|---|
| GRAPHIC MATERIALS | FINE LINE BOARD/LETRASET/DRAFT FILM | 22·50 | 25 | 00 |
| TYPESETTING | APPROX 2 HOURS | 60·00 | 70 | 00 |
| PRINT | AS ABOVE (PLUS GOLD BLOCKED LOGO) | 1000·00 | 1200 | 00 |
| PHOTOGRAPHY | TWO COMMISSIONED SHOTS | 300·00 | 330 | 00 |
| FREELANCE | COPYWRITING | 480·00 | 500 | 00 |
| PMT's | 8 (210 x 297mm) | 48·00 | 48 | 00 |
| TRAVEL | 1 TAXI (4·80) 3 COURIERS (12·00) | 16·80 | 16 | 80 |
| TELEPHONE | — | | | |
| MISCELLANEOUS | Various props for photography (flowers and cutlery loan) | 13·75 | 13 | 75 |
| | | **TOTAL** | 2803·55 | |

This is an example of a job sheet – it is very important to fill one of these in if you are working as a freelance graphic artist. Always give your client a detailed breakdown of these costs, including your own time, before you take on a job. It is a good idea to overestimate slightly when working out the budget so that the client is not presented with an unexpectedly inflated bill when the work is finished. If the budget has already been determined, then it is your job to apportion the costs.

to commission typesetting and illustration, find out whether these can be billed directly to the client. A graphic studio would be expected to bear interim costs and cover them from the overall fee.

**Presenting roughs**

The client will wish to see visual presentation of your ideas before committing to finished artwork. Roughs should convey the idea clearly but need not be highly detailed at the outset. Work up from thumbnail sketches, and in the early stages try not to get too attached to one style or form of presentation – on the other hand do not give your client too many choices; be selective. You must be prepared to accept modifications from the client – in fact the whole idea may be rejected and you may be asked to devise a new concept.

When you have discussed the first roughs and settled on styling, you can work up the image in more detail. Check with the client before commissioning "live" artwork or photography, but present your second roughs in a more descriptive form than the preliminary samples, to actual scale and showing detail of color, selected typography, and basic styling for illustration or photography. For a package or point-of-sale display, do a mock-up of the shape and proportions of the object. Make sure all the important details are agreed and that the client has given a signature of approval to the final rough before you go on to the full realization of the project.

Keeping to schedules and budgets can be frustrating, but these are inevitable conditions of the job; your ability to stick to the limitations affects not only the project in hand but your future prospects with this client, and your chance of being recommended for other work in which you may be given a freer hand.

Kodachrome
Kodachrome
MADE IN GT. BRITAIN REXEL CUMBERLAND Derwent Studio
Deep Cadmium 6
Made in Germany
rotring T 20
rotring rapidograph ISO
UNIQUE
MADE IN ENGLAND

# DESK AND STUDIO EQUIPMENT

# · RULERS ·
# · PROTRACTORS ·
# · TRIANGLES ·

(**1**) A **straight edge ruler** is very heavy and therefore good for cutting mats or thick cardboard. It is rubber backed and so will not move or slip.

(**2**) A **clear plastic ruler** is useful for lining up type and is also easy to keep clean.

(**3**) A **centering rule** has a zero in the middle and is most useful for centering type during paste-up.

(**4**) The **parallel ruler** will produce lines at varying distances that are always parallel.

(**5**) The **protractor** is used for dividing sections of a circle and working out angles for diagrams and percentages.

(**6**) **Right-angled triangles** are essential for squaring up work and keeping accurate consistent angles. (**7**) The **adjustable triangle** is particularly useful for diagrams and graphs.

(**8**) The **pica measure** calculates the number of lines per page of any given size of type. (**9**) The **metal conversion type ruler** performs the same function but can also be used for calculating how long a given size of type will be. (**10**) A **gabled printer's rule** is a metal depth scale, also for measuring lines of text.

It is a good idea to put masking tape on the back of your triangle or ruler. This raises the edge and prevents technical pens from bleeding underneath. It also gives you a cleaner line and prevents the triangle from moving.

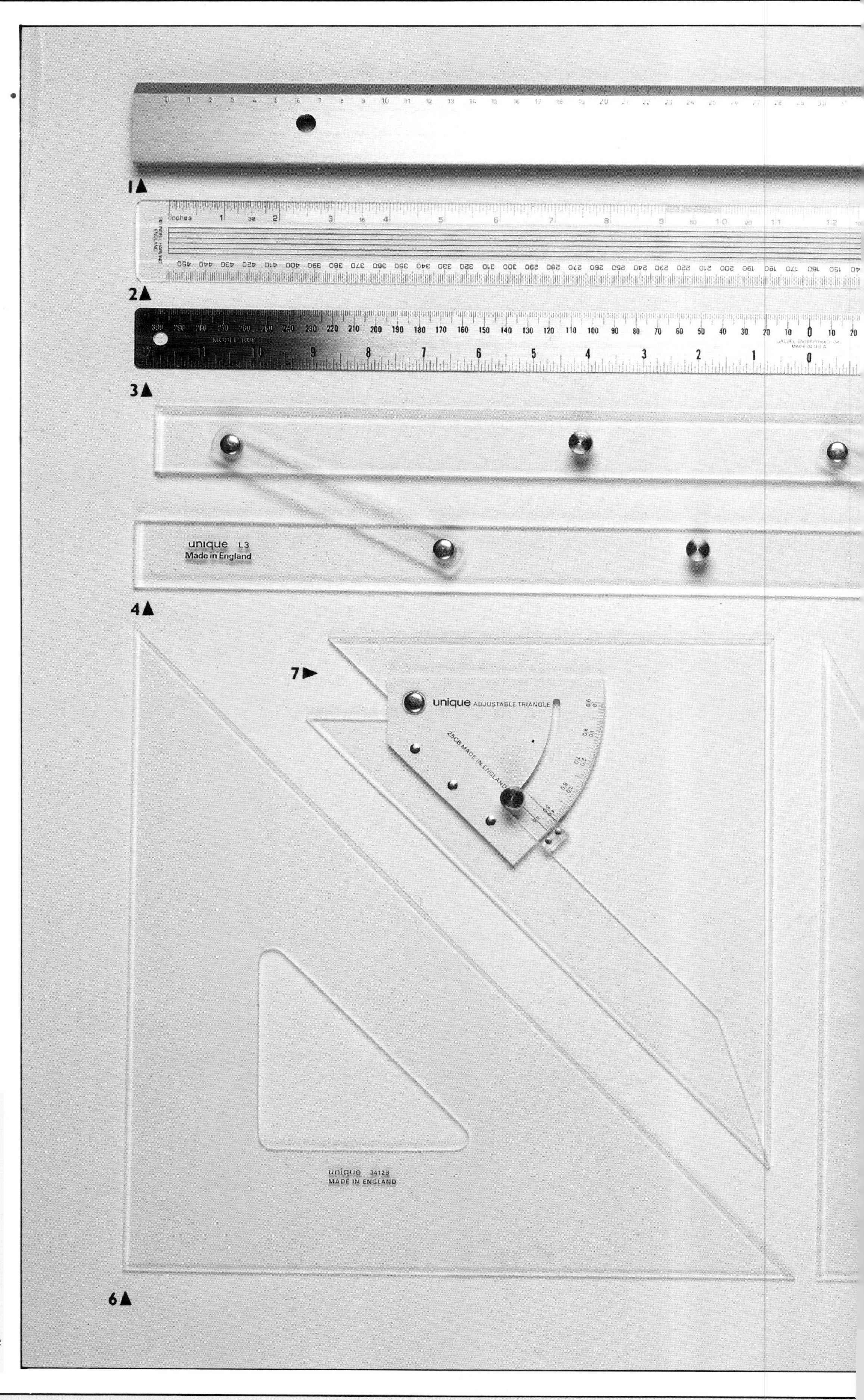

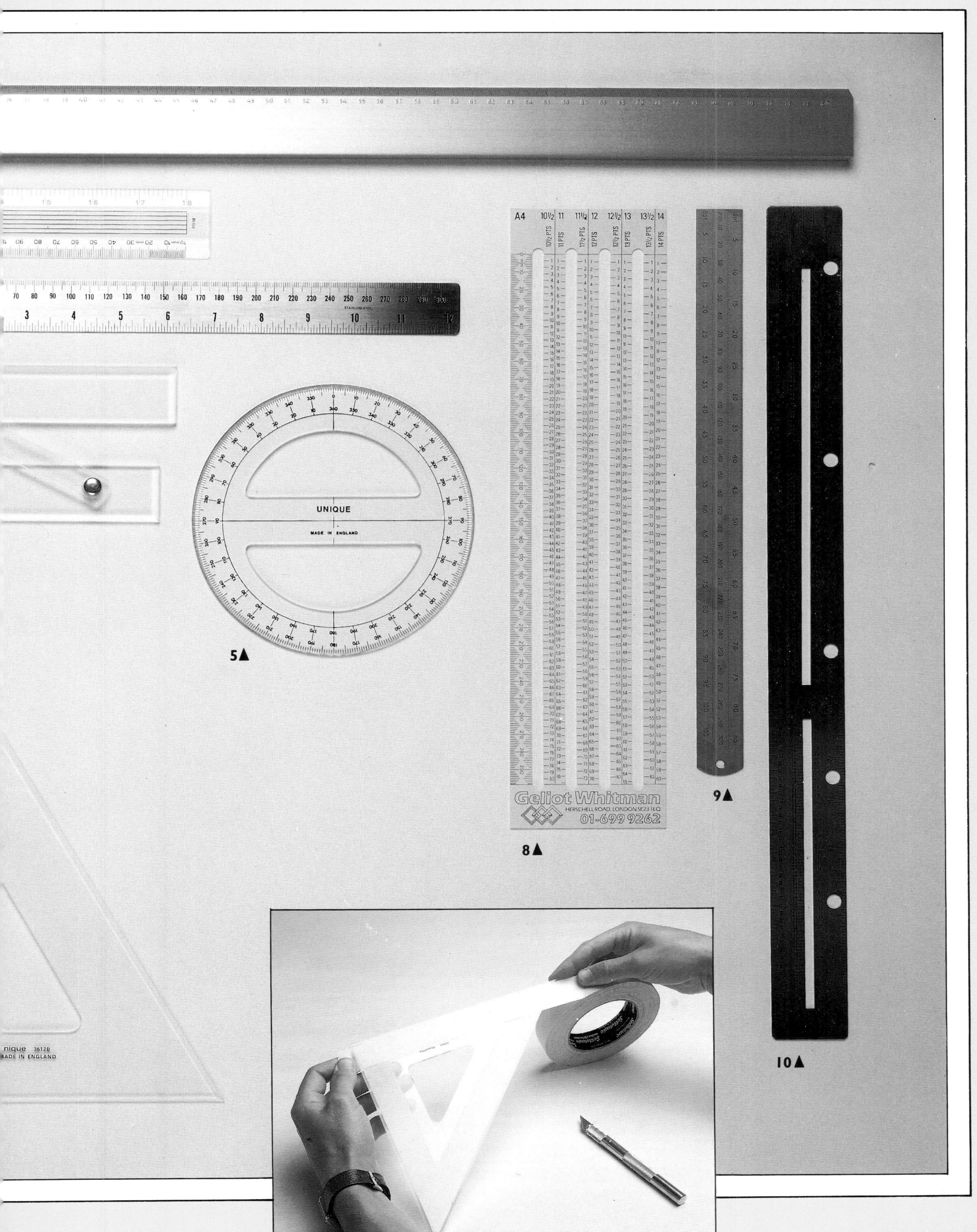
UNIQUE
MADE IN ENGLAND
Geliot Whitman
HERSCHELL ROAD, LONDON SE23 1EQ
01-699 9262
nique 36128
ADE IN ENGLAND
STAINLESS STEEL

5▲

8▲

9▲

10▲

# · COMPASSES · DIVIDERS · RULING PENS ·

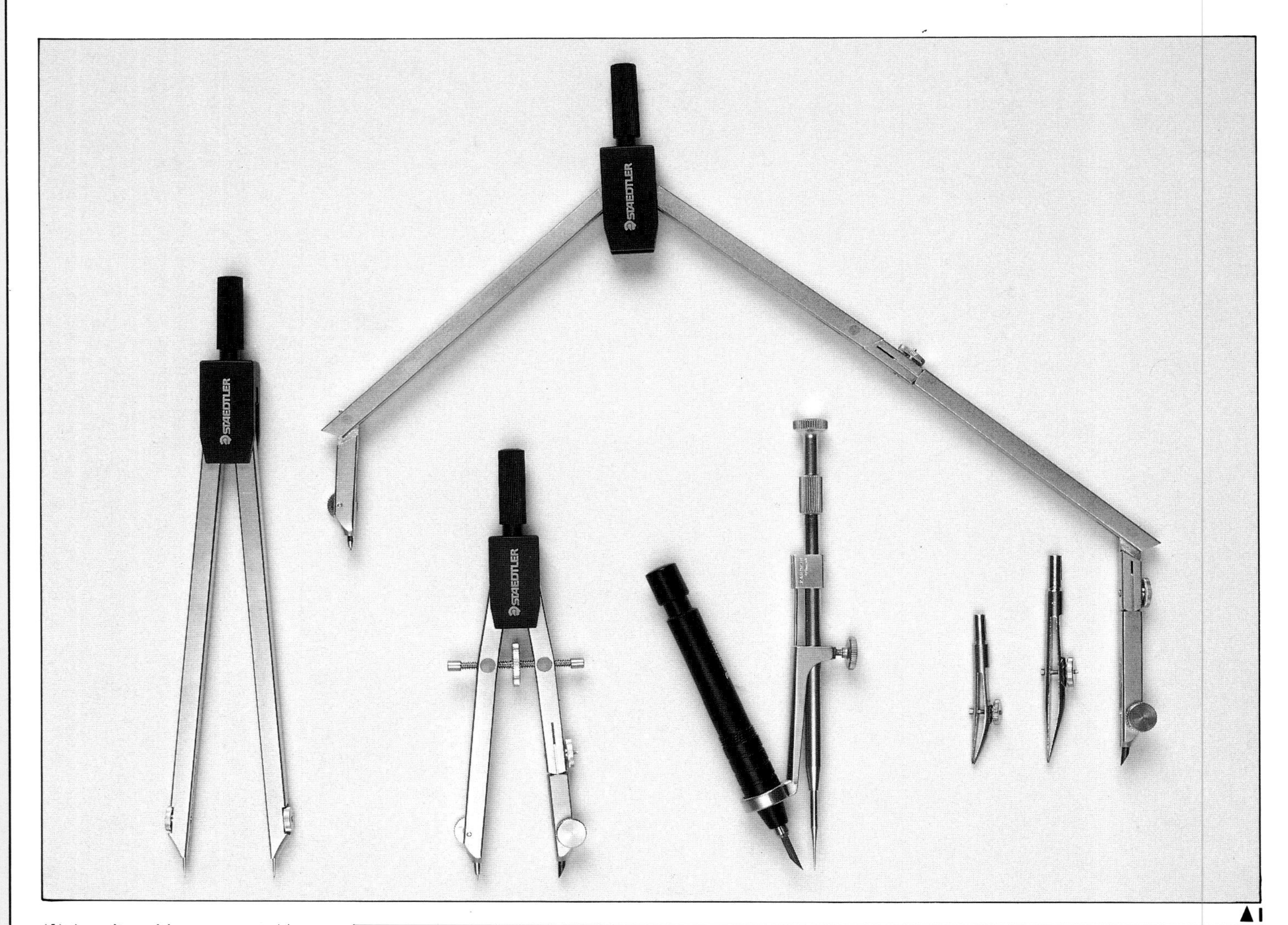


▲1

(**1**) An **adjustable compass** with an extension arm is useful if you wish to produce a large circle, since it enables you to keep the pen or pencil point at a consistent angle of 45° to the paper; but the **smaller compass** has a better locking device for repeating the same circumference. The **attachments** enable you to fit technical pens to the compasses.

(**2**) A **beam compass** is used to draw any large circle. There is no limit to the radius since you can just keep adding extensions.

▲2

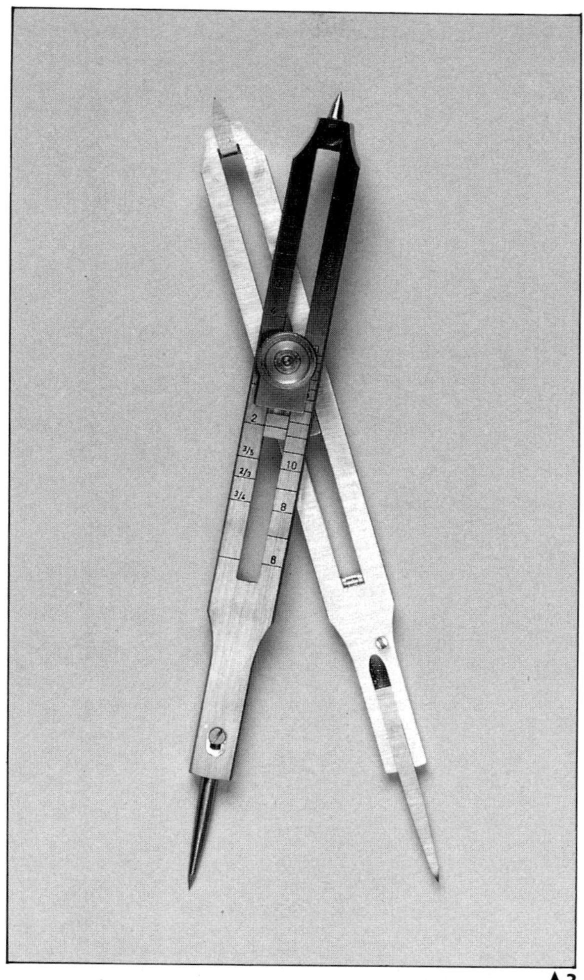


▲3

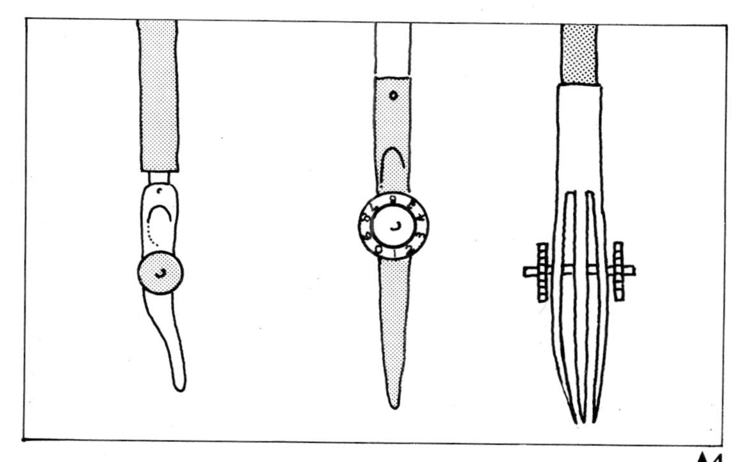

▲4

(**3**) **Proportional dividers** are for taking a measurement and calculating whatever proportions you wish.

(**4**) **Ruling pens** hold all kinds of paint, enabling you to produce a line of a chosen thickness in any color you wish.

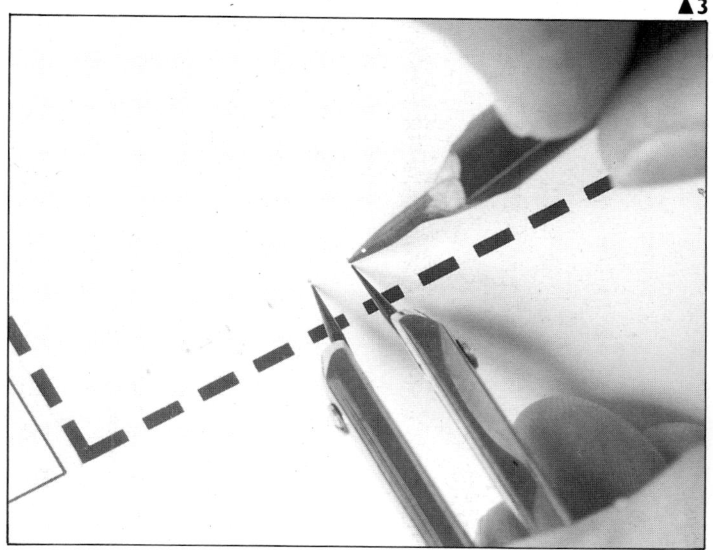

▲5

(**5**) **Dividers** allow you to make repeated and accurate measurements. (See p. 110.)

(**6**) A **pump compass** can draw very small circles of less than 1/16" in diameter.

▲6

Keep your compass lead sharpened for a line of the best quality – an emery board is the easiest way.

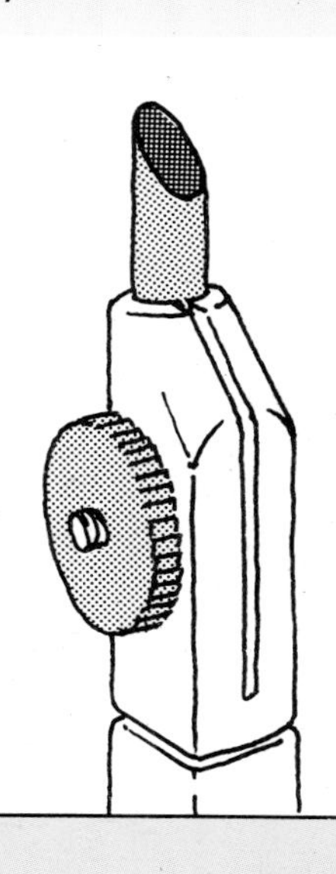

## · TEMPLATES · CURVES ·

(**1**) These **templates** are designed to give you a number of curves and circles. They can be placed directly on artwork and traced around, giving a quick, curved line which is the same size every time. **Templates** with elipses and circles of varying projection degrees range from very small to very large and show the verticals and horizontals of each elipse.

1▲

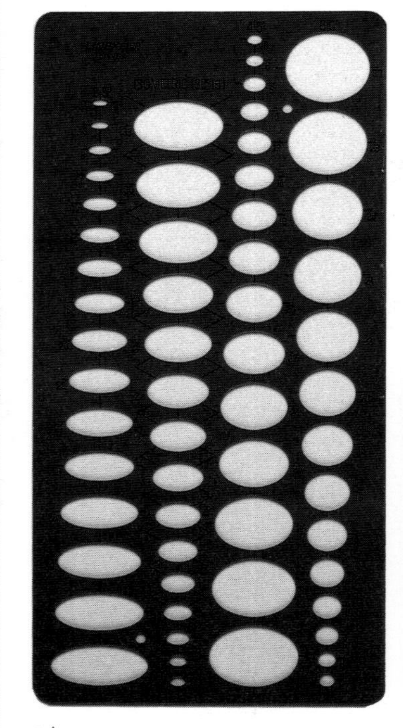

1▲

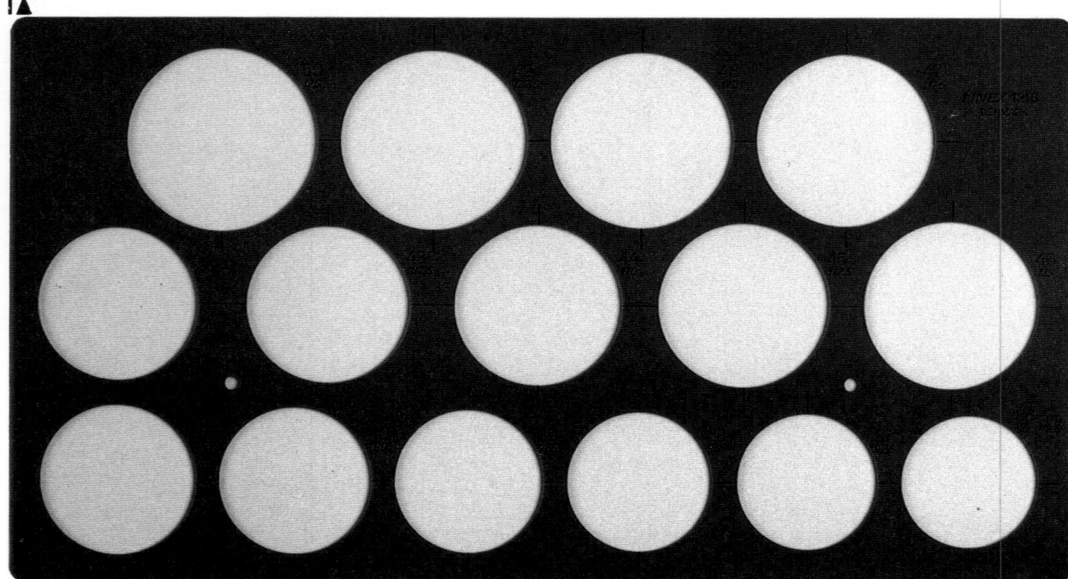

1▲

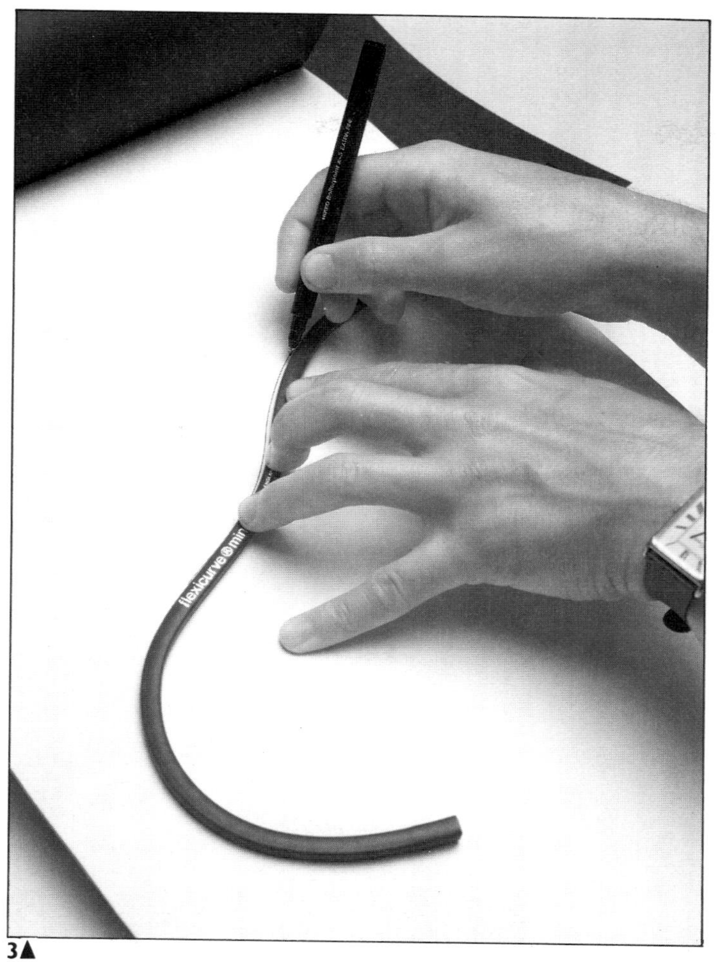


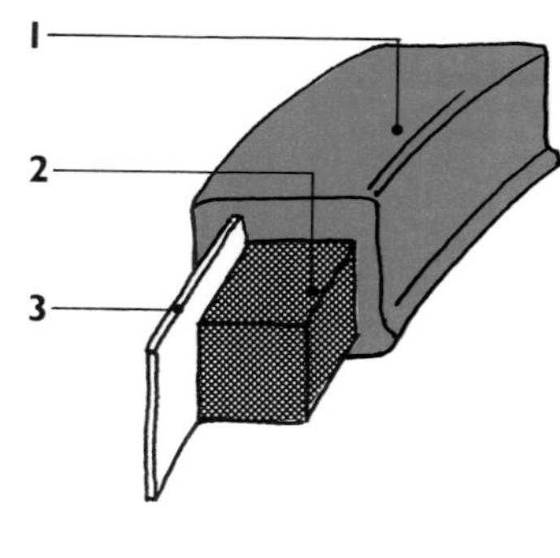


(**2**) Although these **French curves** look as though they may provide only a small number of shapes, the curve itself can be manipulated to produce almost any shape – the problem is remembering the movements when you wish to repeat it!

3▲

(**3**) A **flexible curve** enables you to create whatever shape you want, and it will hold its position. It has lip so that you can produce a clean line from it without bleeding.

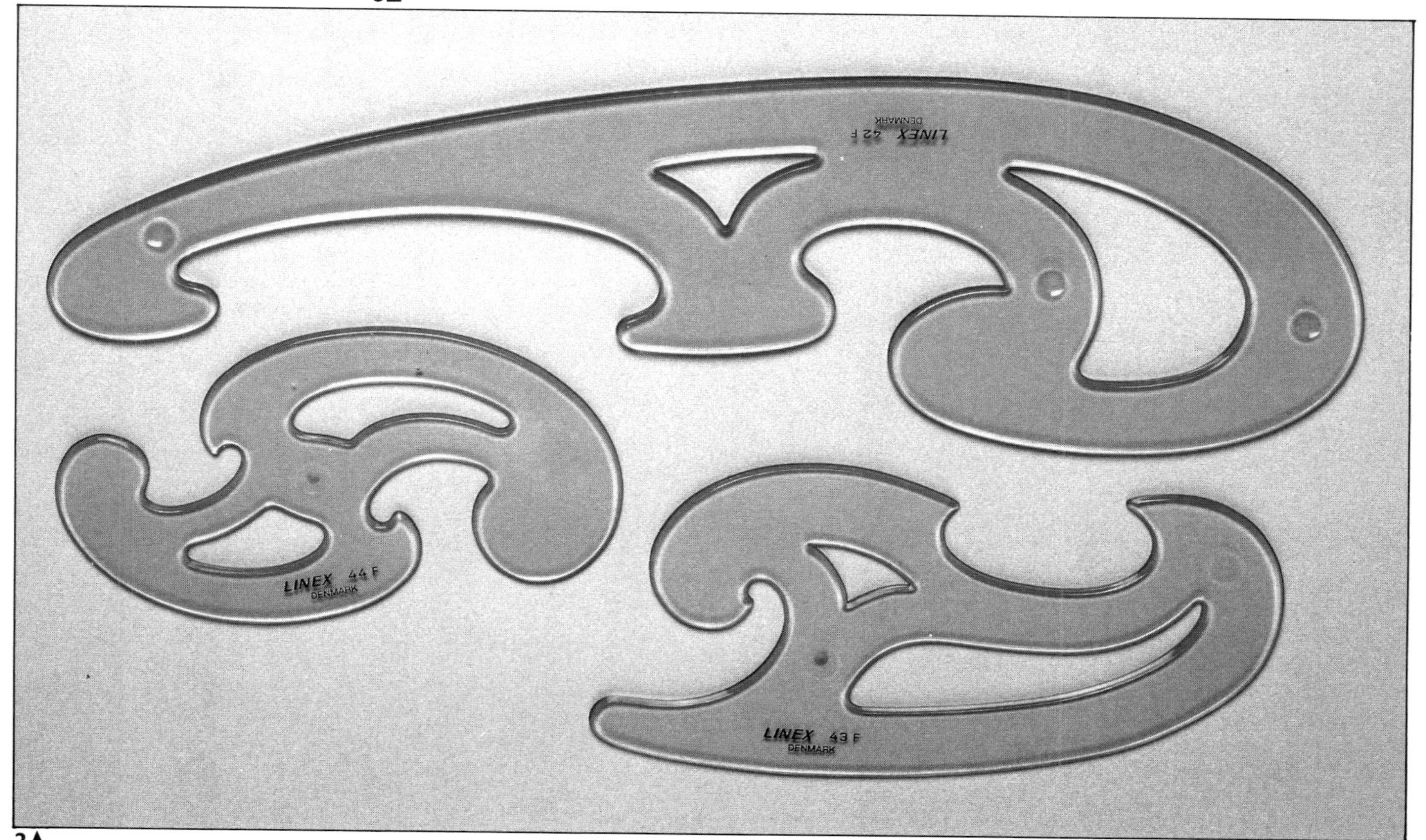


2▲

# · MARKERS · TECHNICAL PENS · PENCILS ·

(**I**) **Magic Marker pens**, **Pantone pens** and **Mecanorma pens** are available in an enormous selection of colors. They are useful for covering large areas with flat color for mock-ups and finished visuals. **Pantone pens** match the Pantone coloring system. Be careful, since most of these pens are spirit-based and so will bleed through normal paper. Apart from the usual colors, **Stabilos** come in fluorescent shades. The **Eddings** come in 2 sizes.

(**2**) **Technical pens** are essential for accurate artwork and detail. Instead of a conventional nib they have a metal tube. The ink is fed through the tube, producing a consistent thickness of line. They also have removable nibs, so that a variety of point sizes can be bought. The pen must be held upright to assist the flow of ink.

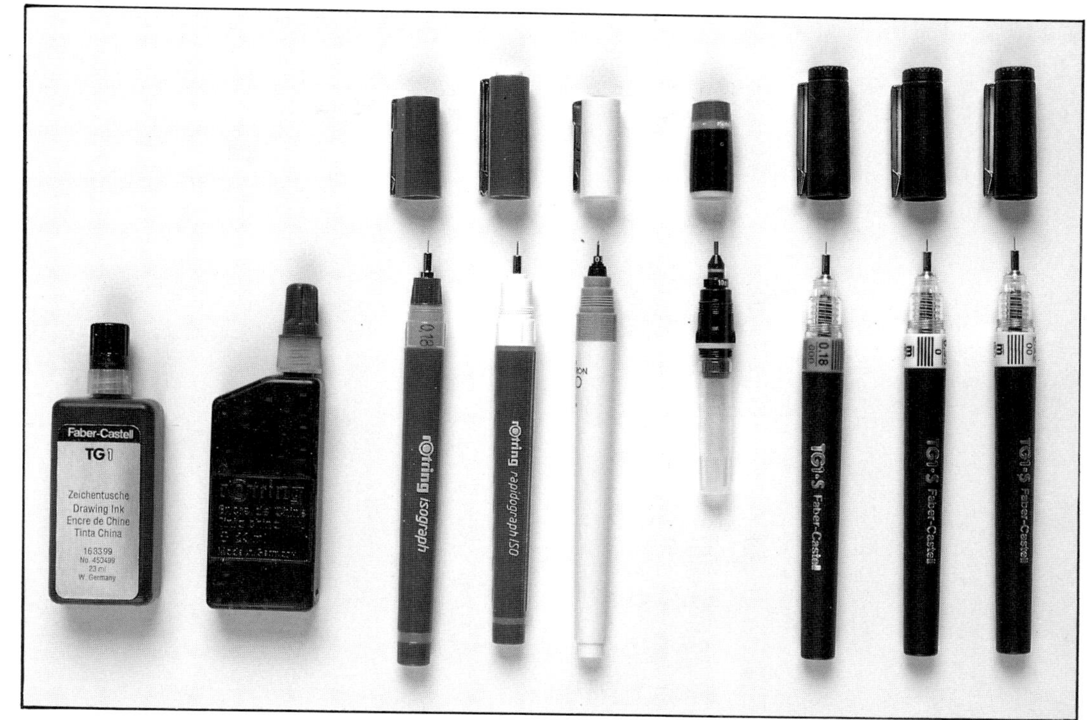


▲2

▲3

(**3**) **Mechanical pencils and lead-holders** hold different thicknesses of leads and have a special sharpener attached. The leads can also vary in hardness – from B to H.

PAPER/GLASS/METAL

CHINAGRAPH

PAPER/GLASS/METAL

FINE ART COLOR PENCIL

FINE ART COLOR PENCIL

COLOR PENCIL CRAYONS

4▲

(**4**) **Pencils, chinagraphs and crayons** are used in the studio for marking transparencies or producing color roughs and mock-ups.

# · KNIVES · BLADES · CUTTING TOOLS ·

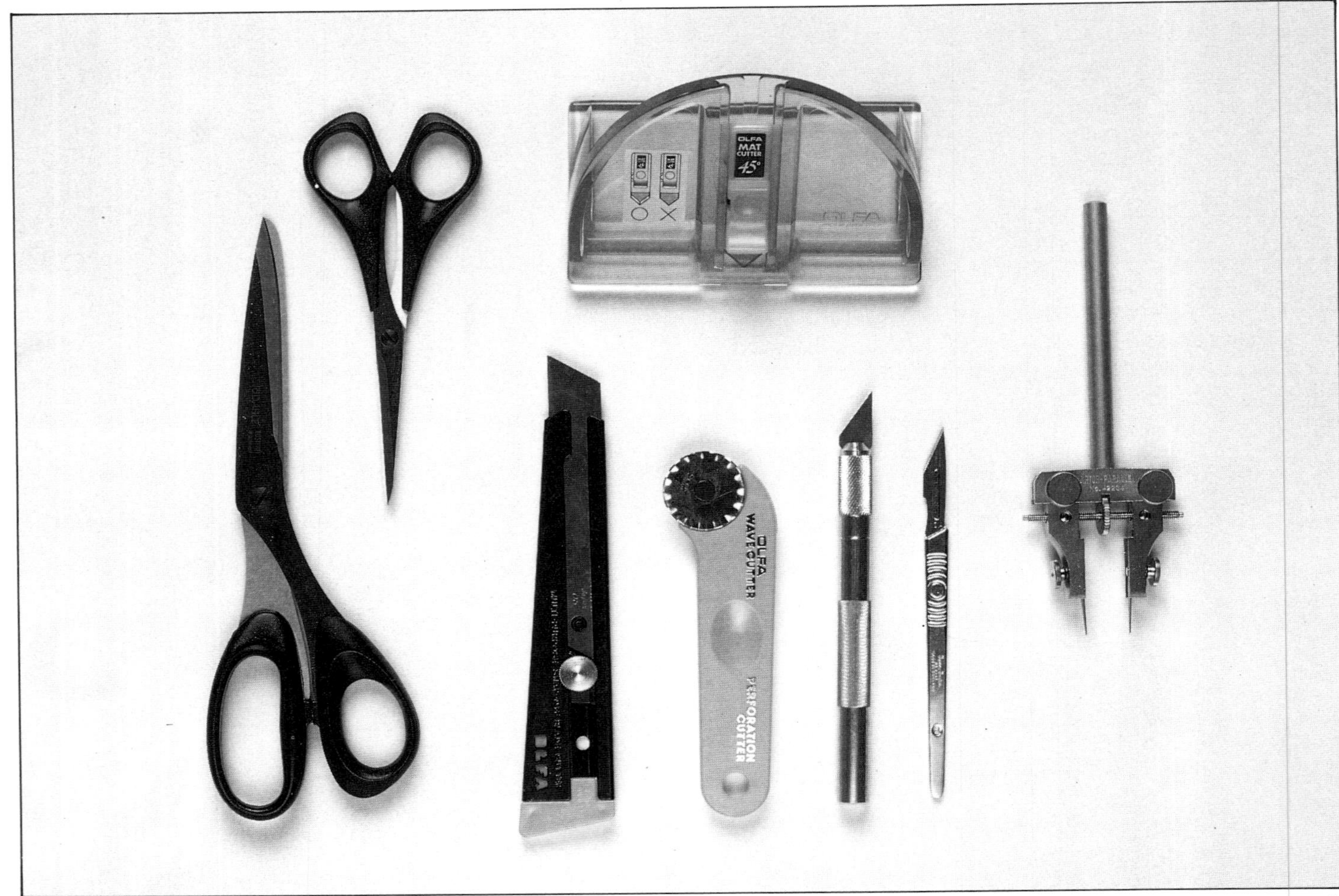


▲1

(**1**) A **sharp pair of scissors**, an **X-acto knife** with a variety of blades and a **larger knife** for cutting heavy cardboard are essential. A **cutting attachment for a compass** is very useful as one often has to cut curves and circles. The **double mounted knife** is adjustable and is for cutting parallel lines.

(**2**) These blades all perform different functions. Never be tempted to pick up your X-acto knife and start cutting without changing the blade first.
(A., B) are for paper, film and thin cardboard.
(C., D) are utility blades for medium weight materials.
(E) This knife has disposable, "snap-off" blades.
The curved blades are better for scraping marks off paper and board.

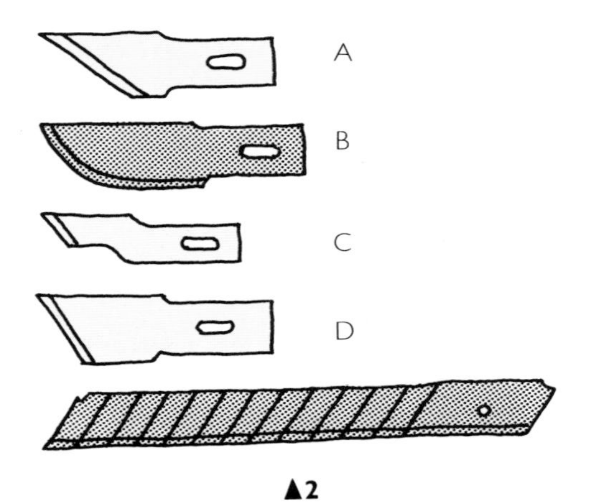


▲2

▲3

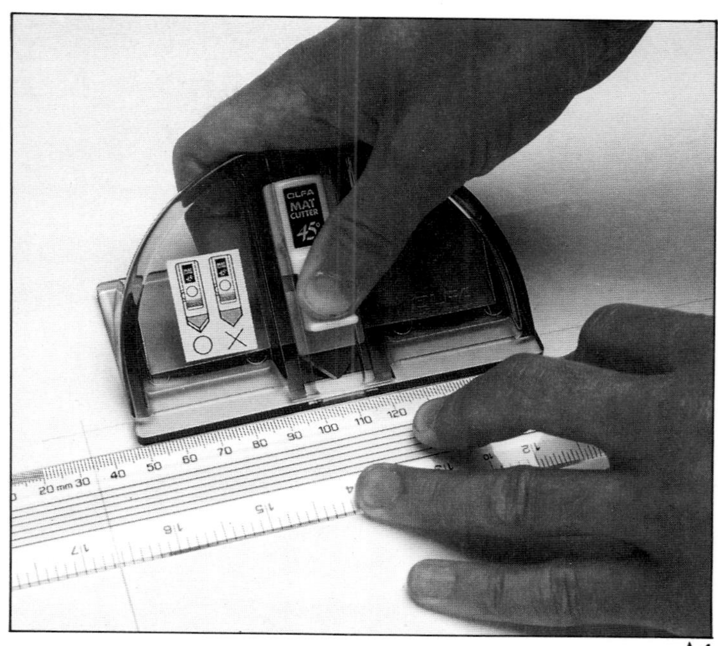


▲4

(**3**) This is a **beam cutting compass** and is useful for cutting accurate circles out of acetate or masking film.

(**4**) This **mat cutter** is for cutting a beveled edge when producing professional mats. It is very difficult to keep a good 45° angle without one.

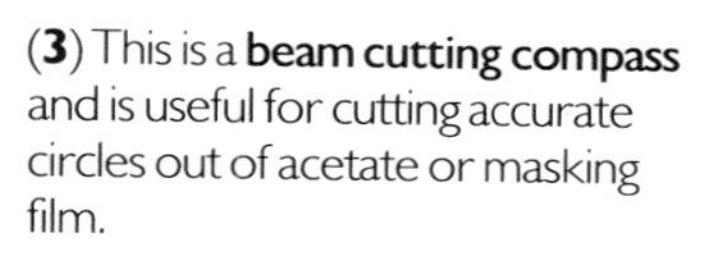

(**5**) **Cutting mats** are either transparent or green. The transparent one is for use on a lightbox and the green one for the desk. The surface does not break down with use and will not blunt the blade of the X-acto knife. There is a grid printed on the surface as a guide for squaring-up photographs.

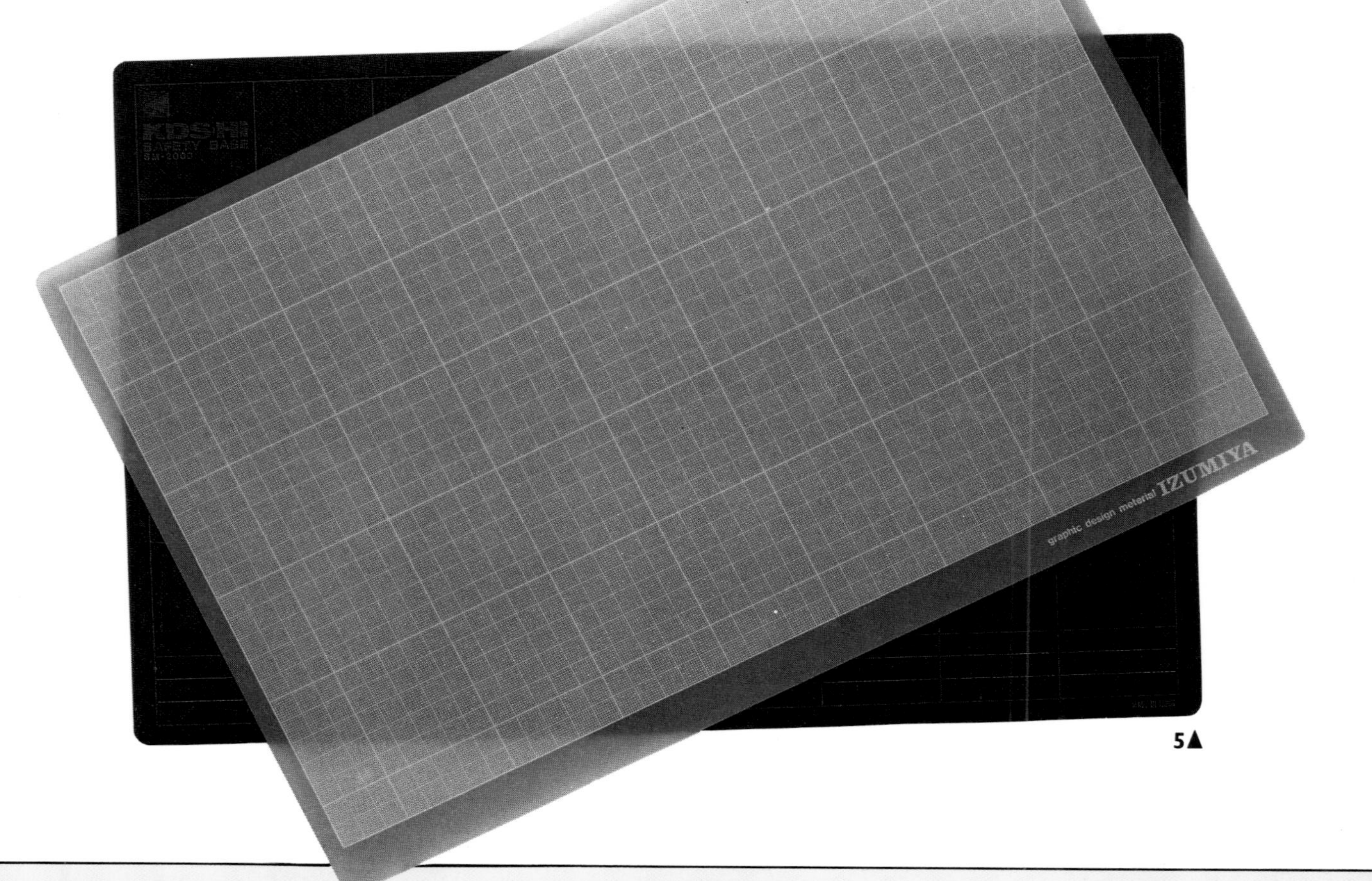


5▲

# · PADS · FILM · BOARDS ·

(**1**) **Marker paper**, as the name suggests, is for Magic Markers; it is impermeable to the ink.

(**2**) **Layout paper** is thin enough to permit design or type underneath to be seen but opaque enough so that drawing on it will block out the work underneath.

(**3**) **Detail Typo paper** is used by the artist for transposing type.

(**4**) **Television storyboard paper** is by far the best paper to use for quick and easy visualizing. It has areas allocated for the visuals, soundtrack and directions.

(**5**) **Graph paper** comes in various sizes and is always useful when working out grids for typography or for diagrams.

(**6**) **Retracing paper** is available in various shades and acts exactly like carbon paper. Colors are easy to either cover up or rub out – as is not the case with carbon paper.

(**7**) **Acetate** is used for presentation as a clear overlay to keep the work clean and for laying over type, transfers, Letraset, etc.

(**8**) **Draft film** takes ink and paint very well and can be scraped clean with an X-acto knife. Because it is film and semi-opaque it can be used for overlays and hand separations.

(**9**) **Airbrush masking** is used for masking out areas that are not to be sprayed. Being only slightly tacky it is repositionable and will not damage artwork.

(**10**) **Block tack** is also used for masking. Cut a piece off, strip off the backing and lay it down on your artwork or overlay. You can then cut it to whatever shape you require. Pen and ink can be used in conjunction with it, and it is transparent on a light box.

(**11**) **Transpaseal** is a single-sided, adhesive, translucent film for protecting folders, maps etc. It gives a laminated appearance and is available in matt or gloss.

(**12**) **CS10 line board** has a very fine, good quality surface. Because it is untextured, technical pens and pencil can be scratched off the surface without damaging it. It will take most masking materials.

(**13**) **Mat board** is available in a variety of colors, and most boards are 22½" by 33", although they do vary according to make. It is important to get the right thickness for your work; otherwise the board may buckle, especially if you are window mounting.

(**14**) **Astralux** is a thin, very shiny cardboard available in a selection of colors and is ideal for mocking up packaging designs or cards, since as the surface has a laminated quality. It does not take all pens and markers and has a good and bad side. To fold it you must score it; otherwise it has a tendency to crack.

(**15**) **Marbled papers** are available in a great number of sizes and colors and are used most often for endpapers or book covers.

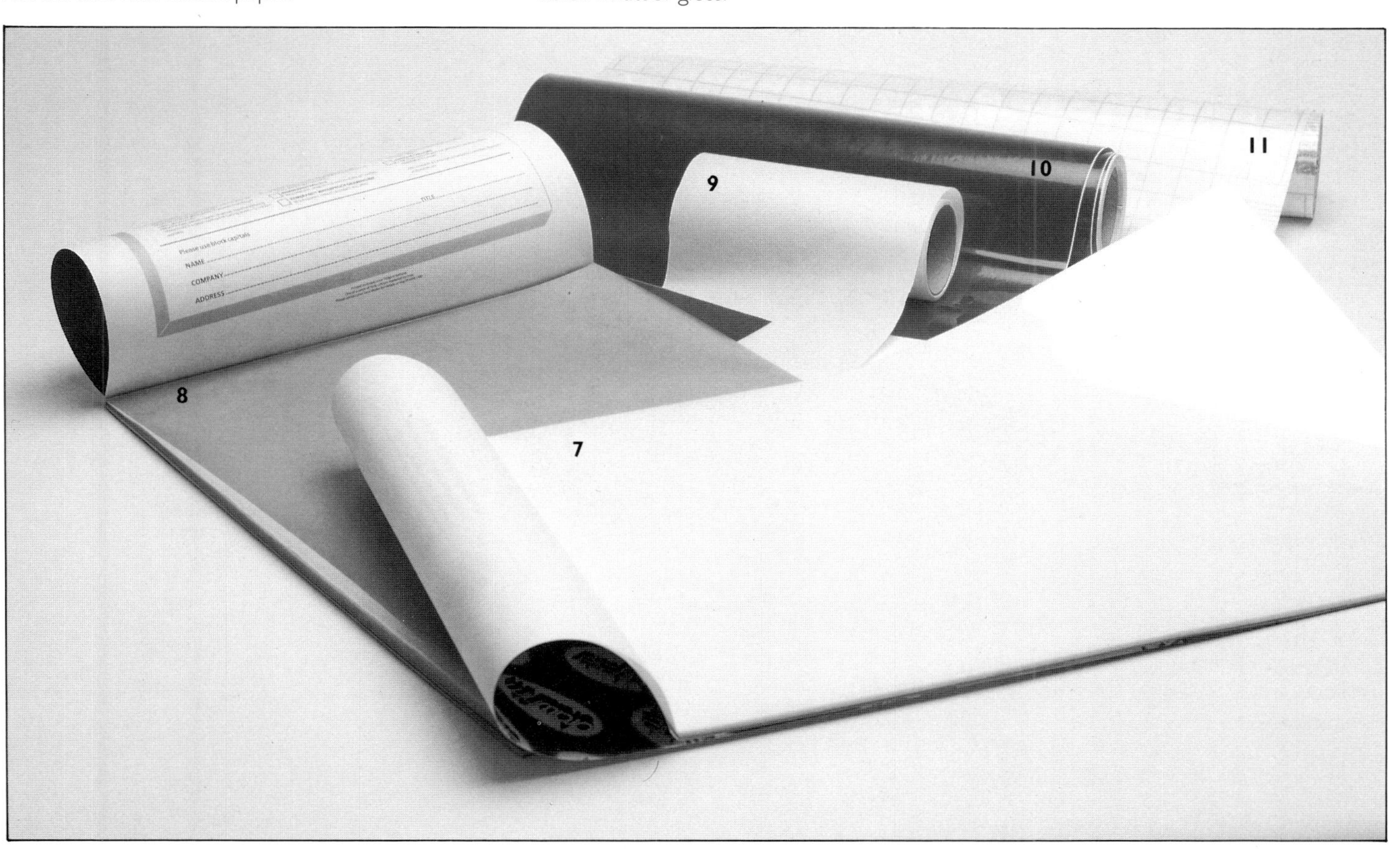

# · INSTANT ART ·

(**1**) **Letraset** is a dry transfer system. It includes a very large range of typefaces in various colors and also rules, borders, symbols, grids, tones and screens, as well as illustrative images.

(**2**) **Letraline** is used when producing graphs and diagrams, in particular, but can also be used for any kind of visual with lines, rules or thin borders.

(**3**) **Letracote** is a protective glossy or matte spray which prevents **Letraset** from being scratched or damaged.

(**4**) **Matt Letrafilm**, (**5**) **black Letraset** and (**6**) **Letrafilm** solvent spray are used together to produce colored type. (**7**) **Pantone colored paper** and (**8**) **Pantone Letrafilm**, which are sticky-backed, are available in a large number of colors and are linked to the rest of the **Pantone** system.

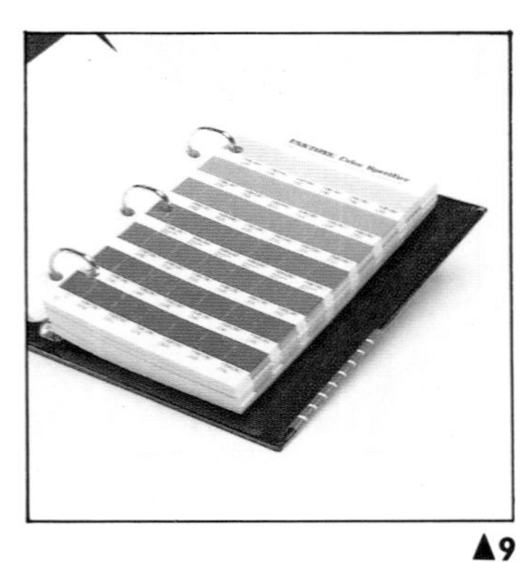

▲9

(**9**) The **Pantone color specifier** holds small samples of all the colors in the **Pantone** range on both coated and uncoated paper and is essential when specifying colors to a printer. Each color has a number and the swatches can be torn out and attached to your artwork.

4066
Letraset symbols
©Letraset Limited 1981. Made in England.
Protected widely by patents & patent applications.
4437
Letraset Architectural Symbols
Scale 1:200 AS1033
Letraset symbols
IL4879
4
Letratone
LT 14
HEAT RESISTANT
a Letraset product printed in England
LT 273
6
LETRAFILM
SOLVENT
3
8
Letraset architecture
ASH 4106
Letraset
Illustration
AA104
ASH 4106

# · ADHESIVES ·

(**1**) **Double-sided tape** is ideal for sticking down small pieces of artwork. It is very secure and not easy to reposition.

(**2**) **Masking tape** is available in various thicknesses and is easy to lift and reposition. It is a good all-purpose tape.

(**3**) **Black cellophane tape** is a block-out tape used when preparing negatives for printing.

(**4**) **Invisible tape** is best for presentations when you wish to attach something such as acetate without the joining being seen. Rub the tape down well to make it invisible.

(**5**) **Rubber cement** is for sticking down large areas. If you need to reposition the work, do not leave the rubber cement to dry before laying the work down. **Artgum** will remove any excess glue.

(**6**) **Rubber cement** is a permanent glue ideal for gluing all types of paper and board.

(**7**) **Blu-tack** is useful for fixing photographs and pictures to most surfaces and can be easily removed and re-used.

(**8**) **Ronsonol** lighter fuel is extremely useful for removing grease and fingerprints from artwork. It will also dissolve certain marker pens and can be used creatively in this way.

(**9**) A **hot wax machine and roller** are the best ways of attaching artwork. It is easy to reposition and petrol will clean away any excess wax.

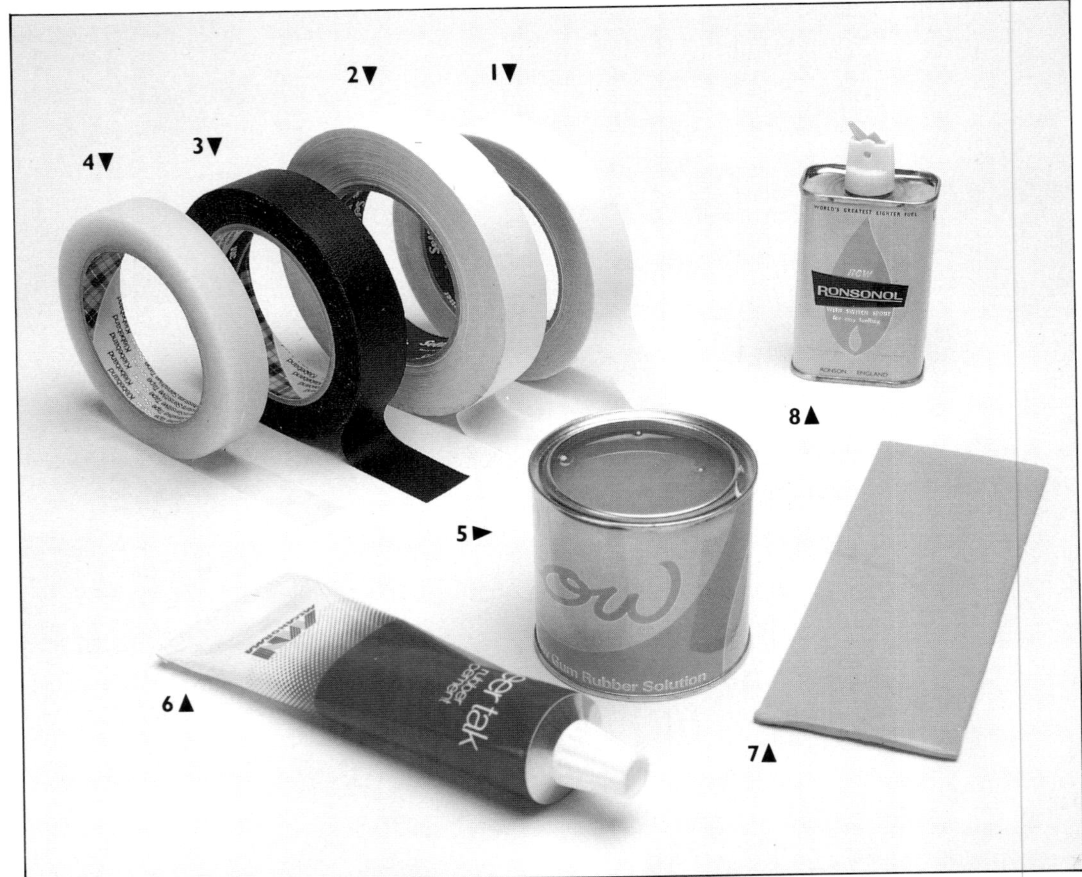

9▲

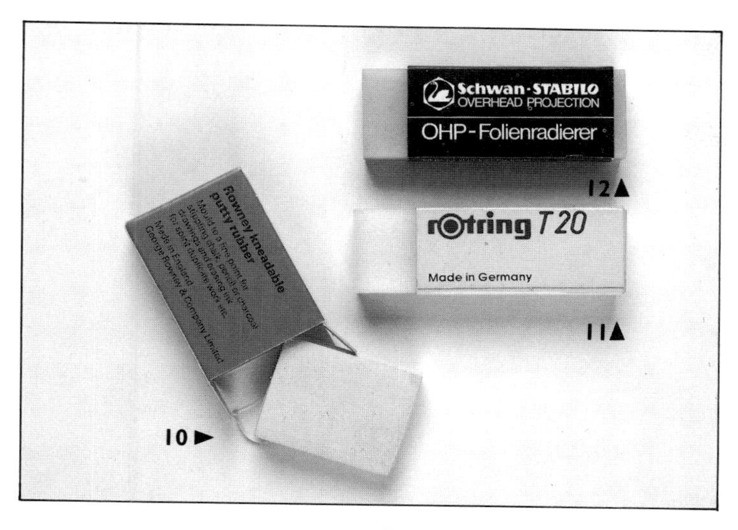

13▲

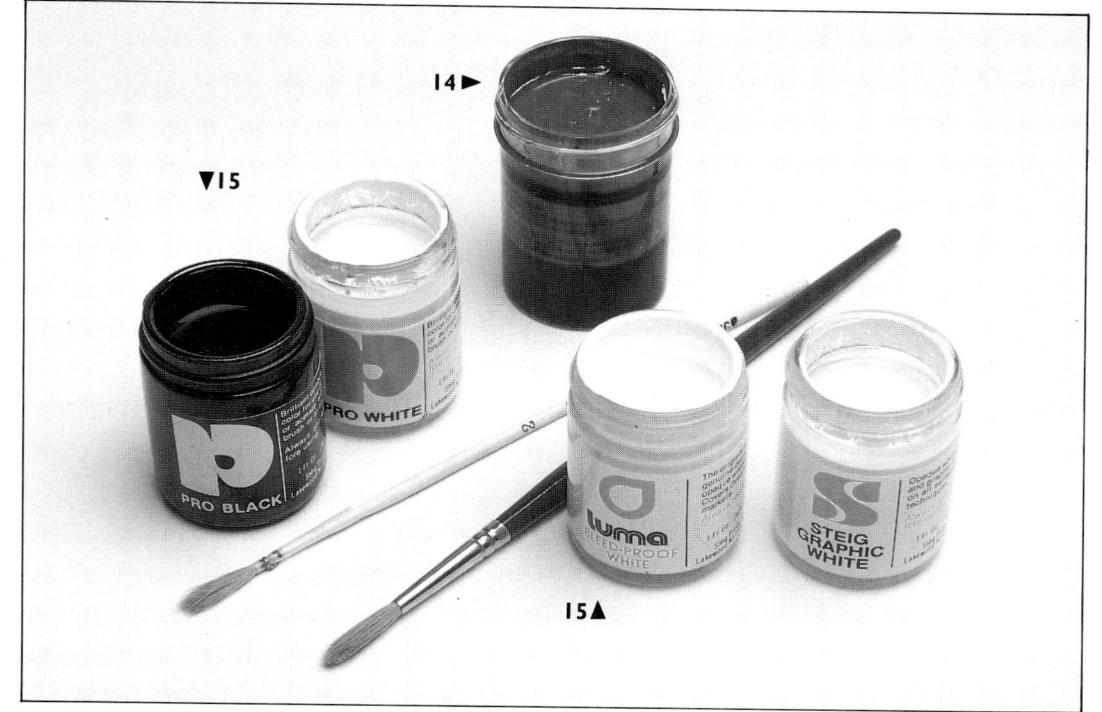


(**10**) A **kneaded eraser** is for soft pencil and for keeping your work surface clean.

(**11**) A **Rotring rubber** is for ink or very hard pencil.

(**12**) The **overhead projection eraser** removes markers from acetate.

(**13**) A **scalograph** is for scaling rectangles up and down in proportion.

(**14**) This **red opaque paint** blocks out separations for artwork, and photographic negatives and positives when it is important that light not pass through.

(**15**) The **black and white paints** are for blocking out, masking and covering up mistakes on artwork. Some are bleed proof.

(**16**) This **roller** is used when sticking something down with wax or any other glue – it gives a smooth surface. The **burnisher** is for pressing down very small pieces.

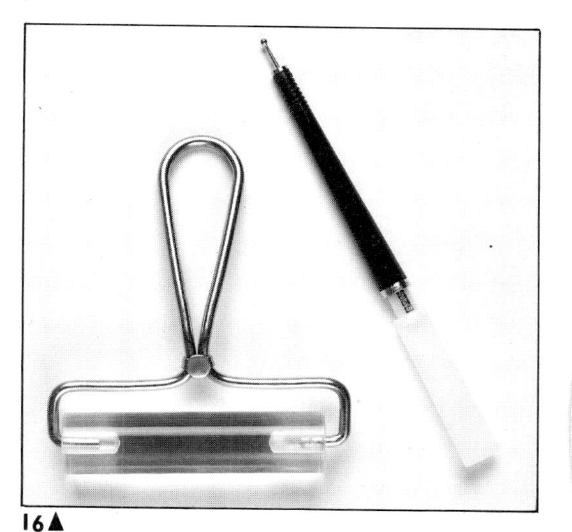
16▲

(**17**) This is a **reproduction computer** and is for scaling images up and down to the required size.

17►

# · AIRBRUSHES ·

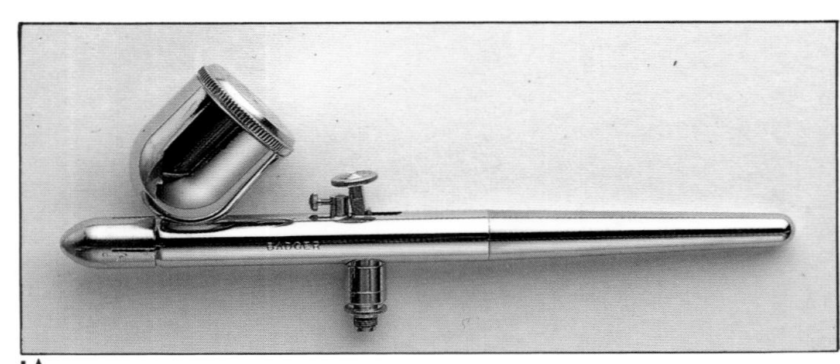

1▲

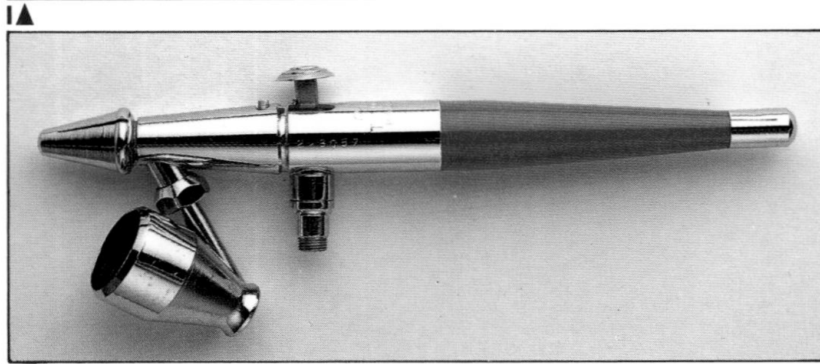

2▲

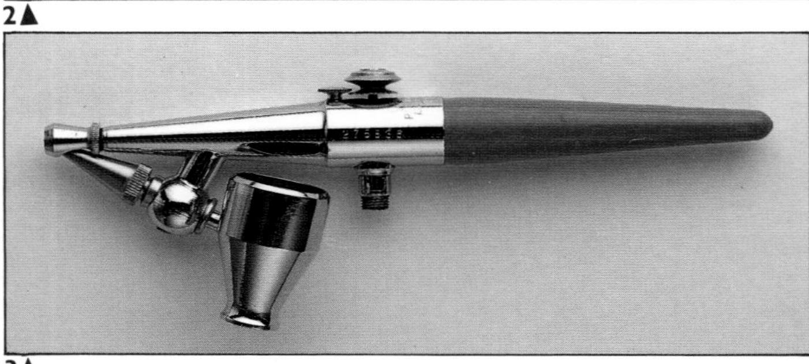

3▲

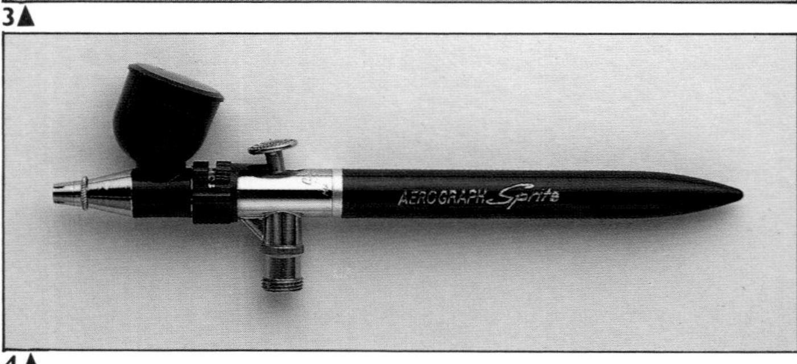


4▲

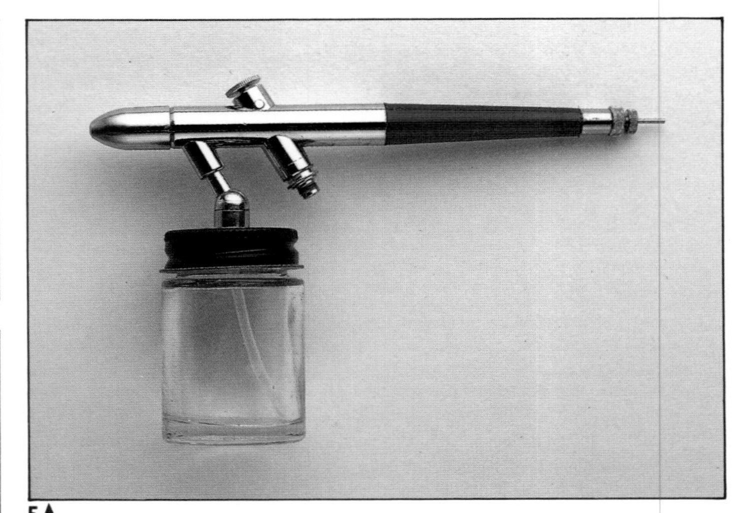

5▲

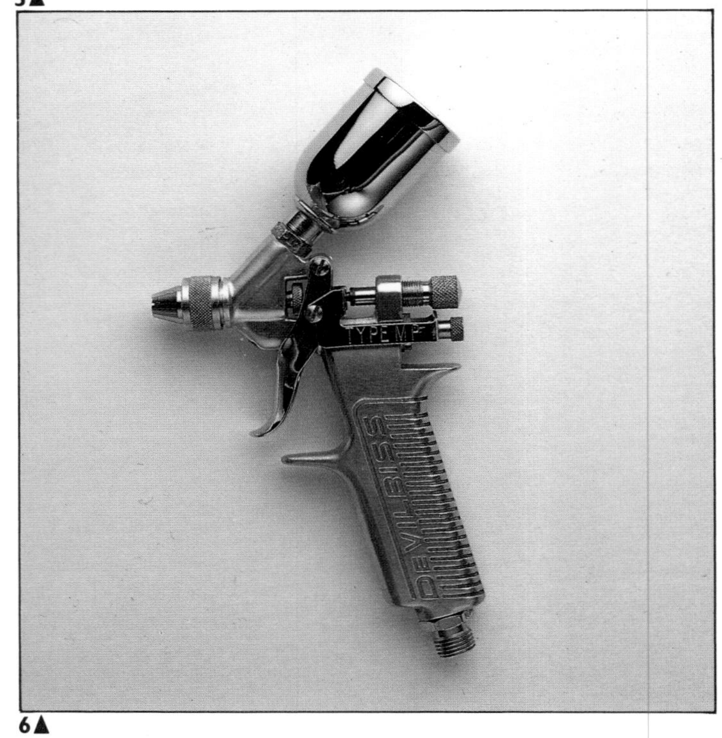


6▲

**1.** The **Badger 100 LG** is a simple two-way gravity-feed airbrush. It is quite cheap and there isn't a great deal of control, but it is suitable for beginners.

**2.,3.** The **Passche H3** is also at the cheaper end of the market. It is for rough work rather than precision and is often used by model-makers. The Paasche VLS is a better, precision, double-action airbrush. Both are slightly larger and heavier than their competitors.

**4.** The **De Vilbiss Sprite** is a medium-quality airbrush. It is a good working model, not too expensive and is suitable for students and hobbyists.

**5.** The **Badger 200** is a model-maker's airbrush, and so is very useful for large areas of flat color but not for detailed work. It has a fixed jet, just on and off – which is why it produces a constant flow.

**6.** The **De Vilbiss MP Spray Gun** is a lightweight industrial airbrush. It is suitable for medium detail work, for spraying large amounts of color and for three-dimensional applications.

7▲

7. The large **SAC 110** and the smaller **SAC 330 Seminar** compressors are the best on the market. The SAC 110 can run two airbrushes at the same time and you can leave it running all day. The SAC 330 is only suitable for one airbrush. The two smaller compressors, the **Badger 180 automatic** and the **Dawson Macdonald** and **Dawson D351 VM** do not have reservoirs and are therefore subject to air pulsing. They are not ideal for low pressures but are suitable for long periods of use.

8▲

**8. Luma Inks** are radiant watercolors and a typical airbrush medium. The dropper in the lid makes it easy to apply the color.

9▲

**9.** The **Letrajet Airmaker** is a simple airbrush driven by an aerosol can and draws its paint from a large marker pen. A wide choice of colors are available from the Pantone range.

# · DRAWING BOARDS · PARALLEL MOTION BOARDS ·

1. A basic **folding steel drawing board stand** with cross bar foot rest. The height is telescopically adjustable and the board can be tilted through 180° either side.

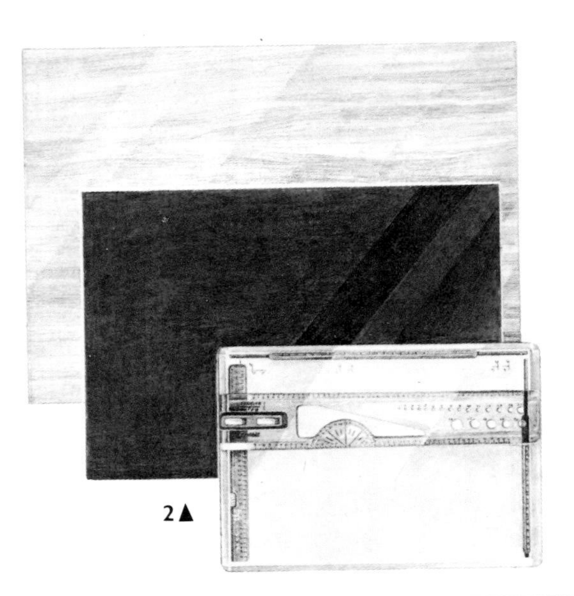

2▲

1▲

2. **Drawing boards** in a variety of sizes and materials. With a plain wooden board (upper) it is often necessary to use a backing sheet. The formica-covered board (middle) can be wiped clean. This adjustable model (lower) has a drafting head which can be fixed in any position.

3. A differently designed **stand**, giving more leg room.

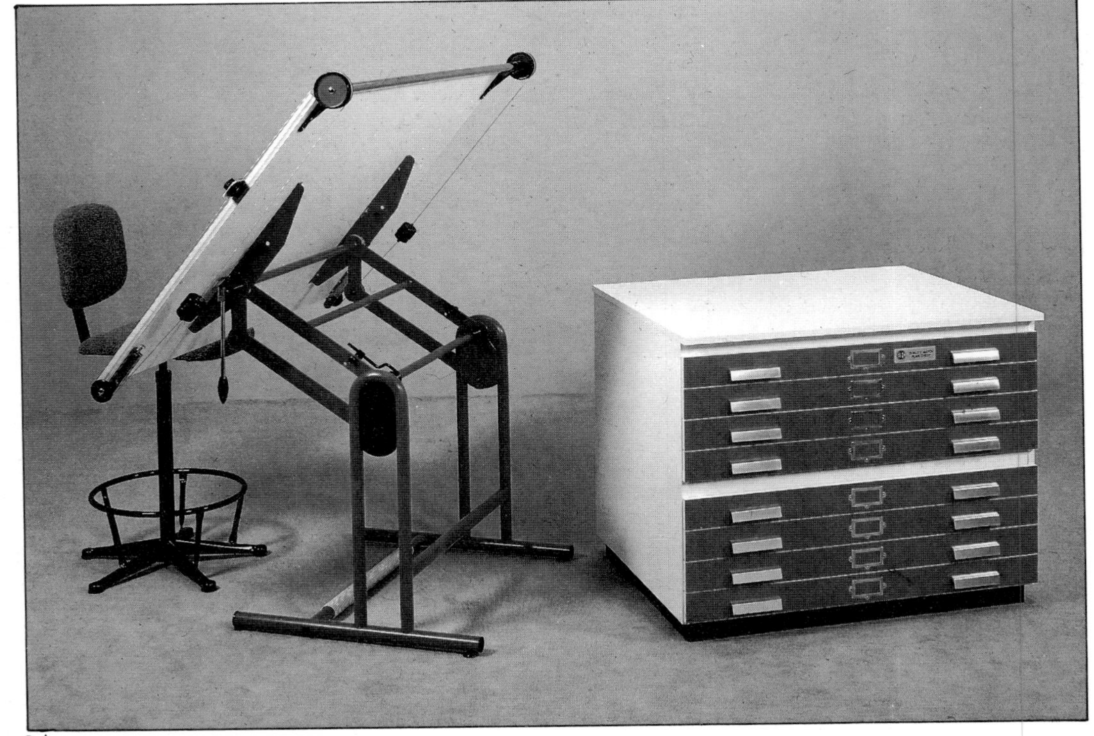

3▲

4▲

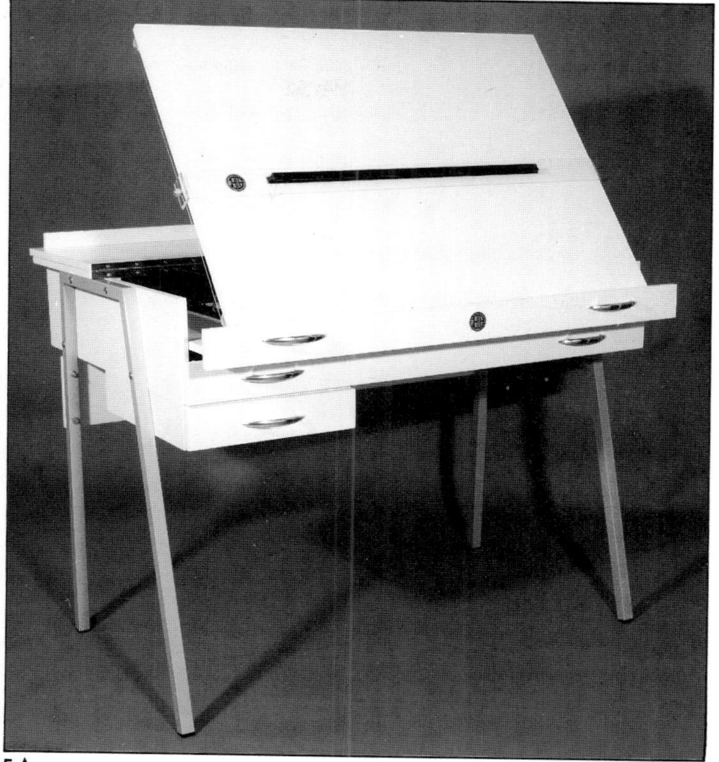

5▲

7▲

**4**. **Double parallel motion assembly unit**, here shown on a stand, used for viewing negatives, positives or transparencies and doubles as a 'spotting' bench.

**5**. **Two-drawer desk with drawing board**, which can be adjusted to the tilt required and folds away when not in use.

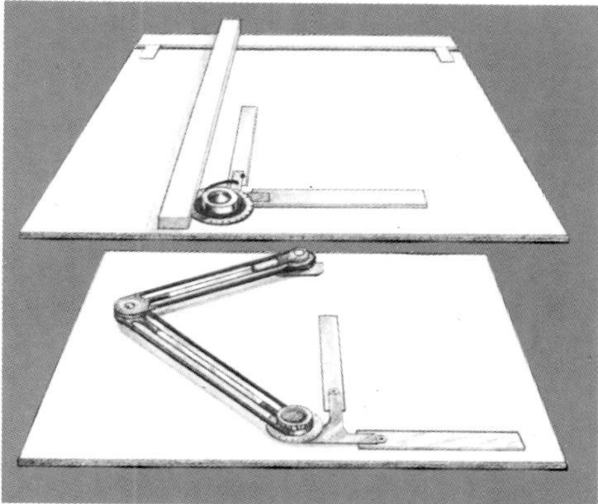

6▲

**6**. **Drafting machines**, used for drawing accurate parallel lines, both horizontally and vertically. More recent models have a fixed bar for increased accuracy.

**7**. This **single pedestal stand** will take board sizes 36″ × 50″ and 36″ × 59″. It has gas compensation height adjustment and will revolve through 360° without any movement of the pedestal.

# · PMT MACHINE ·

**1**. The **PMT machine** is very versatile: it can reverse images from black to white, enlarge and reduce, make acetate overlays and screens and convert lettering and artwork to autotype. Most are automatic; you put in your requirements and the camera automatically adjusts itself. The machine and paper are expensive, but once bought will enable you to do practically everything yourself.

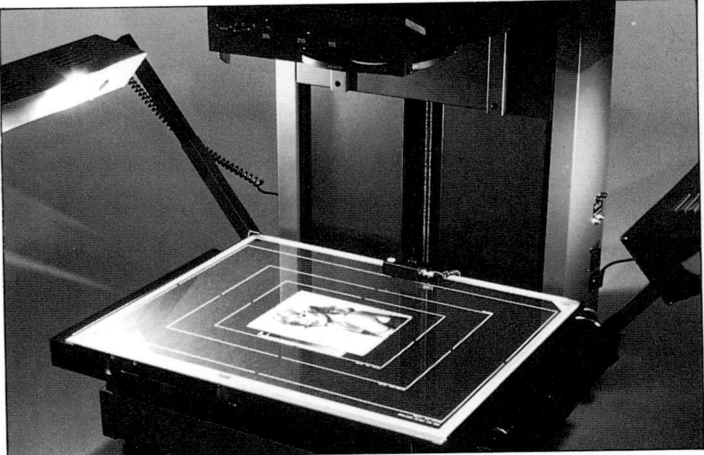

2▲

▲1

**2**. The **copyboard** is spring-loaded to accommodate originals of different thicknesses, and has a vacuum, which when switched on holds the original to be copied in place. A framing guide is printed on it and the copyboard itself is reversible – continuous tone originals are usually placed on the black side to minimize the flare, line originals are usually placed on the white side to provide a black surround to the negative. The PMT machine can be used like a Grant enlarger.

◄3

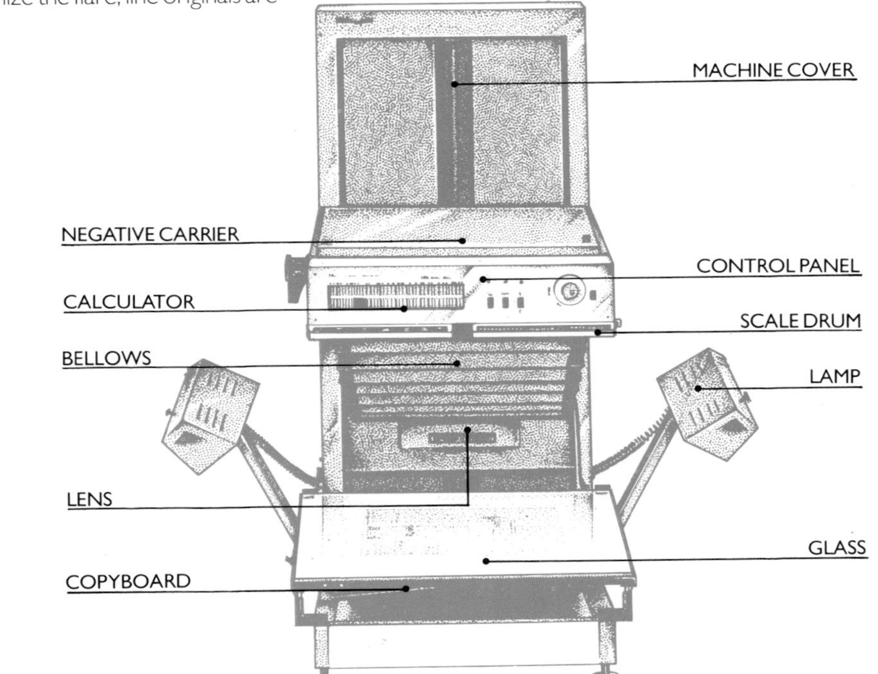


**3**. This manually-focused machine still includes an **electronic control panel**, which enables you to calculate different exposure times for different reproduction ratios, including automatic correction of maximum and minimum density in one-third stop increments. The LED lights and scales readouts can be switched off when using panchromatic film.

**4**. The PMT machine must be used in a darkroom, since the paper used is light sensitive. It is useful to keep a good pair of scissors and some tape available so that you can mark where your paper is to go on the glass, for although there is a framing guide, it is difficult to see in the dark.

▲5▼

▲5▼

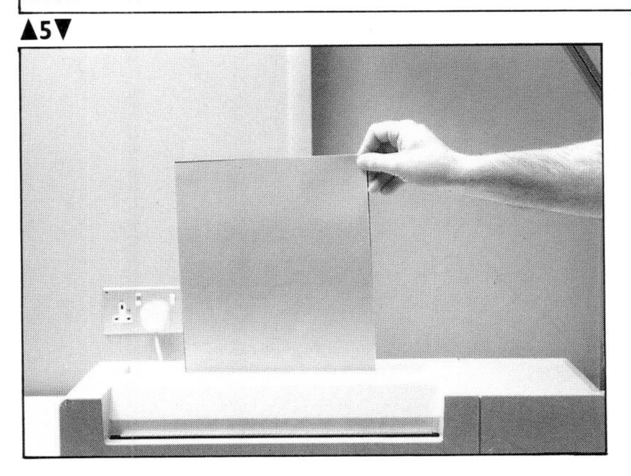

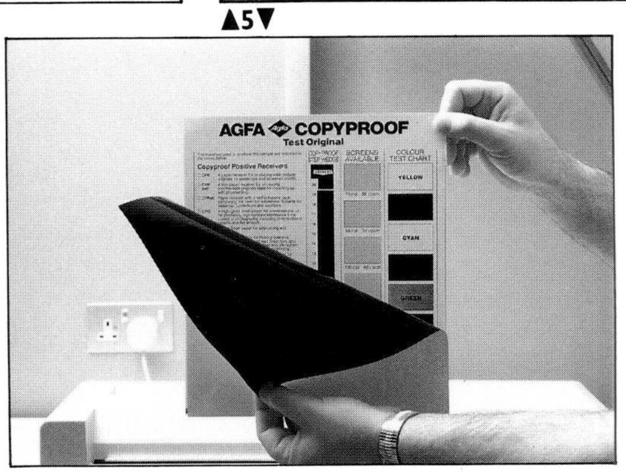


**5**. There are many types of paper for the PMT machine: **reversal paper**, **gloss** and **matt paper**, etc. The paper is very expensive, so calculate your requirements carefully and cut the paper accordingly, remembering, however, that the developing machines will not take pieces that are too small. Do not peel the papers apart immediately but leave for the specified time, e.g., 45 seconds for half-tones; otherwise the picture will not develop.

# · PROJECTORS · LIGHT BOXES ·

**1**. This is a simple **slide projector.** It is useful for enlarging 35mm colour transparencies.

1▲

**2**. A **light box** is essential in the studio for viewing transparencies, tracing through images or type and doing separations for artwork. It is quite easy to make your own, but use strip lighting as ordinary bulbs do not give an even light source and get very hot.

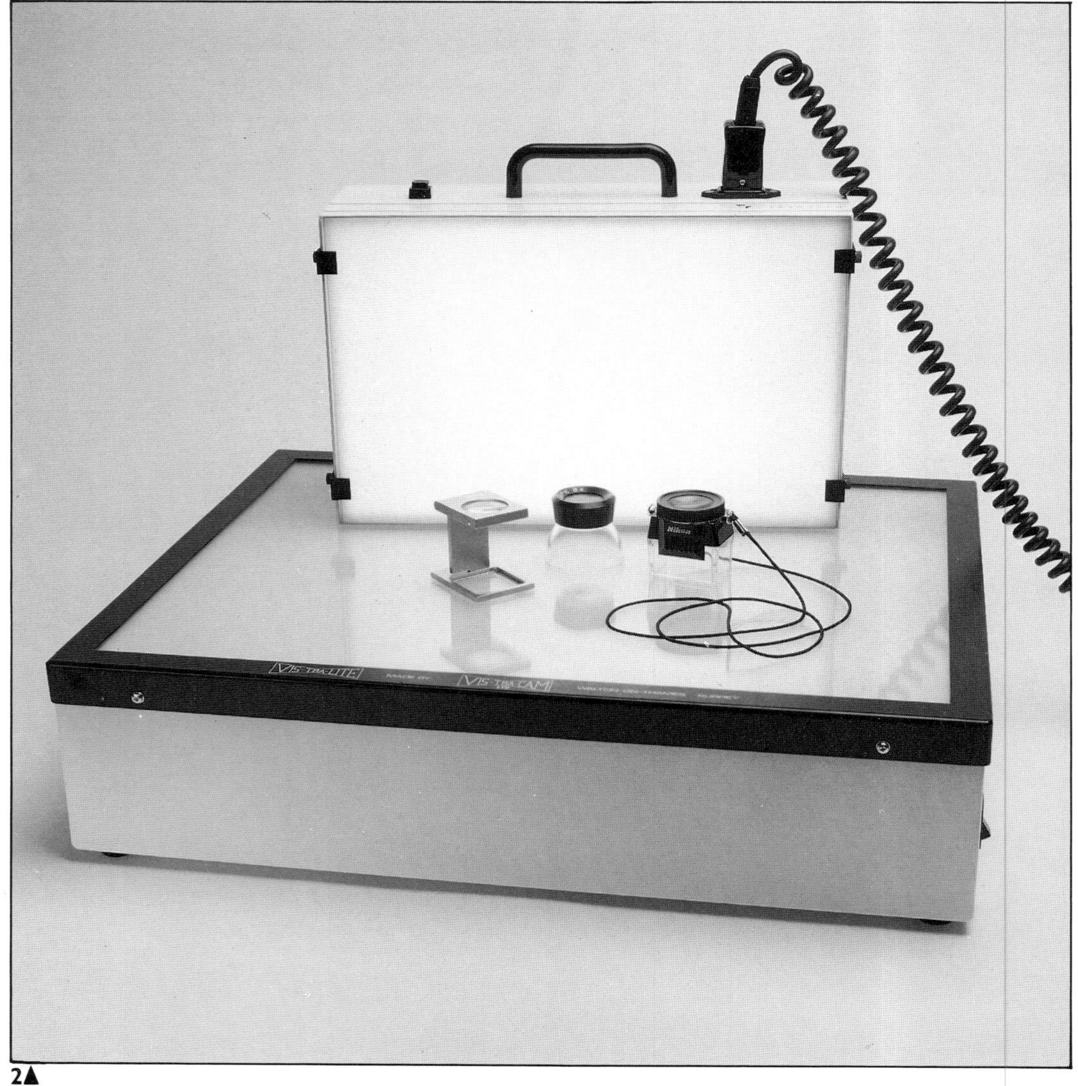

2▲

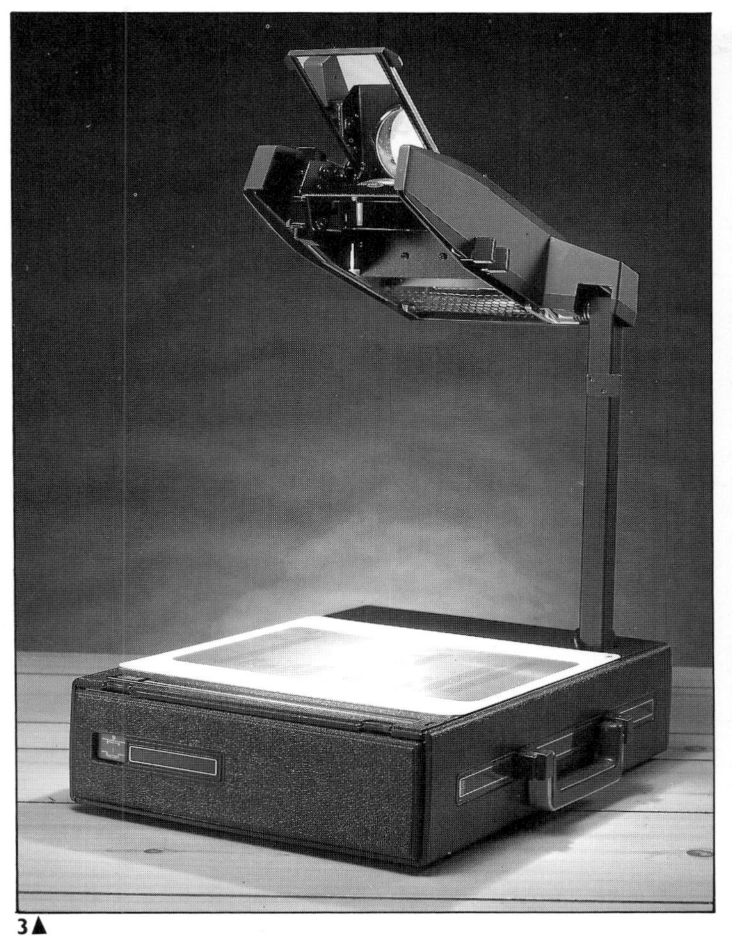

3▲

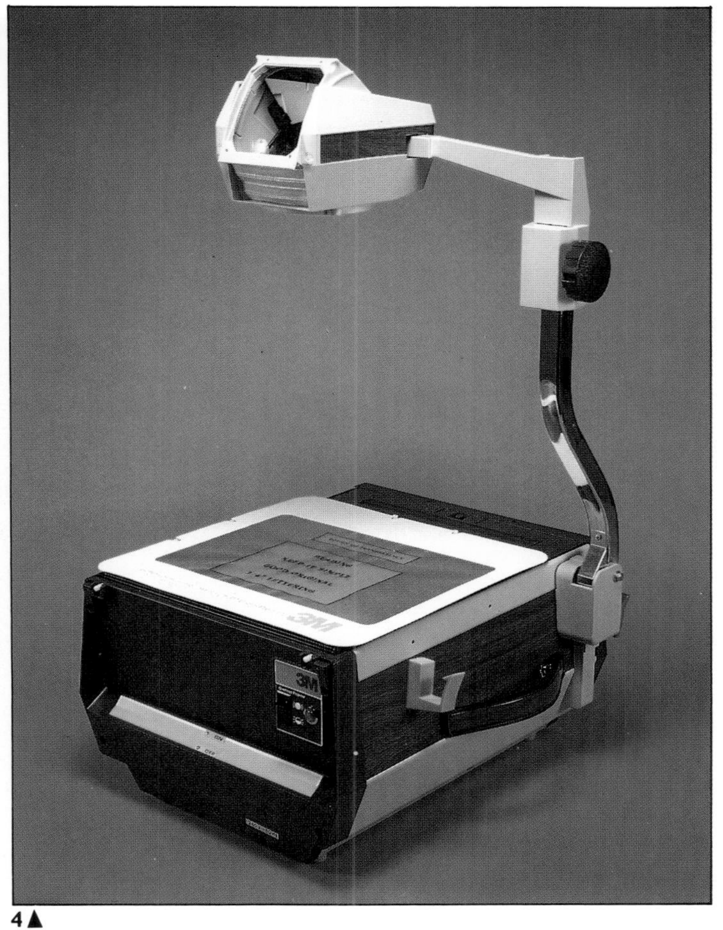

4▲

**3**.,**4**. An **overhead projector** is useful for presentations as you can place transparencies and your own visuals on the machine and make alterations as you go along. Many are portable and some have external color timing.

5▲

6▲

**5**.,**6**. **Camera Lucidas**, although rather large, are the easiest way to scale photographs, typography or any image for artwork up or down. The handles adjust the size and focus and you trace the image off the top sheet of glass using tracing paper. Most enlargers have a light box fitted into the base for tracing off transparencies. These are the "Grant Dual Purpose" models and they combine the normal functions of a Grant camera with the simplest form of a dark-room process camera.

The two models of photocopier shown on this spread use the latest in microprocessors and fibre optics to combine a wide range of features in a small space. Both will reproduce in red, brown, and blue as well as black, can copy onto a wide range of materials, and are especially convenient for double sided and two-color copying.

The more expensive model will enlarge or reduce copies in 1% stages from 65% to 154%, and can be programmed with your 2 most commonly needed ratios.

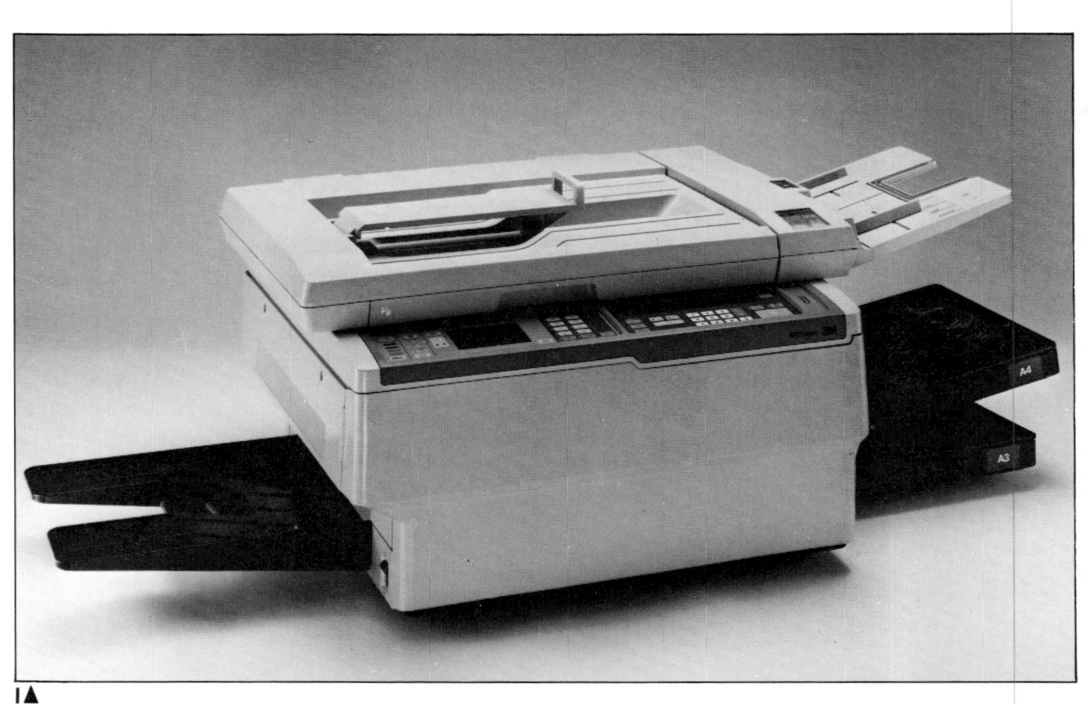

1▲

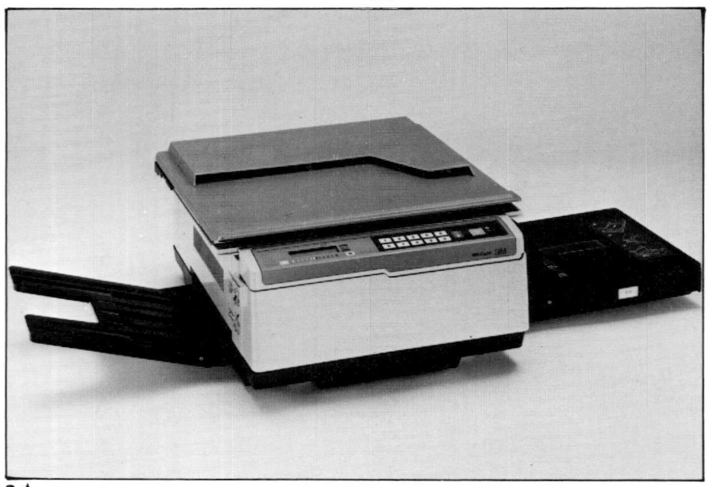

2▲

**1.** The **3M copier** is a high-volume copier that will reproduce to virtually any size and can be pre-programmed with 8 reduction and enlargement settings.

**2.,3.** The more compact **3M 6010 copier** has a pocket for storing originals and is hinged for easy access in case of jams.

3▲

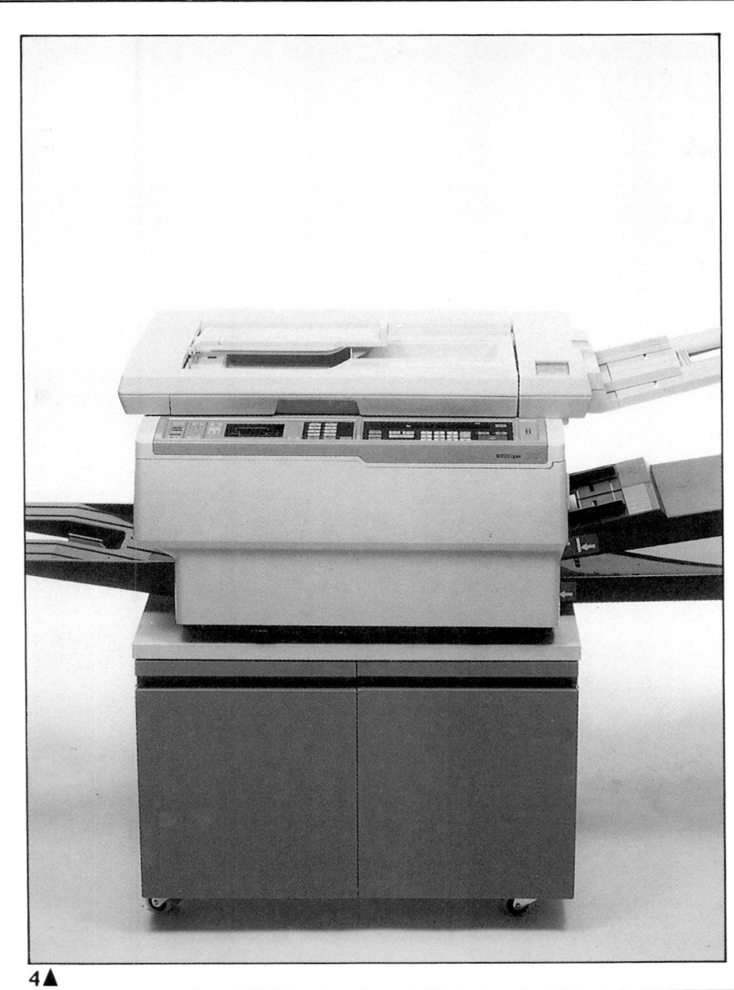

To calculate the enlargement percentage you require, divide the height of the final image (B) by the height of the original (A), and multiply by 100.

4▲

For enlargements over your machine's capacity, multiple enlargements are used. This pencil drawing has been enlarged 400% in 4 stages.

Kodachrome
Kodachrome
MADE IN GT. BRITAIN REXEL CUMBERLAND Derwent Studio
MADE IN GT. BRITAIN REXEL CUMBERLAND Derwent Studio Deep Cadmium 6
Made in Germany
rotring T20
rotring rapidograph ISO
UNIQUE
MADE IN ENGLAND

# THE BASIC SKILLS

# · PREPARATION OF ARTWORK ·

Typography is, fundamentally, the art of fitting words into a given space in a way that is readable, understandable and visually complementary to their content. It is therefore essential for the artist to have an understanding of the two major elements involved in typographic design, which are the varying widths of the alphabetic characters and the spaces between them. Both of these depend largely on the equipment that is used. For example, a manual typewriter produces consistent letter spacing by using wide serifs on letters such as 'i' and 'l'. This reduces the amount of white space, resulting in words of a far more even appearance. Typesetting machines, however, are capable of producing type to practically any specifications. This in turn affords the artist far greater scope to experiment and come up with new ideas.

Graphic artists today require a much greater understanding of the technical aspects of typesetting than they did in the past. New technology is developing rapidly, and the systems can now be operated by people with no typographical knowledge – so the artist has to know the capabilities of the machine and has to keep an eye on the quality of the typeset copy.

The most important factor when asking about a typesetting system is the quality of the characters reproduced on paper or film; how sharp is the image and does the density vary? Below is a list of questions which you should ask about a system, especially if you are thinking of using a particular typesetter for a number of jobs.

- How many fonts are available at any one time and how many characters in each font?
- If it is a CRT machine, what are its distortion capabilities?
- Character positioning – is it possible to select a tighter or looser fit and, if so, by what increments?
- Can characters be kerned automatically?
- Can the machine condense or expand type?
- What pi facilities exist; i.e. what extraneous characters are there which are not normally in a font, like * or &?
- What is the size range of the machine, how true are the type sizes, and what is the complete size mixing ability?
- What is the maximum line length and is it applicable to all sizes? (Check that there is no image distortion across line length.)
- What is the claimed output speed and what is the actual output speed on various kinds of work?
- What is the leading increment?
- Is there any reverse leading? If so, by what increments and how accurate is it?
- What is the galley output?
- What is the consistency of image on all sizes?

This spread involves full color, so the artist will mark exactly on the board where all the illustrations and images will appear. This is what the platemaker will use as his guide. An overlay of plastic film is secured over the board and registration marks are made. Registration marks show how each overlay fits together with the base artwork, and they enable you to re-align the overlay if you move it for any reason. The overlay will hold everything that is to be printed black. PMTs are taken of all the type, line drawings, headings, etc. and pasted down using rubber cement, which will not cockle the paper. When pasting up finished artwork, always start at the top and work down. You will stand more chance of keeping your work clean if you are not leaning across the sections you have already pasted down.

Black and white artwork can be made to appear in four-color by the use of mechanical tints which are laid by the printer or origination house. These can be selected from a process color tint chart since they can be specified as combinations of specially mixed colors. These areas can be pre-

·QDOS

·QDOS

WHAT

THE EMPHASIS ON design in corporate communications is greater today than ever before.

Companies now need to communicate to a variety of audiences. Institutions, shareholders, trading partners, employees and the media must all be reached effectively and economically. Good design plays a vital part in this process.

All too often, however, what passes today for sophisticated design fails to deliver a discernible benefit for the client. Corporate design and presentation go far beyond visual impact for its own sake, rather they have to convey the substance of a message in a way that enhances its meaning and resonance and relates to market needs.

**An individual stamp** Imaginative design can and should be as effective a means of communication as the more traditional expressions of a company's performance such as the review of operations or even the figures in the balance sheet.

Above all, it should animate a company's strengths, performance and objectives so that they lodge securely in the minds of all those vital target audiences.

Such an undertaking requires marketing insight; the skills required to bring to life complex information; the ability to orchestrate and follow through large projects; and the flair to place an individual stamp on contenders in a crowded marketplace.

The team at QDOS offers all these qualities and our past performance is confirmation of our ability to deliver.

Only marketing skills of the first rank could have carved out a large and profitable market for Quarto in the highly competitive international illustrated book market.

**Visual information** The presentation of complex material in a striking, visual form was the key quality of QED, beginning with the still famous *Sunday Times Facts of Life* series in 1975. Winner of The Designers' and Art Directors' Association Silver Award, QED's graphics were hailed as a breakthrough for their depiction of the human brain and body in an accessible, accurate, detailed and attractive way.

This was among the first of many such assignments. Our *Radio Times* and *Sunday Times Magazine* covers combined explanation with impact. We broke new ground with the *Macdonald Guidelines* series of books by portraying industrial and commercial processes in a way that could be absorbed and understood immediately.

A further boost to our ability to tackle complex information visually, and one that answers a need for many companies, came with our purchase of *Geographical Projects*: a complete library of relief maps encompassing the whole world, oceans, seabeds and land masses, which enables us to depict geographical information with unique accuracy. Our relief maps for the *Reader's Digest Great World Atlas*, for example, were produced from this source.

**Seeing projects through** The experience we have gained in seeing through major international book projects has taught us how to initiate and realise workable concepts and, through tight control of all the elements in production, bring them in on time, on budget and to the highest creative standards. Our recent win of the *Times Educational Supplement* Information Book Award is testimony to this ability.

All our products carry an individual stamp, for example our work for a discriminating and professional client such as The English Tourist Board, for whom we devised and produced *Let's Go* magazine and the successful *Mini-Guide* series as well as a series of holiday brochures. Our own publications such as *The Complete Guide to Illustration and Design*, *The Design Source Book* and the best selling *New Classic Cuis*… winner of the Glenfiddic… book award, by the celebrated Roux brothe… are equally distinguish… *New Classic Cuisine* is… another example of h… make the hitherto ren… and accessible. The a… of *Le Gavroche* and … Michelin's top-rated … be associated only … matched their own…

**Design a…** from the… portfoli… commu… recentl… *to Adv…* practi… desig… some authority… independent d… be placed on t… Our expertise as outstanding desig… have the experience of running a large company is the first and major benefit that QDOS has to offer to its clients.

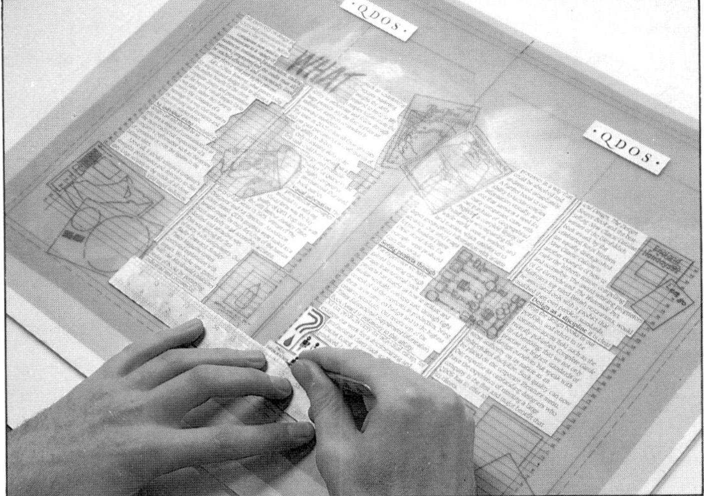



pared either with one overlay, with keylines defining each area to be tinted, or by using a different overlay for each combination. The first is more convenient but more expensive since it involves a considerable amount of handwork at the origination stage.

Here we see how the finished artwork translates to a printed page.

Marking up copy for the typesetter involves specifying the fonts and the general style of the type. The exact words, headings or paragraphs to be italicized, set in a bold face, or different size must be clearly indicated. These instructions should be attached to the copy as a permanent reference. If the instructions are complicated and become too dense to follow, use a coding system of letters or numbers and key them into a master style sheet.

Try to confine the type mark-up to the manuscript and the layout instructions to the layout – there will be more than one operator keying in the copy and a completely different team of people will do the page make-up.

Numbers can either be non-aligning or aligning. Non-aligning numbers are small with ascenders and descenders; aligning numbers are same size and align on the base line. It is best to specify which you want as in many fonts there is a choice available.

1234567890
1234567890

The x-height of small caps is the same as that of lower case characters. Designed small caps are of even weight. Photographically reduced small caps tend to look lighter when set with normal type.

Designed SMALL CAPS
Reduced SMALL CAPS
A variation on SMALL CAPS

When two or more characters are joined and set as a single unit they are termed ligatures. Common examples are ff, fi, fl and ffl. They should not be used when letterspacing is tight, as the result may look gappy.

fi fl ff ffi ffl
*fi fl ff ffi ffl*

**The form typography is to take**
**The form typography is to take**
**The form typography is to take**
**The form typography is to take**
**The form typography is to take**
1▲

VAULT VAULT

AT AY AV AW Ay Av Aw
FA TO TA Ta Te To Ti
Tr Tu Ty Tw Ts Tc LT
LY LV LW Ly PA VA Va
Ve Vo Vi Vr Vu Vy RT
RV RW RY Ry WA Wa We
Wo Wi Wr Wu Wy YA Ya
Ye Yo Yi Yp Yq Yu Yv
2▲

12pt 11.75pt 11.5pt 11.25pt 11pt 10.75pt
10.5pt 10.25pt 10pt 9.75pt 9.5pt 9.25pt
9pt 8.75pt 8.5pt 8.25pt 8pt 7.75pt
7.5pt 7.25pt 7pt 6.75pt 6.5pt 6.25pt
6pt 5.75pt 5.5pt 5.25pt 5pt 4.75pt
4.5pt 4.25pt 4pt 3.75pt 3.5pt 3.25pt
3pt 2.75pt 2.5pt 2.25pt 2pt 1 75pt
1.5pt 1.25pt 1pt 0.75pt 0.5pt 0.25pt
Broken
3 point shaded or total
3▲

**1**. Letterspacing is the space between letters, which can be adjusted depending on the artist's requirements. The type of spacing required is normally specified as normal, loose, tight and very tight. In phototypesetting, these instructions are translated into units or half units, depending on the system.

**2**. When the spacing between specified characters is deliberately reduced, leaving the rest of the setting the same, the result is called kerning. The technique is frequently used with certain letter combinations, such as Yo, Te, Ly and la. When these are set, there is often too much space between them, compared to the rest of the setting. Kerning solves this problem.

**3**. Rules can be used to help visual organization by providing form and structure; they can also provide a sense of character for what would otherwise be straight type. In common with line spacing, rules are defined in points or fractions of a point. Some also have names – a ¼-point rule is usually referred to as a hairline rule, while a ½-point rule is a fine rule. Lengths are normally specified in picas.

When using rules, there are two important points to remember. Firstly, specify the spacing required below and above them. Secondly, when continuous rules have been specified, check proofs carefully for breaks and jaggedness.

| Instruction to printer | Textual mark | Marginal mark |
|---|---|---|
| Correction is concluded | none | |
| Leave unchanged | typeface groups | STET |
| Remove unwanted marks | typeface groups | × |
| Push down risen spacing material | typeface groups | lower |
| Refer to appropriate authority | typeface groups | ? |
| Insert new material | groups | typeface |
| Insert additional material | typgroups | A |
| Delete | typeface groups | |
| Delete and close up | typeface groups | |
| Substitute character or part of one or more words | tpeface grops | y u |
| Wrong font replace with correct font | typeface groups | wf/fix |
| Correct damaged characters | typeface groups | × |
| Transpose characters or word | groups typeface | tr. |
| Transpose characters (2) | yptface groups | tr. |
| Transpose lines | the dimension of is disastrous when | tr. |
| Transpose lines (2) | the dimension of is disastrous when | tr. |
| Center type | typeface groups | center |
| Indent 1 em | typeface groups | indent 1em |
| Delete indent | tyepface groups | flush left |
| Set line justified | typeface groups | Justify |
| Set column justified | | Justify col |
| Move matter to right | typeface groups | ] |
| Move matter to left | typeface groups | [ |
| Take down to next line | Typeface groups | break |
| Take back to previous line | typeface groups | move up |
| Raise matter | typeface groups | |
| Lower matter | typeface groups | |
| Correct vertical alignment | typeface groups | ‖ |
| Correct horizontal alignment | typeface groups | Align |
| Close up space | t ypeface groups | |
| Insert space between words | typefacegroups | # |
| Reduce space between words | typeface groups | reduce # |
| Reduce or insert space between letters | ty pe face groups | # |
| Make space appear equal | typeface groups | equal # |

| Instruction to printer | Textual mark | Marginal mark |
|---|---|---|
| Close up to normal line spacing | typeface groups | normal #ing |
| Insert space between paragraphs | aerobic movement The dimensions of | # |
| Reduce space between paragraphs | aerobic movement The dimensions of | reduce # |
| Insert parentheses or brackets | (typeface groups) | ( ) or [ ] |
| Figure or abbreviation to be spelled out in full | 12 point twelve pt | sp. out |
| Move matter to position indicated | are called the set points dimension | tr. |
| Set in or change to italics | typeface groups | ital |
| Set in or change to capitals | typeface groups | CAP |
| Set in or change to small capitals | typeface groups | SC |
| Capitals for initials small caps for rest of word | typeface groups | cap + SC |
| Set in or change to bold type | typeface groups | bf |
| Set in or change to bold italic type | typeface groups | bf + ital |
| Change capitals to lower case | typeFACE groups | lc |
| Change small capitals to lower case | tyepface GROUPS | lc |
| Change italics to roman | typeface groups | rom |
| Invert type | typeface groups | 9 |
| Insert ligature | fimsetter | fi |
| Substitute separate letters for ligature | fimsetter | fi |
| Insert period | typeface groups | ⊙ |
| Insert colon | typeface groups: | : |
| Insert semicolon | typeface groups; | ; |
| Insert comma | typeface groups, | , |
| Insert quotation marks | "typeface groups" | " / " |
| Insert single quotation marks | 'typeface groups' | ' / ' |
| Substitute character in superior position | typeface groups | sup |
| Substitute character in inferior position | typeface groups | sub |
| Insert apostrophe | typeface groups' | ' |
| Insert ellipses | typeface groups . . . | . . . |
| Insert leader dots | . . . typeface groups | |
| Substitute or insert hyphen | typeface groups | = |
| Insert rule | typeface groups | 2pt rule |
| Insert virgule | typeface groups | / |
| Start new paragraph | are called points The question is | ¶ |
| New paragraph run in | are called points The question is | no ¶ |

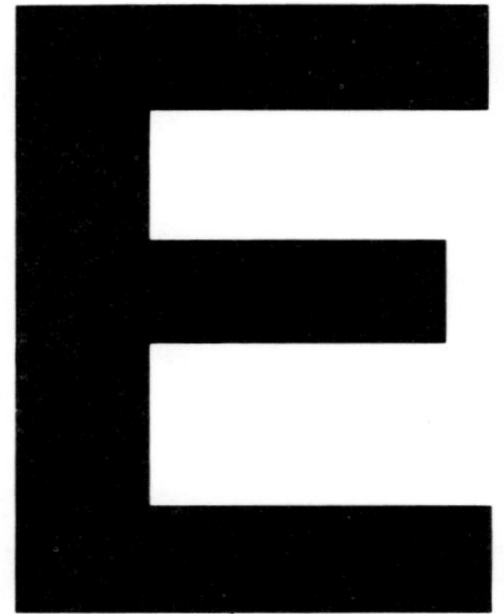

These are examples of a serif typeface *(above left)* and a sans serif typeface *(above right)*. Sans serif type is more legible in smaller sizes and so is often used for text setting. The serif typeface is most often used for display headlines.

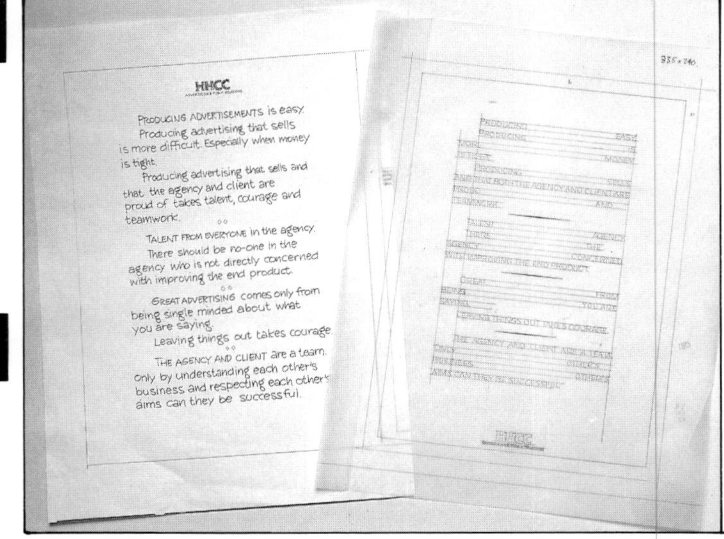

Typesetting is always expensive, so the artist decided to write the copy out in full, following the same style as the chosen typeface to check that the design worked. Once satisfied, he drew up an accurate layout was drawn up for the typesetter to follow. This is done by drawing the page and indicating the x-height of the type with parallel lines. The type is flush left but indented at the start of a paragraph, so these two points of alignment were also shown. The artist is determined to avoid any mistakes in the type-setting, so the first few words of a line and the last word are penciled in.

PRODUCING ADVERTISEMENTS IS EASY.
PRODUCING ADVERTISING THAT SELLS IS MORE DIFFICULT. ESPECIALLY WHEN MONEY IS TIGHT.
PRODUCING ADVERTISING THAT SELLS AND THAT BOTH THE AGENCY AND CLIENT ARE PROUD OF, TAKES TALENT, COURAGE AND TEAMWORK.

TALENT FROM EVERYONE IN THE AGENCY.
THERE SHOULD BE NO-ONE IN THE AGENCY WHO IS NOT DIRECTLY CONCERNED WITH IMPROVING THE END PRODUCT.

GREAT ADVERTISING COMES ONLY FROM BEING SINGLE-MINDED ABOUT WHAT YOU ARE SAYING.
LEAVING THINGS OUT TAKES COURAGE.

THE AGENCY AND CLIENT ARE A TEAM. ONLY BY UNDERSTANDING EACH OTHER'S BUSINESS AND RESPECTING EACH OTHER'S AIMS CAN THEY BE SUCCESSFUL.

HHCC

DECORATIVE RULES

*A way of separating paragraphs to make them individual features and add more interest to the page. Typesetters always hold a stock, but they are also available in Letraset.*

WORD SPACING

*Adds importance to words by turning them into individually considered units through wider spacing.*

INITIAL CAPS

*Used to attract the attention of the reader, thereby directing the eye to the information.*

Producing advertising is easy. ¶Producing advertising that sells is more difficult. Especially when money is tight. ¶Producing the kind of advertising that sells and that the agency and client are proud of takes talent, courage and teamwork. ¶Talent from everyone in the agency. ¶There should be no-one in the agency who is not directly concerned with improving the end product. ¶Great advertising comes only from being single minded about what you are saying. ¶Leaving things out takes courage. ¶The agency and client are a team. Only by understanding each other's business and respecting each other's aims can they be successful. HHCC

tising c / minde / ¶Leav / ¶The / Only b / busines / aims c

tising con / minded a / ¶Leaving / ¶The age / Only by u / business a / aims can t

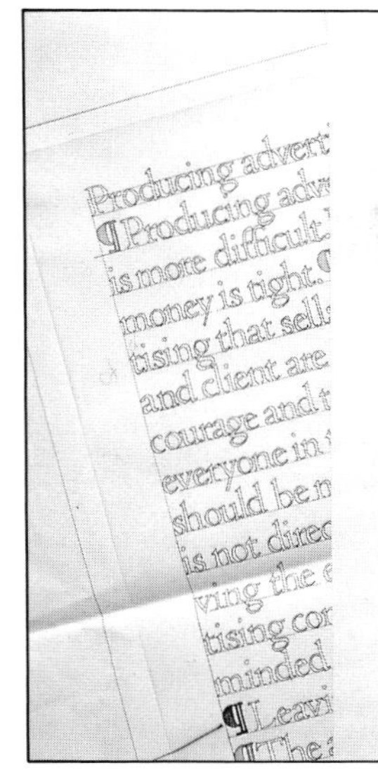

Producing advertisements is easy. ¶Producing advertising that sells is more difficult. Especially when money is tight. ¶Producing the kind of advertising that sells and that the agency and client are proud of takes talent, courage and teamwork. ¶Talent from everyone in the agency. ¶There should be no-one in the agency who is not directly concerned with improving the end product. ¶Great advertising comes only from being single-minded about what you are saying. ¶Leaving things out takes courage. ¶The agency and client are a team. Only by understanding each other's business and respecting each other's aims can they be successful.

This demonstrates how changing the typographical approach to the same piece of copy can create a totally different visual image and mood.

¶Producing advertisements is easy. ¶Producing advertising that sells is more difficult. ¶Producing the kind of advertising that sells and that the agency and client are proud of, takes talent, courage and teamwork. Talent from everyone in the agency. ¶There should be no-one in the agency who isn't directly concerned with improving the end product. ¶Great advertising comes only from being single-minded about what you are saying. ¶Leaving things out takes courage. ¶The agency and client are a team. Only by understanding each other's business and respecting each other's aims can they be successful. **HHCC**

HYPHENS AND DASHES

*Offers the eye a "breathing space" and prevents all the words running into each other. Here they have been used to mark the beginning of a new sentence and emphasized further by pulling them out in a second color.*

DECORATIVE DEVICES

*In justified setting they are a very good way to complete the line length, but here the choice of an unconventional angled style has added extra visual interest.*

WORD BREAKS

*In a solid block of type it is virtually impossible to avoid word breaks. However, the words must be broken logically, and it is important that one-word widows are avoided, i.e., a single word standing as the last line of a paragraph. Here again, a decorative style was chosen to enhance the manuscript.*

Preparing camera-ready artwork requires a great deal of care and attention to detail. Any imperfections or specks of dirt will be picked up by the camera during plate-making and will, in turn, reproduce in printing, so remember to keep your artwork clean. Before pasting onto the board dust the surface with a soft brush and even if you only have to leave the artwork unattended for a few minutes always cover it.

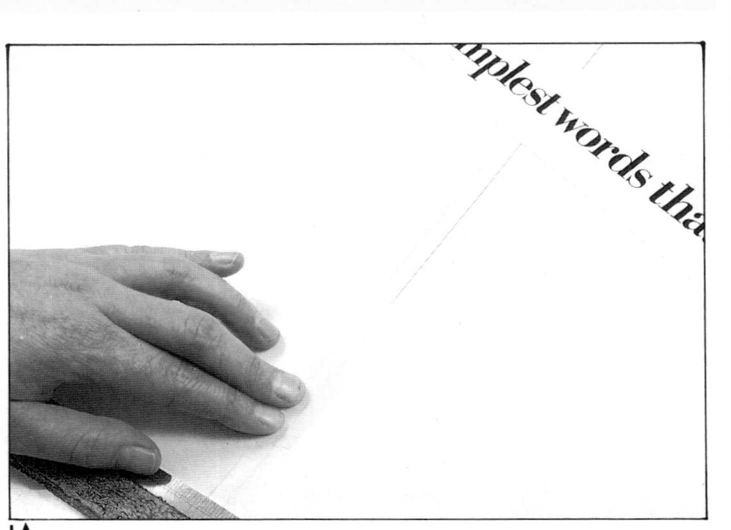


1▲

2▲

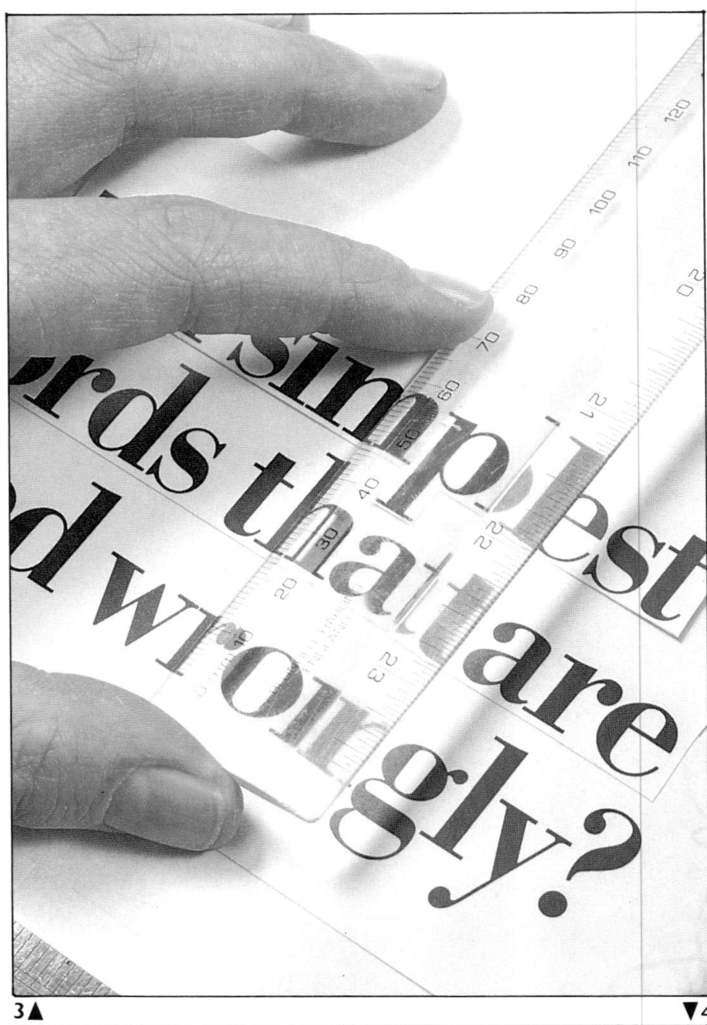


3▲

▼4

**1.,2.,3.,4.** The headline has been set in a single strip, so it will have to be cut and positioned by the artist. The strip is divided into four before it is trimmed. When doing this always place the ruler on top of the image so if your cutting hand should slip you cut into the waste. The descenders are cut around closely as they will have to drop below the cap height of the line below – in this particular case it is easier to work from the bottom up.

**5.,6.,7.** On trying to centre the top line a spacing error is discovered in the line below which caused the descender of the 'y' to clash with the ascender of the 'h'. The 'h' is cut out with a scalpel and moved very slightly towards the centre. Now that it all fits a PMT is taken and pasted onto a piece of board. Check that the PMT is clean and if there are any specks remove them by applying a drop of water (with a small brush) to the blemish and after a few seconds gently scrape it off with a scalpel. It will come away easily without damaging the surface of the paper. Place a sheet of tracing paper over the artwork and give the whole area a final burnish.

5▲

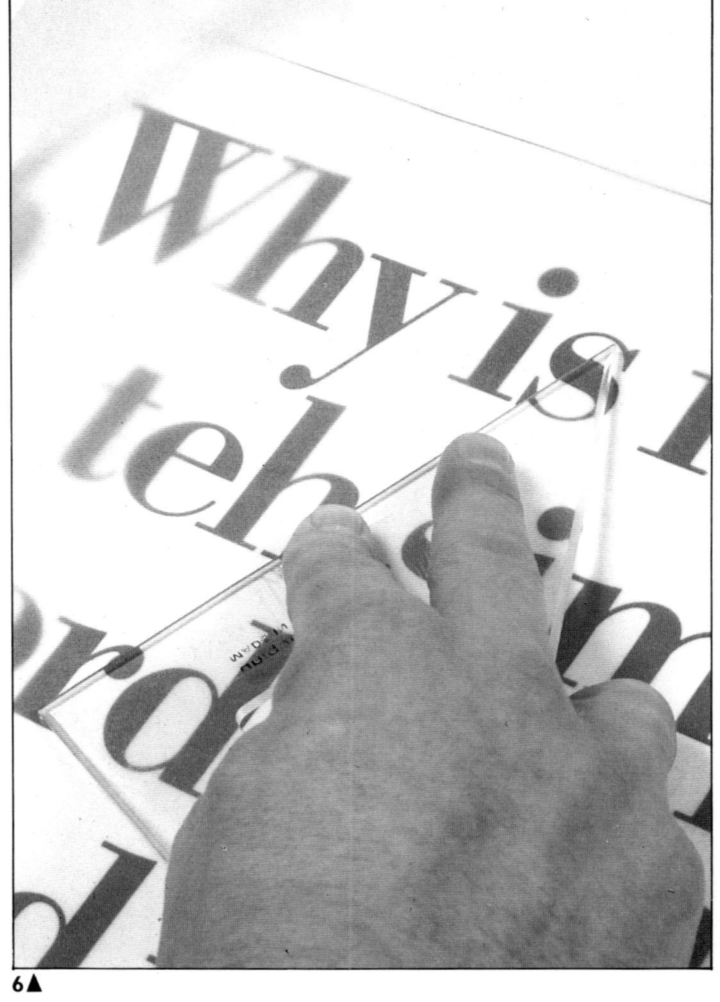

6▲

## CURVED HEADLINES AND CIRCLES

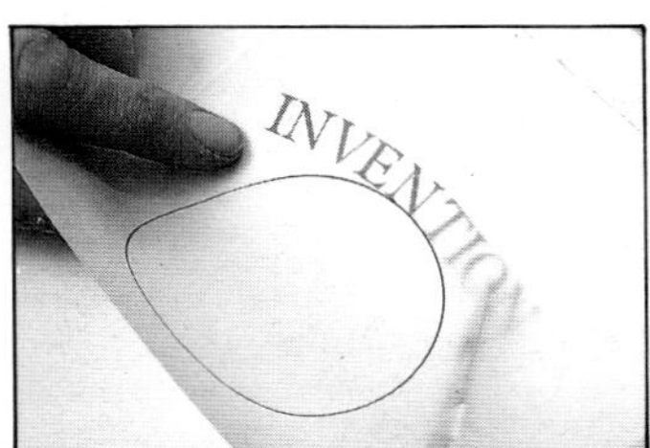

Take the strip of setting and apply adhesive to the back as it is going to be cut several times and so will need to stay secure. Cut down between each letter, leaving them joined at the bottom edge. Move the strip onto the board and attach an overlay with the drawn curve, which will act as the guide over the board. The bottom edge is cut through as each letter is teased into position. When complete a PMT can be made for the finished art.

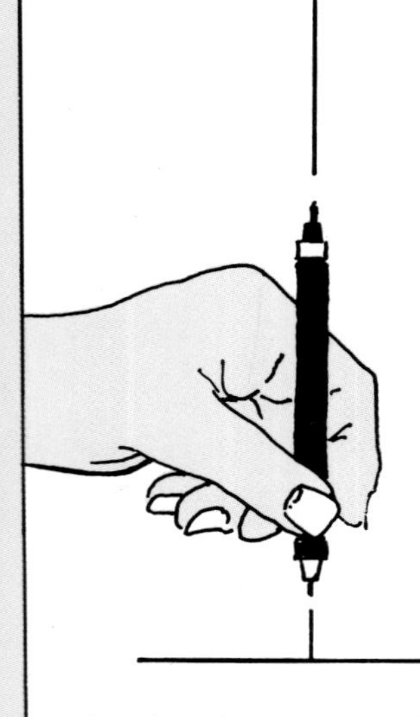

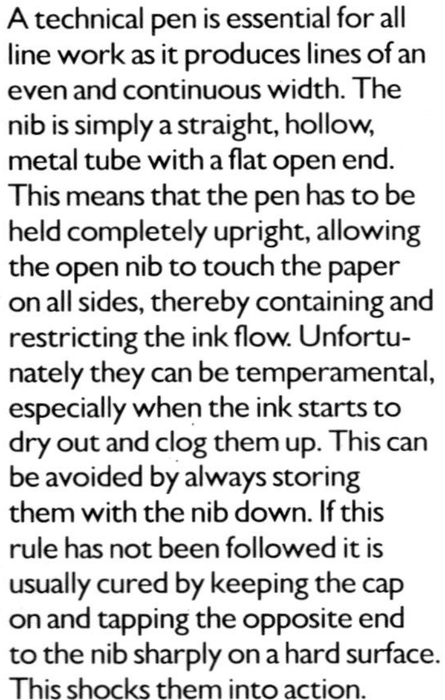

A technical pen is essential for all line work as it produces lines of an even and continuous width. The nib is simply a straight, hollow, metal tube with a flat open end. This means that the pen has to be held completely upright, allowing the open nib to touch the paper on all sides, thereby containing and restricting the ink flow. Unfortunately they can be temperamental, especially when the ink starts to dry out and clog them up. This can be avoided by always storing them with the nib down. If this rule has not been followed it is usually cured by keeping the cap on and tapping the opposite end to the nib sharply on a hard surface. This shocks them into action.

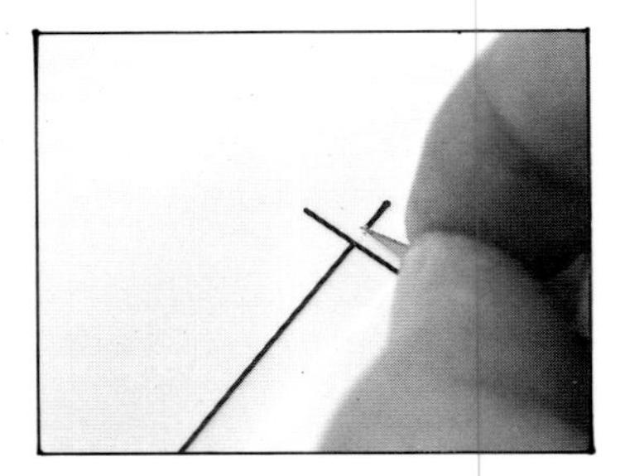

**REPEAT LAYOUTS FOR ARTWORK**

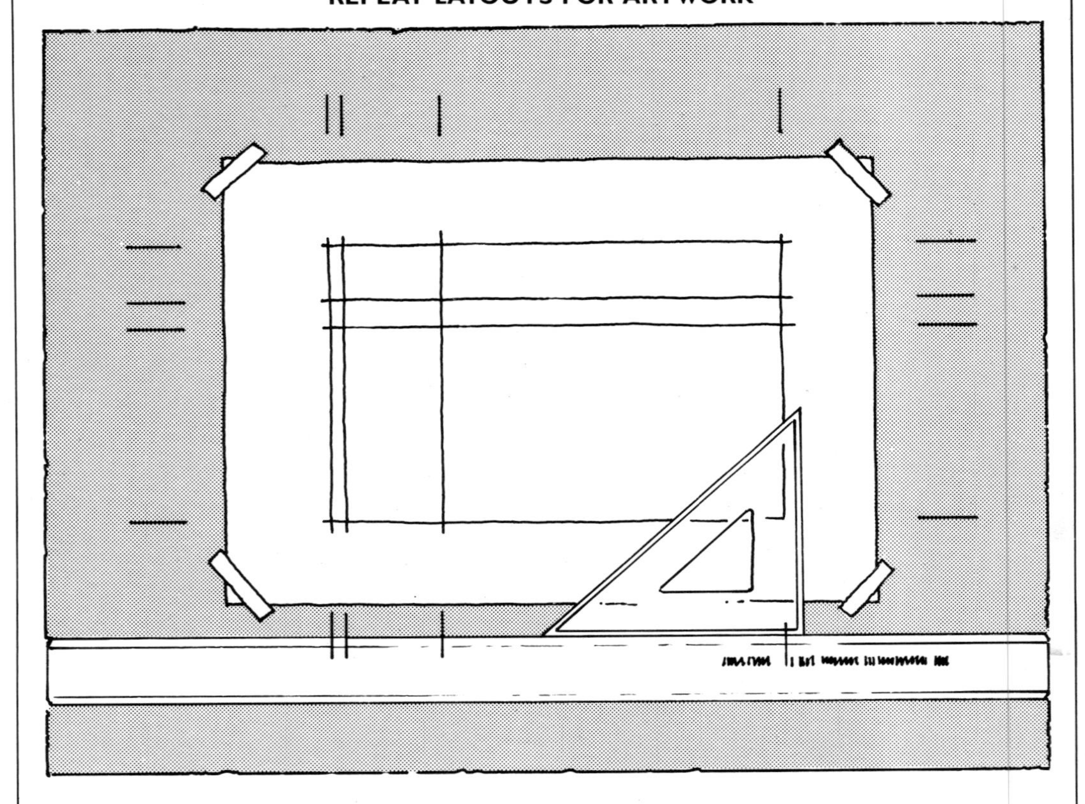

The three pictures at the top of the page show how to achieve a neat square edge when drawing a box rule by extending the lines beyond the point at which they meet, then scraping the overlap back with a scalpel.

*Above:* When working with repeat layouts, to save time and avoid having to measure each one individually, mark up your drawing board. Attach the layout to the board and with a T-square and set square extend the lines past the edges onto the board. Mark the corners, then remove the layout, replacing it with your clean sheet. Draw the layout onto this by simply following the lines on the board.

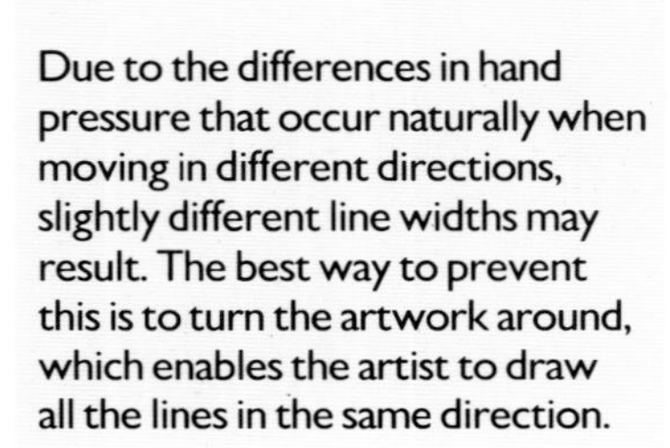

Due to the differences in hand pressure that occur naturally when moving in different directions, slightly different line widths may result. The best way to prevent this is to turn the artwork around, which enables the artist to draw all the lines in the same direction.

In the preparation of camera-ready artwork always follow this sequence of assembly.

**1**. Separate all the individual components.

**2**. Secure the layout guide over the board.

**3**. Position all the larger and most straightforward components first.

**4**. Drop in the illustrations.

**5**. Finally add all the small details.

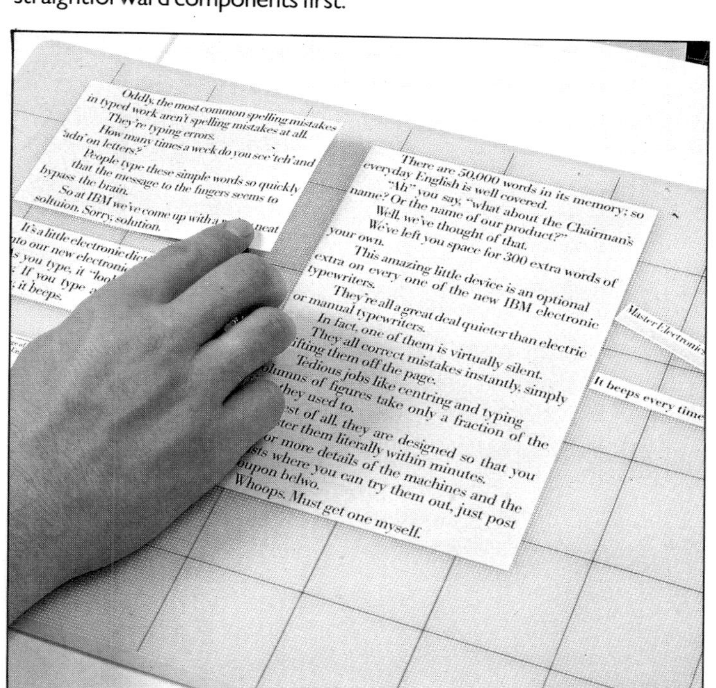


1▲

3▲

4▲

▼2

▼5

## PROTECTIVE OVERLAYS

Always protect your work, whether it is a rough or finished art, with two overlays – a transparent one first, to note any changes at the rough stage or instructions to the printer on finished art, and an outer cover for extra protection. It is worth using attractive, colored paper as neatly presented work shows professionalism. It is also useful to have a form, with the name and date of the presentation and a space for the client to sign when the job has been approved. This saves any arguments at a later stage.

**1.,2.,3.,4.,5.** To protect and present your artwork secure the two overlays at the top with double-sided tape. Place the artwork face down with the top edge parallel to the top edge of the layouts. Cut at a 45° angle from the corner of the artwork to the top edge of the layouts and fold the flap over, securing it with double-sided tape. Finally trim the excess from the other three sides.

3▲

1▲

4▲

▼2

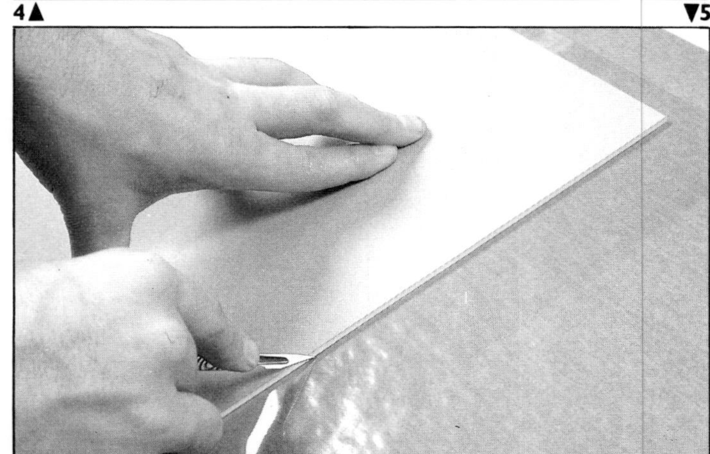

▼5

## CUT-OUT PHOTOGRAPHS

To help the client visualize how effective a cut-out image can be, it is best to make a mask. Using white paint follow the outline of the image and fill in any gaps, such as between the wheel spokes in this example.

**1**. Place a sheet of tracing paper over the image and pencil in the outside outline.
**2**. Remove the trace and secure it in the centre with double-sided tape onto a sheet of cartridge paper.
**3**. Leaving 0.3175mm (⅛in) from the pencil line follow the trace with a scalpel, cutting through both sheets. Always take great care when handling scalpels, but if you should be unlucky and cut a bit of finger off put it in a clean plastic bag packed with ice and take it to the hospital with you.
**4.,5**. Lift out the image area and you now have a mask, which is placed over the original image.

1▲

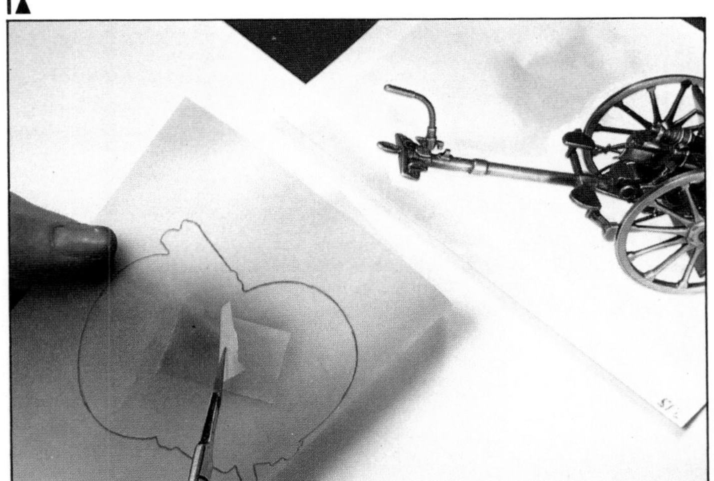

2▲

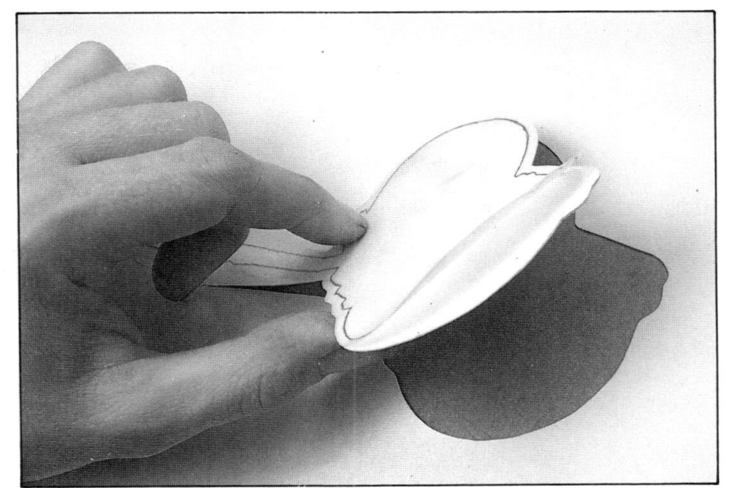

4▲

▼3

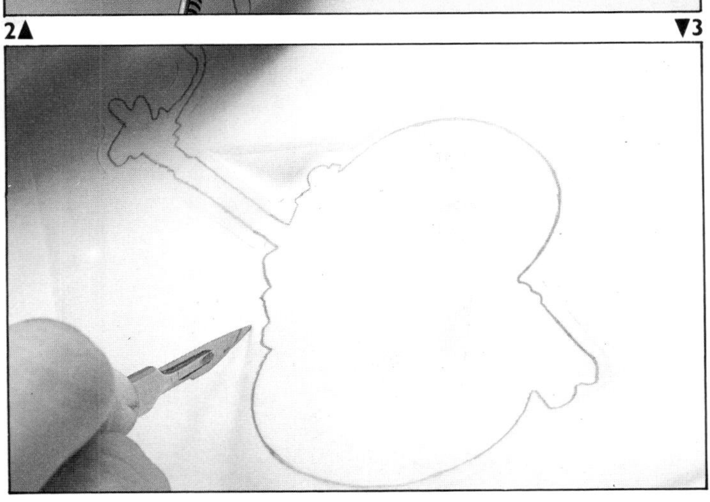

▼5

# · DRAWING & ILLUSTRATION ·

Illustrations are concerned with conveying specific information, are subject to economic demands and yet rely heavily on traditional art skills. It is "commercial art" and although a modern studio will use a specialist for a brief which involves illustration, the graphic artist should be aware of the different techniques and styles as he or she will often be involved in the commissioning.

The main areas of illustration are analytical and descriptive drawing and the demand for technical work is growing. The same basic skills, however, still apply – the ability to observe and to transform what is seen into an accurate two-dimensional representation of the three-dimensional object.

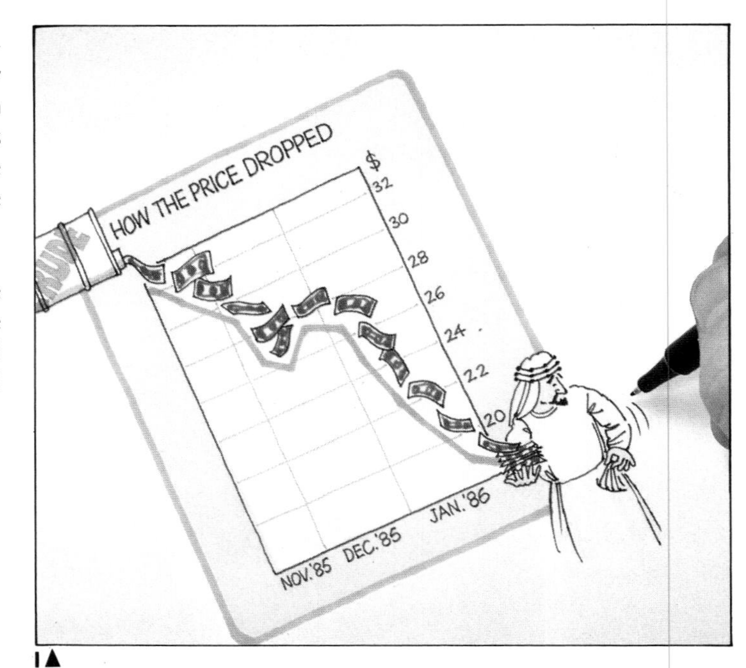


1▲

These examples show different types of illustrations:

**1.** This is a pictogram, a combination of factual detail and illustration which conveys the message in a simple and visual way.

**2.** This is a storyboard for a proposed television commercial.

2▲

3▲

4▲

5▲

**3**. This is a highly finished Magic Marker visual, and **4**. is the printed result.

**5.** This is a full-tone airbrushed illustration of a dumptruck.

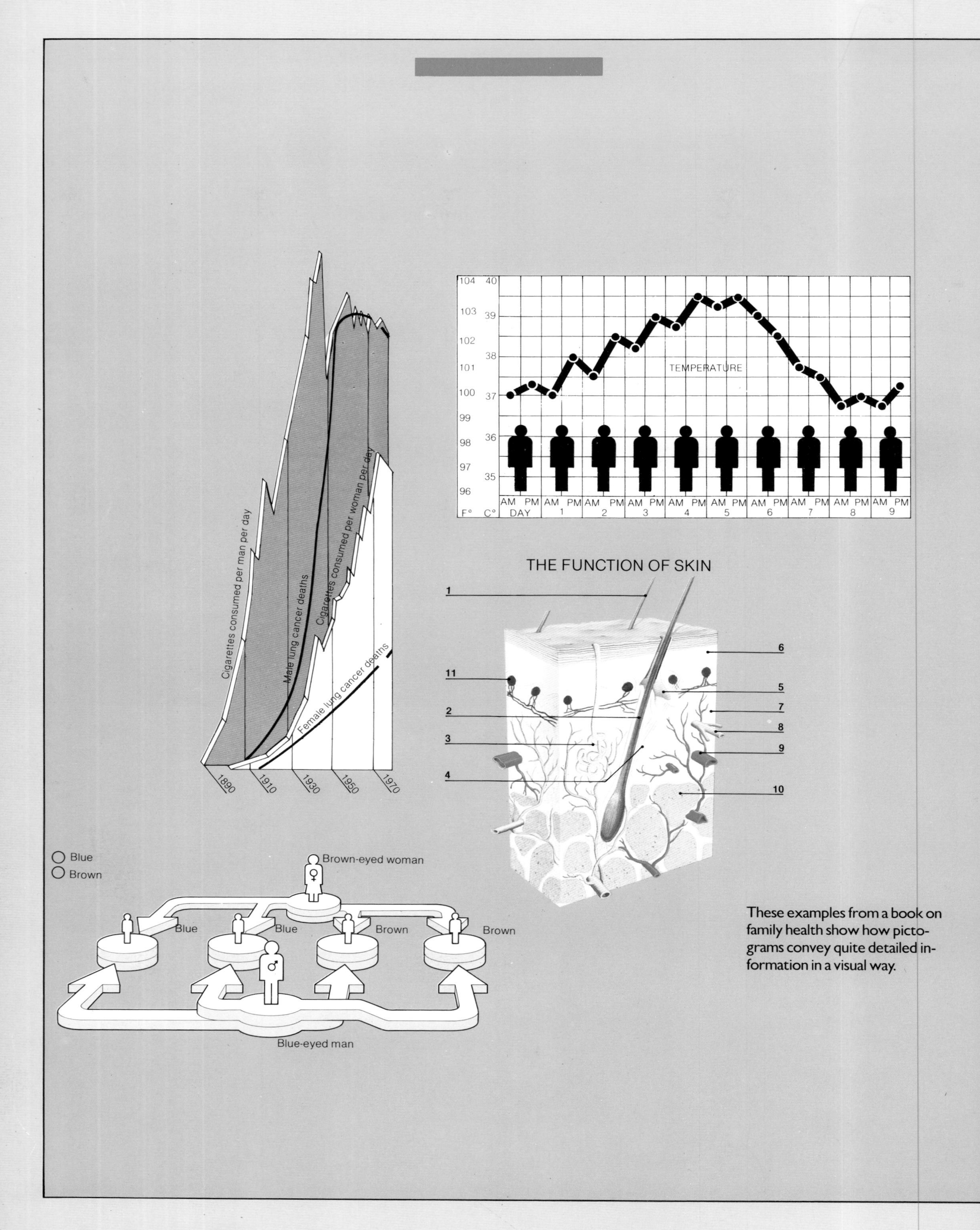


These examples from a book on family health show how pictograms convey quite detailed information in a visual way.

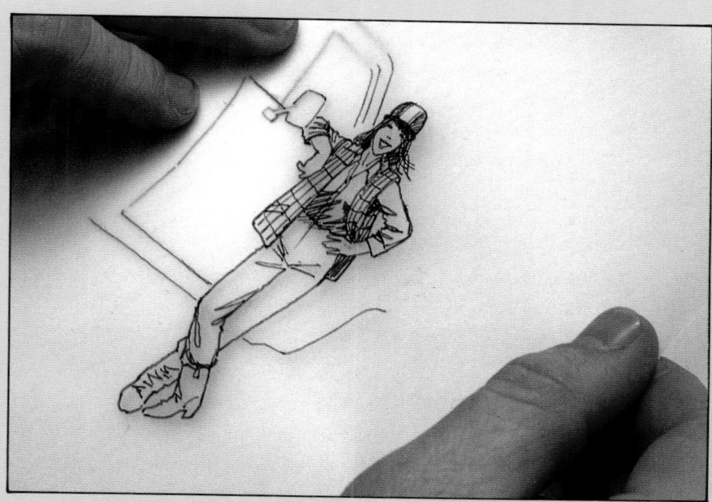

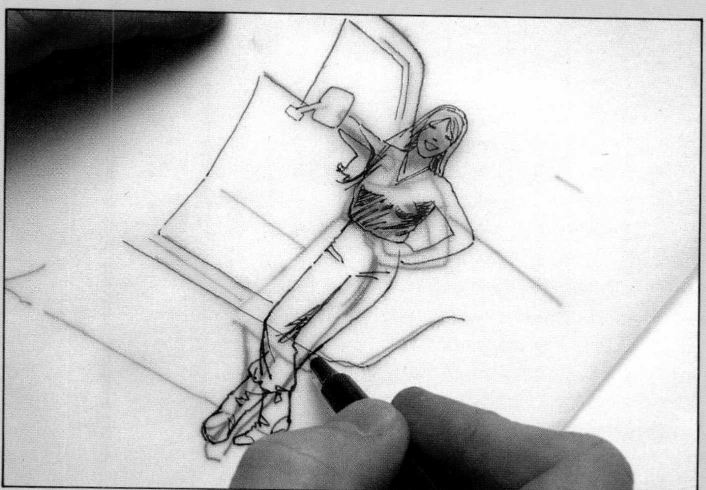

Just as the editor's dictionary is his "bible," a comprehensive reference library is vital to the graphic artist. Start with mail order catalogs for general reference. They will supply endless figures in all positions, different facial expressions and examples of how materials fold and hang, as well as a good range of everyday objects and manufactured goods. Do not just keep a catalog by your side. but break it down logically so that you can find what you want quickly without frantic searching.

Use the alphabet rather than numbers for your reference system, as letters are easier to remember. For example, under "F" you would have faces, which would then be broken down further with craggy, smiling, crying, etc. Apply this method to every file and if you practice a bit of self-discipline and replace it in its correct place after use, the end result will be a very efficient and indispensable working reference library. These pictures show how such material is put to use.

# · GRAPHIC REPRODUCTION ·

The best way to achieve high quality color printing is to provide the printer with the best originals possible. Most printers prefer transparencies, because they can be separated photographically or electronically, they are easy to handle and they can be ganged-up to reduce costs. Remember that it is cheaper if your originals are "in pro", i.e., to be reduced or enlarged by the same percentage and of a similar density, since they can be scanned together.

The only way to get a really good transparency is to work with a good photographer; however, the graphic artist should be aware of which defects are correctable and which are not. Check transparencies carefully and do not retouch them yourself, for the retouching will show on the separations. The best way to overcome the deficiencies is to reshoot the original artwork. Another way is to send the transparencies to the engraver along with a black and white print on which the corrections are marked.

The most important thing to remember is that it is impossible to reproduce the full contrast range of a transparency – you must look at an original knowing that its tonal gradation will be altered during the origination process. A decision to bias the contrast or color will also affect the gray balance – so beware of side effects.

View small transparencies on a color-corrected light box (one which has had its light source balanced to give the correct type of light for viewing color film) with most of the lighted surface masked out by black cardboard. Judgment on the suitability of small transparencies, however, can best be made by projecting them.

It is important to understand the relationship between light and color.
Light contains all the colors of the spectrum. These colors can be broken down into three areas, red, green and blue. These three colors, when projected on top of one another, create white light. If one color is removed, leaving the other two overlapping, then a new color is created – e.g. red and blue with green removed produce magenta, green and blue with red removed produce cyan, and red and green with the blue removed produce yellow.

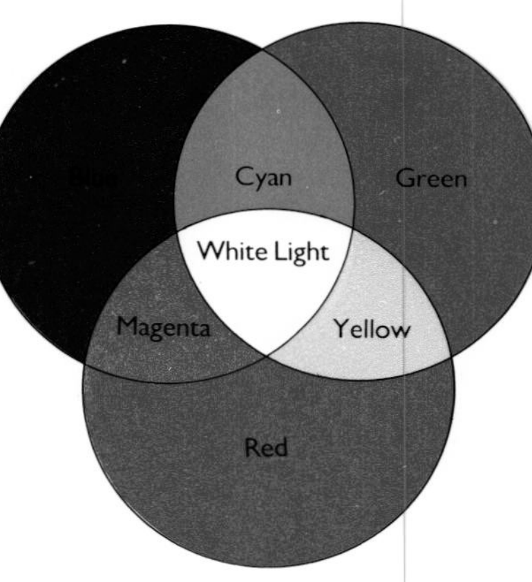


Red, green and blue are called additive primaries because they combine to produce white light. Yellow, magenta and cyan are produced by taking away one of the additive primaries and so are called subtractive primaries.

When two subtractive primaries are added together they create an additive primary: cyan and yellow make green, yellow and magenta make red, and cyan and magenta make blue. The three subtractives together make black.

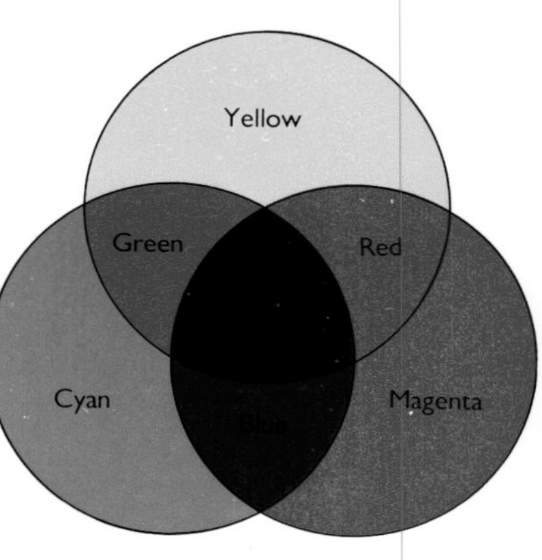


Before an illustration can be sent for origination it must be made to fit the specified area:
**1**. First, square up the picture on a transparent overlay.
**2**. Use the overlay to draw a diagonal line on the layout across the area the picture is intended to fill.
**3**. This shows how much of the picture can fit into the space.
**4**. Mark the layout dimensions on the overlay and shade in the area to be cropped.

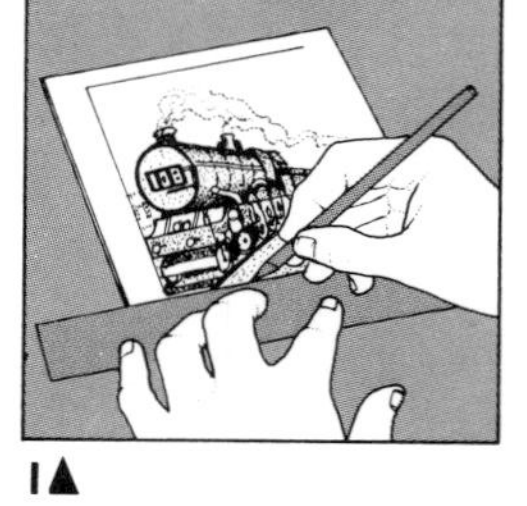

**1▲**

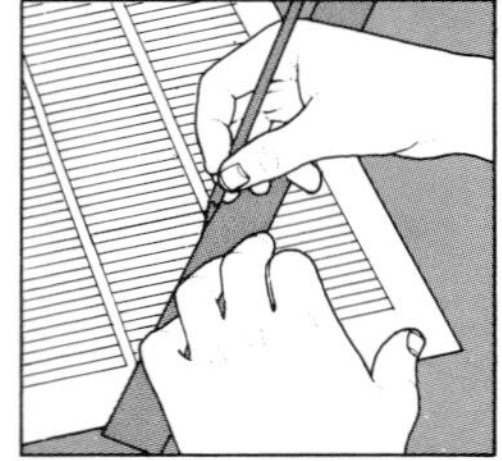

**2▲**

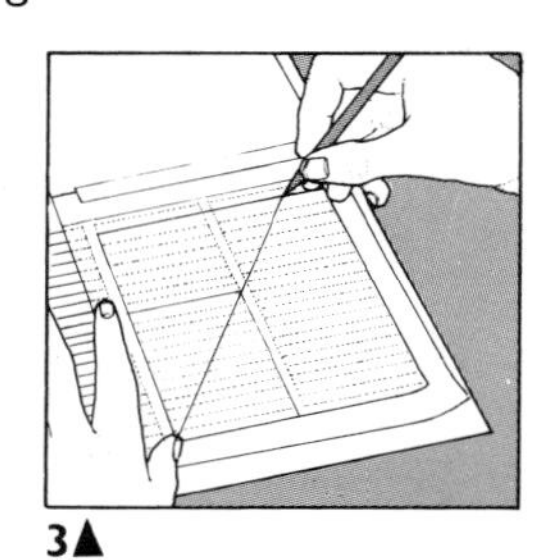

**3▲**

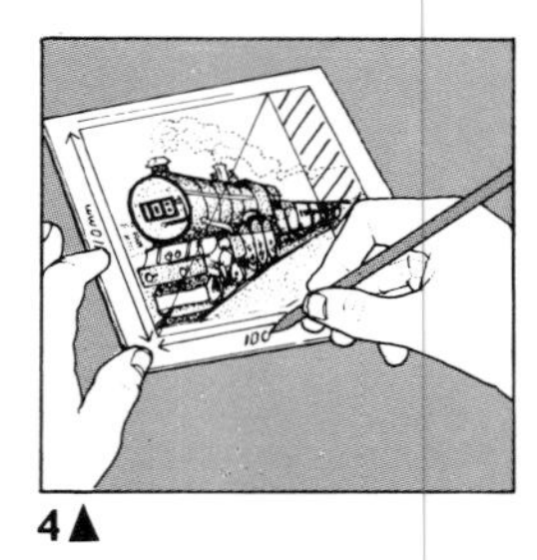

**4▲**

To calculate reproduction percentage

$$\frac{\text{Size of final image}}{\text{Size of original}} \times 100 = \%$$

The percentage of enlargement has to be marked on the overlay for the origination house. Same size is 100 per cent, so a reduction in size from 3″ to 2″ square would mean a reduction of 66%.

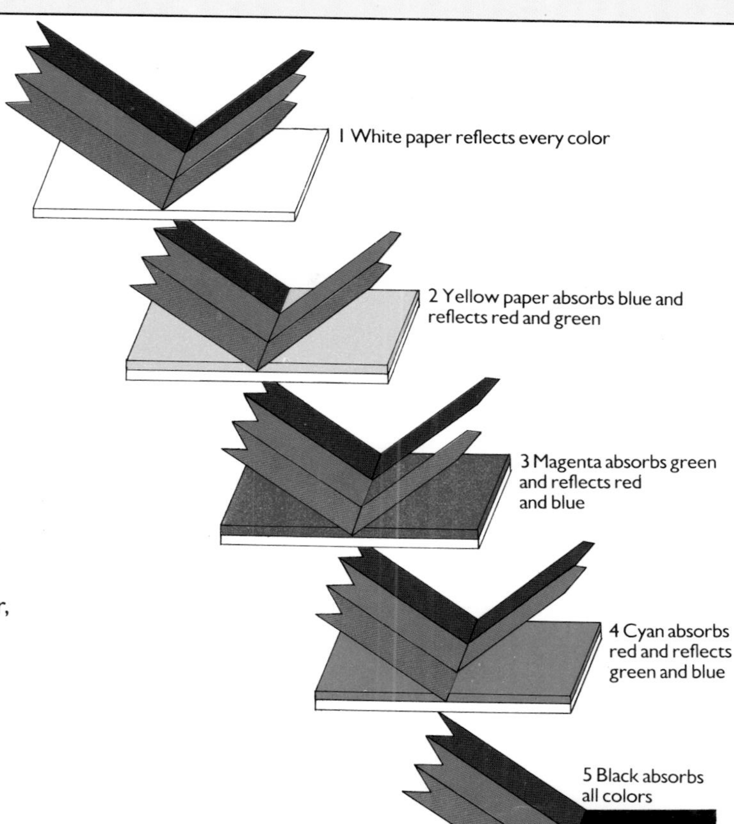


The quality and color of the paper used in printing influences the quality of the color printed on it. Process inks are transparent so that the light that is reflected from the paper's surface supplies light to the ink. Let's look at cyan printed on a sheet of paper as an example. Cyan absorbs red (the color it is not) and allows green and blue to pass through (the color it is). The green and blue reflect off the paper and back up through the ink, so what the eye perceives is cyan. Obviously the brighter and smoother the paper, the more evenly the light will reflect.

Yellow printer negative

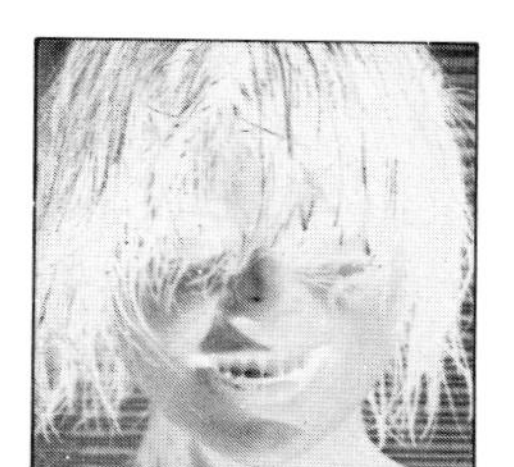
Magenta printer negative

Cyan printer negative

Black printer negative

Yellow proof

Magenta proof

Cyan proof

Black proof

Yellow proof

Yellow plus magenta

Yellow magenta plus cyan

Yellow, magenta, cyan plus black

Using inks in the three subtractive primaries, yellow, magenta and cyan, it is possible to re-create all the colors of the spectrum. In order to do this one must photograph the image three times, through filters of the respective additive colors. For instance, when the image is photographed through the red filter the green and blue are absorbed and a negative recording of the red is produced. By making a positive of this we obtain a record of everything that is not red, i.e., a record of the green and blue – and green and blue combined produce cyan.

Since each filter covers one third of the spectrum, a record is eventually made of all the colors in the original image. Unfortunately in practice printing inks are not "pure" and so absorb other colors. Color corrections must be made on the separations to compensate for the deficiencies in the ink. Black improves the overall contrast and shadow density and is the last color to be added. A black separation is made by using either a yellow filter or a combination of all three filters.

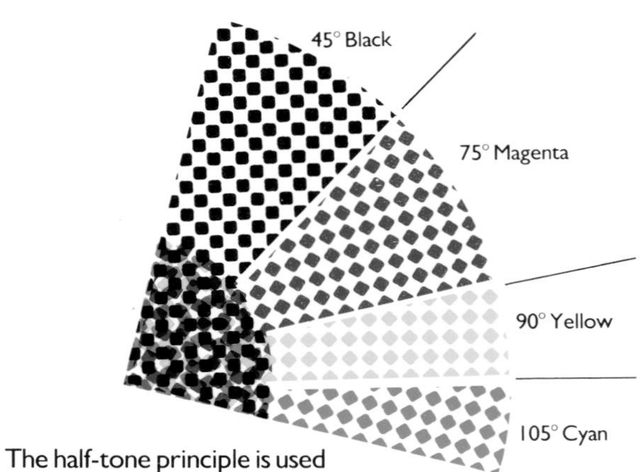


The half-tone principle is used whether color originals are transparencies or "flat-copy." To prevent the screens from clashing and producing a "moiré" effect the screen lines are set at different angles to each other – there are normally 30° between each screen. Making sure that they are all positioned correctly is very important.

The four process colors overlap to give a full-color reproduction of the original image. The dots in this diagram have been greatly enlarged to show how the principle works. At their normal size the individual dots cannot be seen.

Quality control strip
Stripper's color identification
Solid yellow
Magenta overprints yellow
Solid magenta
Cyan overprints magenta
YMCK
120-L
0123456789
starf
40% tints of solid colors
120 line screen colors section
10% tints of solid colors
Originating house identification

This is a color bar, used by the printer for quality control. It is independent from the artwork in hand and so is consistent from job to job. The printer can tell at a glance if the correct amount of ink is being carried on each plate. He can also see printing errors such as dot gain and ink trapping.

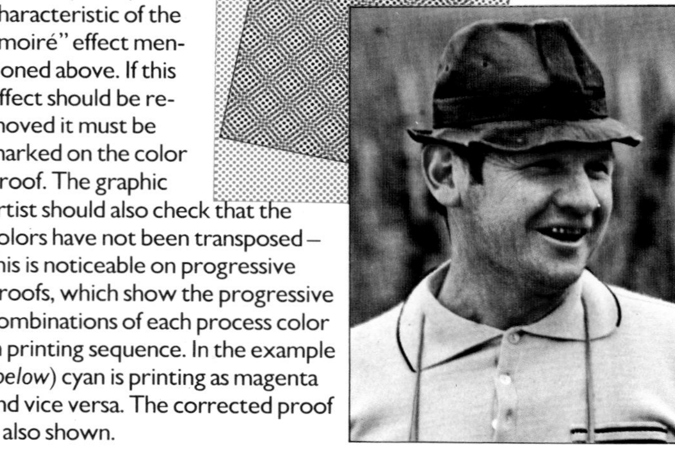

This checkered pattern (*above*) is characteristic of the "moiré" effect mentioned above. If this effect should be removed it must be marked on the color proof. The graphic artist should also check that the colors have not been transposed – this is noticeable on progressive proofs, which show the progressive combinations of each process color in printing sequence. In the example (*below*) cyan is printing as magenta and vice versa. The corrected proof is also shown.

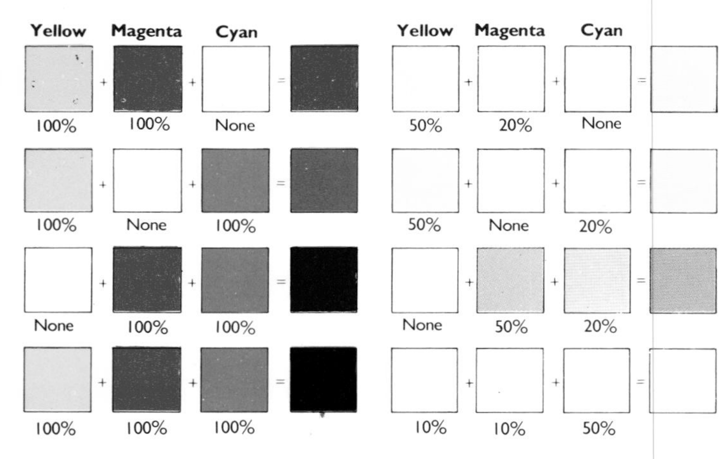


The process colors are mainly used to reproduce full-color, continuous-tone originals, but they can also be used to reproduce black and white line copy in color. Various combinations of tints of the four process colors can be used to approximate any flat color. The total percentage of tints should not exceed 240%, because when using tints, the more ink applied to the paper, the muddier the colors become.

In the first four columns (*above*) a few of the combinations and the colors they produce are shown. The four columns to the right show some of the tints available and the combinations that produced them.

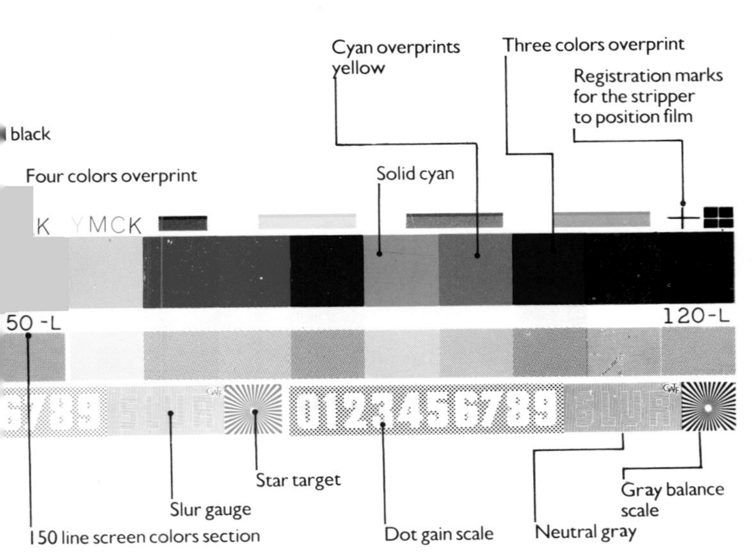


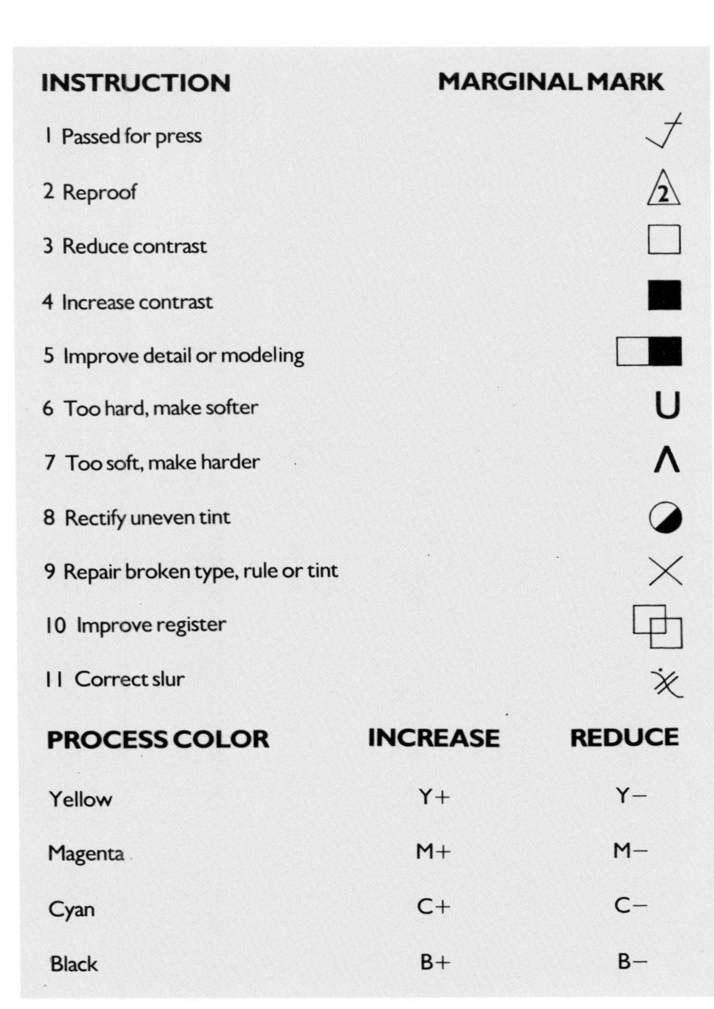

| INSTRUCTION | MARGINAL MARK |
|---|---|
| 1 Passed for press | ✓ |
| 2 Reproof | △2 |
| 3 Reduce contrast | □ |
| 4 Increase contrast | ■ |
| 5 Improve detail or modeling | □■ |
| 6 Too hard, make softer | U |
| 7 Too soft, make harder | Λ |
| 8 Rectify uneven tint | ◐ |
| 9 Repair broken type, rule or tint | ✕ |
| 10 Improve register | ⧉ |
| 11 Correct slur | ✕ |

| PROCESS COLOR | INCREASE | REDUCE |
|---|---|---|
| Yellow | Y+ | Y− |
| Magenta | M+ | M− |
| Cyan | C+ | C− |
| Black | B+ | B− |

The correct version (1)

Too much contrast (3)

Not enough contrast (4)

Loss of detail (5)

Detail too hard or sharp (4)

Detail too soft (7)

Too much yellow

Too much cyan

Too much magenta

Too little yellow

Too little cyan

Too little magenta

can occur.

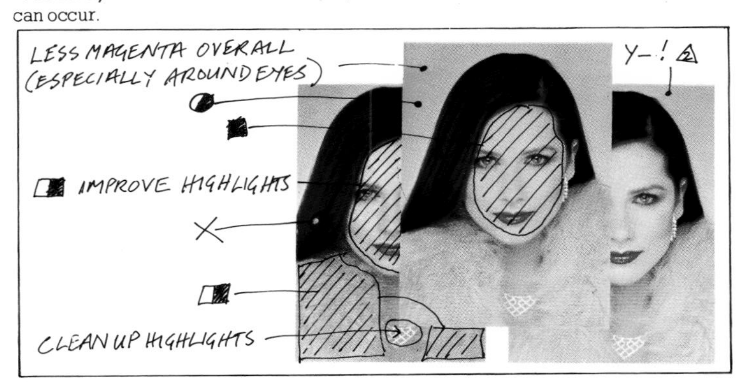


Color proofs should be checked for sizing and color quality. These are color proof correction marks. (**5**) refers to the highlights and details that need enhancing. Hardness and softness are used to describe subjects where the edges of color, shape or tone are too sharp or indistinct respectively. If the image is out of register then the films for one or more of the colors have been misaligned. If the edges of the image are not in register then the film has been positioned incorrectly on the plate.

Slur is a proofing defect which elongates the half-tone dots.

When viewing proofs the important thing to remember is to say what effect you want, not how you think it should be achieved. Do not seek out areas where the proof departs from the original unless they are important; where the side effects of emphasis are tolerable, accept them.

## IMPOSITION

This is the positioning of the pages on each side of a printed sheet so that they will emerge in the right order with the intended margins for cutting, folding and trimming. The printer will work out the imposition scheme, which is based on the fact that most presses print 8, 16 or 32 pages (or multiples of these) at a time. This does not usually concern the artist or client except when a publication is, say, half in four-color and half in two-color. In these cases the imposition scheme must be known, since the artist will have to plan the layout around it.

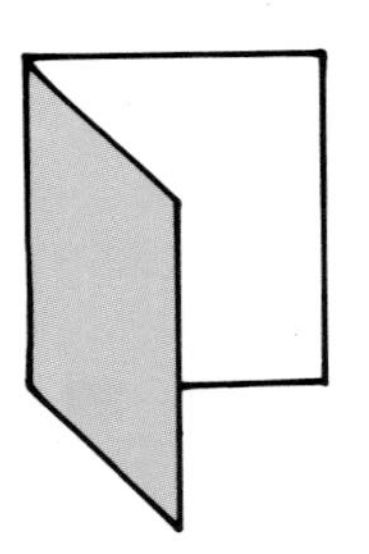

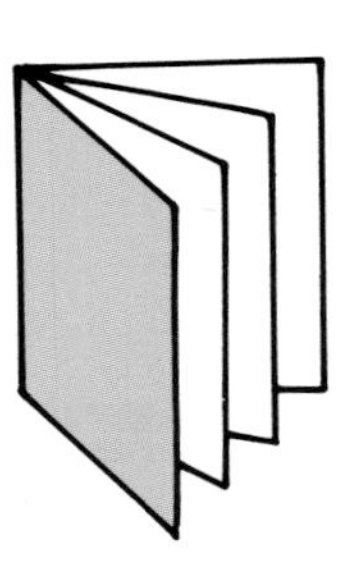

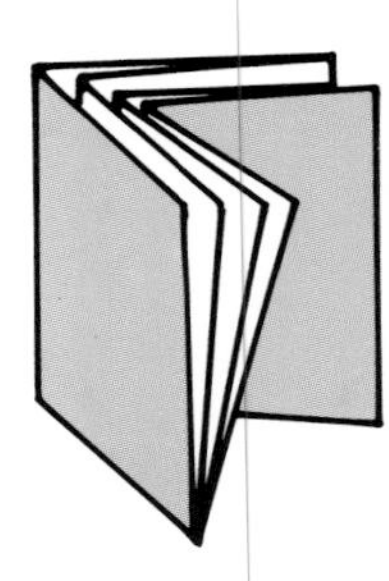

*This is how the pages fold for the first three imposition schemes, but to gain real understanding the best thing to do is to take a sheet of paper, fold it, number the pages and make up your own dummy.* ***"Work and turn"*** *is when the sheets are turned over left to right, so the same gripper edge on the printing press is used for printing both sides. In* ***"work and tumble"*** *the sheets are turned over during printing so that the opposite edge becomes the gripper edge.*

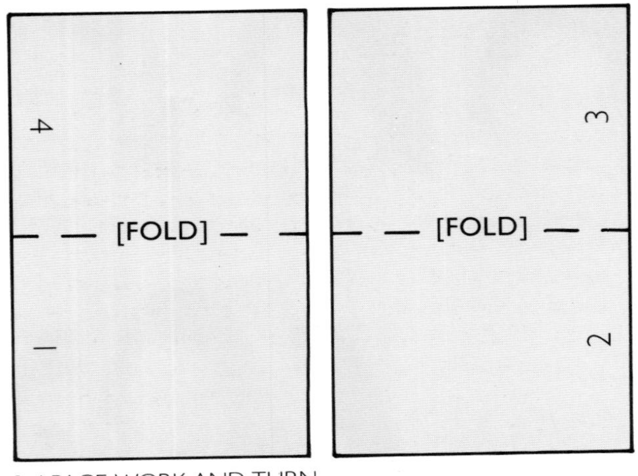


**1:**4 PAGE WORK AND TURN

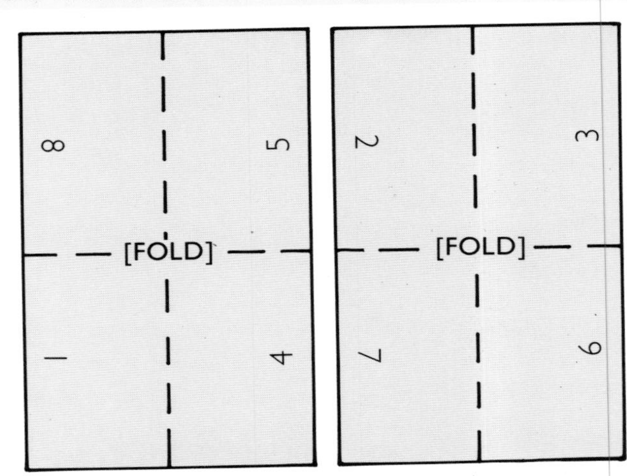


**3:**8 PAGE WORK AND TUMBLE

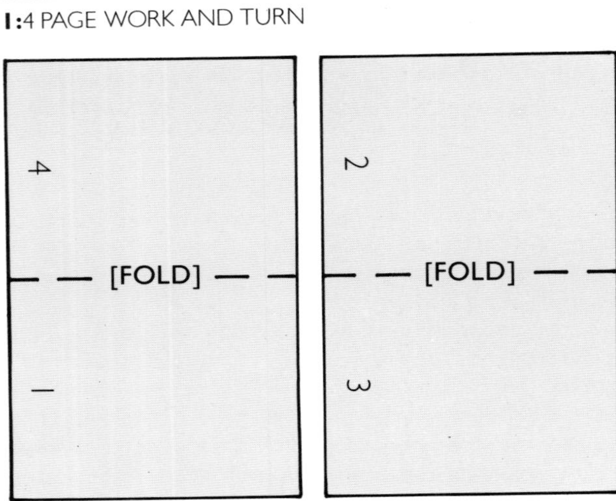


**2:**4 PAGE WORK AND TUMBLE

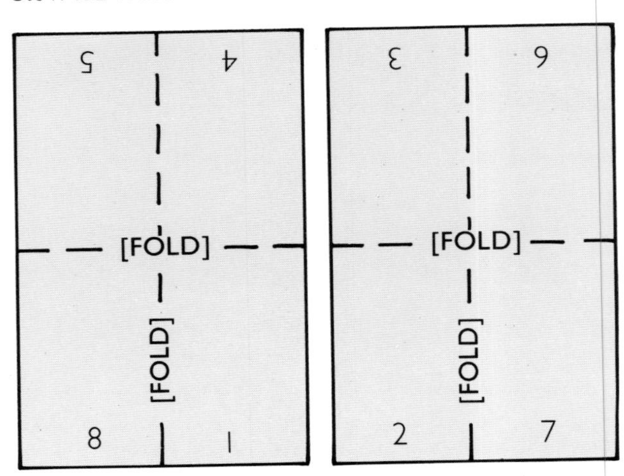


**4:**8 PAGE WORK AND TURN

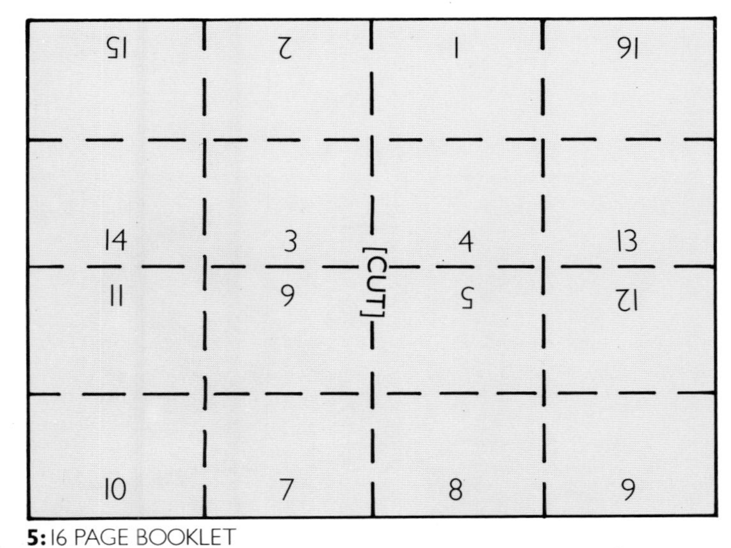


**5:** 16 PAGE BOOKLET

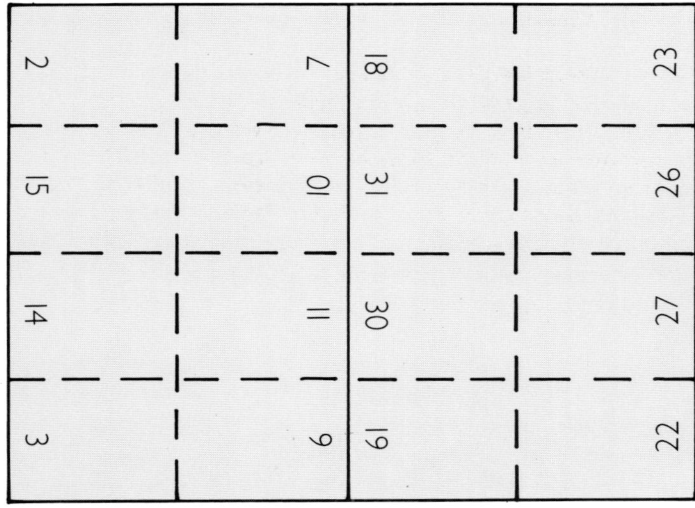


**6:** 32 PAGE SECTION (16 TO VIEW)

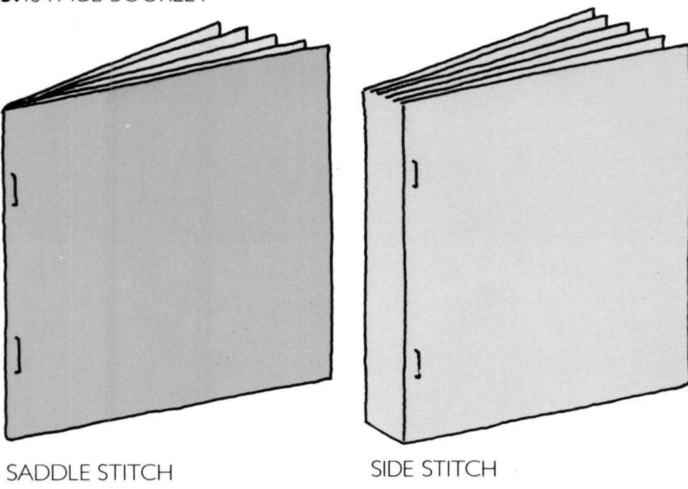

SADDLE STITCH

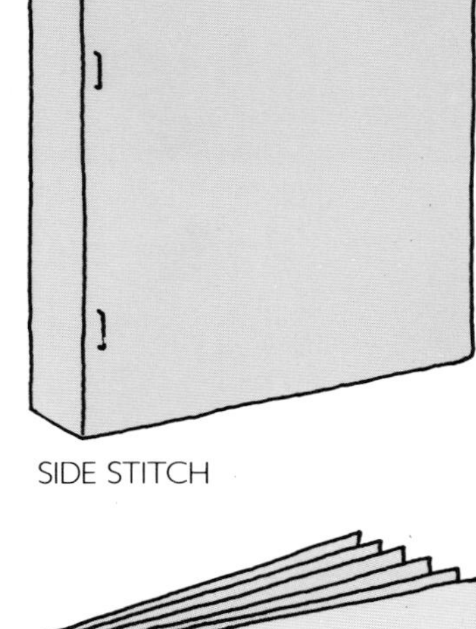

SIDE STITCH

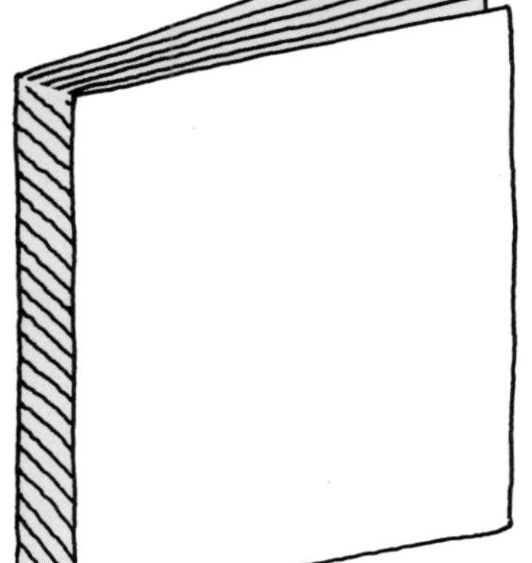

PERFECT BINDING

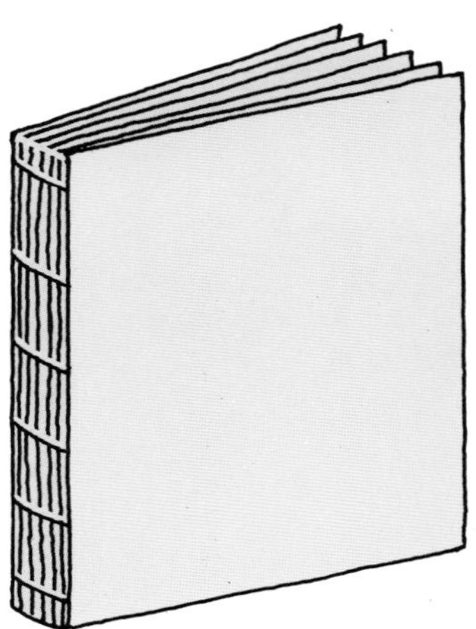

THREAD SEWN

## BINDING METHODS

There are four main methods of binding used for paperbacks and magazines. In **saddle stitching** the booklet is opened over a metal 'saddle' below a head that inserts wire staples through the spine. **Side stitching** is used for thicker publications where the staples are inserted through the front about 1/4 inch/6 1/2cm from the back edge. With this method the pages do not lie flat. **Perfect binding** is the most widely used method, and most paperbacks and magazines are bound in this way. The folded sheets are gathered and the back folds trimmed and roughened so that the binding glue adheres strongly. This leaves individual pages, which are glued together and attached to the cover before trimming the other three sides. Some paperbacks are thread sewn. Each signature, or section of 16 pages, is sewn and then the gathered signatures are sewn together. The cover is then glued to the spine and the books trimmed. The **comb**, **spiral** and **wiro** are mechanical methods of binding and are used mainly for manuals or when it is imperative that the pages lie flat. Holes are drilled through the cover and pages, which are then joined by a wire or plastic spiral coil. **Wiro** uses wire fingers that push through slots, and the **comb** method is simply its plastic equivalent.

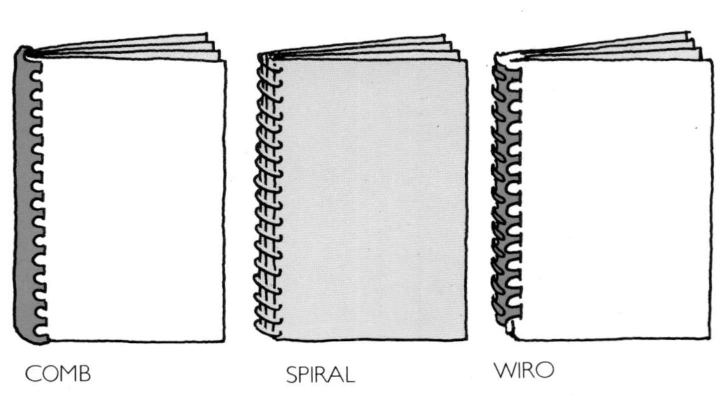

COMB SPIRAL WIRO

# · HAND LETTERING ·

In a world so full of technology it is understandable that an artist specializing in lettering might be assumed to be something of a "dinosaur." However, even though a resident lettering artist is not necessarily a permanent member of a studio team, he or she still plays a very important role.

With an ever-increasing choice of dry transfer lettering and photosetting it is not always necessary to hand draw all the larger scale work used for headlines, posters and advertising material. Expertise is essential, though, when original and distinctive lettering, such as an individual logo, needs to be created.

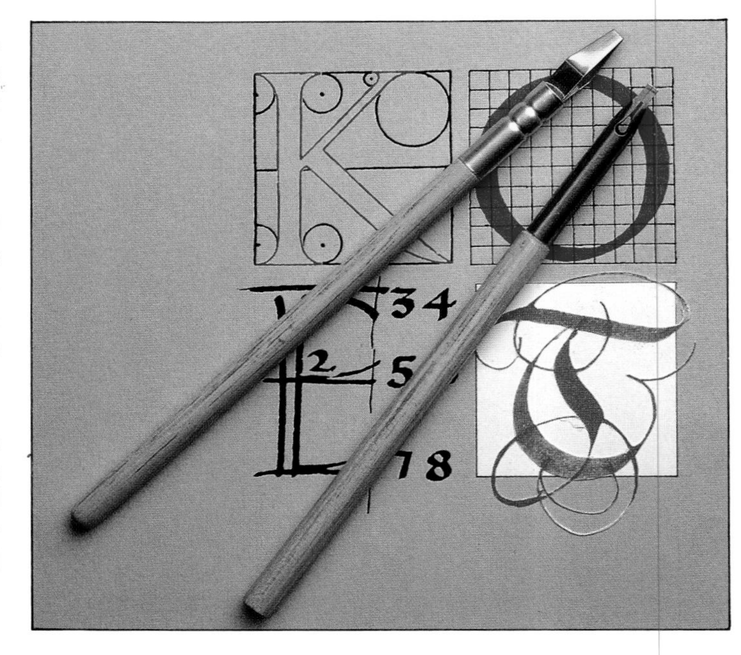

There is still some confusion as to the difference between calligraphy and hand-drawn lettering. The word "calligraphy" is derived from the Greek word "kaligraphia," meaning beautiful writing, whereas hand lettering is the construction of letter forms. Artists often like to make use of calligraphy's fluid spontaneity when designing letter forms, by using it as a basis, rather like a thumbnail sketch.

1▲

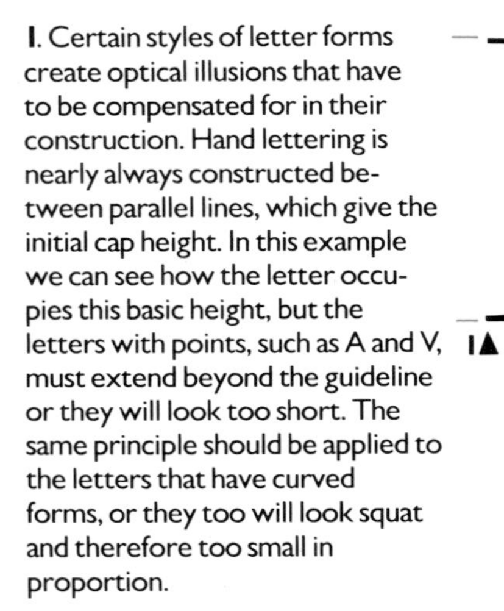

**1.** Certain styles of letter forms create optical illusions that have to be compensated for in their construction. Hand lettering is nearly always constructed between parallel lines, which give the initial cap height. In this example we can see how the letter occupies this basic height, but the letters with points, such as A and V, must extend beyond the guideline or they will look too short. The same principle should be applied to the letters that have curved forms, or they too will look squat and therefore too small in proportion.

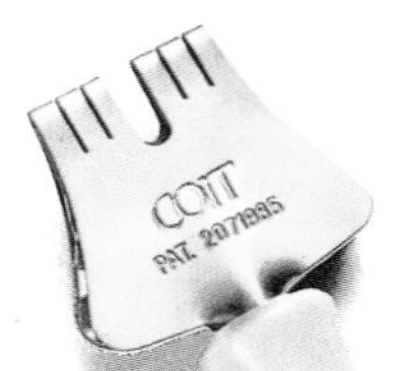

2►

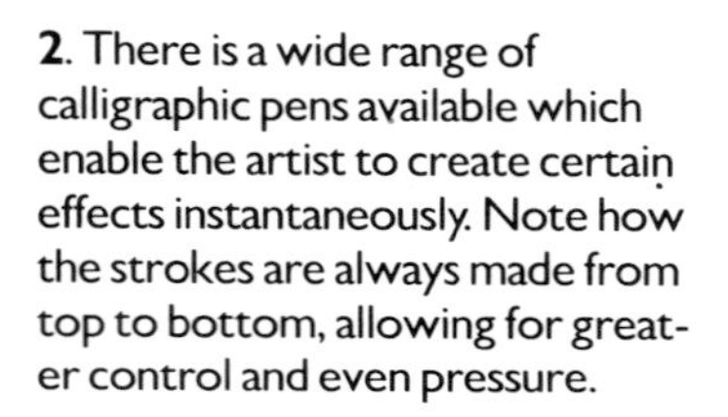

**2.** There is a wide range of calligraphic pens available which enable the artist to create certain effects instantaneously. Note how the strokes are always made from top to bottom, allowing for greater control and even pressure.

3▲

3▲

4▲

5. This is a very clever adaption of existing type. UFO was drawn and the flash created by cutting out the center of the letters and finishing the zigzag by hand.

5►

3. From this close-up it is possible to see how the lettering was achieved for the artwork. The lettering was masked while the surround was stippled with a coarse spatter cap fitted to an air-brush. The double effect for the New York Dolls logo was created by reversing out a second version of the lettering.

4. This is a very simple and effective technique created with drawn type. The type is photocopied and the image smudged with solvent. This is then photocopied again and again until the image breaks up.

**1**. This is the initial felt tip rough as presented to the client.

**2**. It is always best to work at least twice up to achieve maximum detail and crispness when the image is reduced for reproduction. The artist will take an enlarged tracing from the rough (with the use of a camera lucida) to use as his initial guide. This is then drawn over in pencil with the help of French curves to insure correct measurements. The pencil should be a soft weight, but well sharpened.

1▲

2▲

3▲

4▲

▼5

**3.**,**4.**,**5**. When complete the tracing is then turned face down onto another sheet of tracing paper and rubbed over in pencil, leaving a mirror image of the lettering on the new sheet. This is now turned over and rubbed down again onto the surface of the final artwork – the lettering will now be the right way up.

**6**. Using a graphics pen with a broad nib the outlines are followed precisely. To avoid any risk of smudging, always use a quick-drying permanent ink.

**7**. In this case the printer will apply the color, so only the keylines are necessary. The shadow area will be defined by a finer line using a technical pen.

**8**. The artist then obliterates any overdraws with white paint and a fine brush.

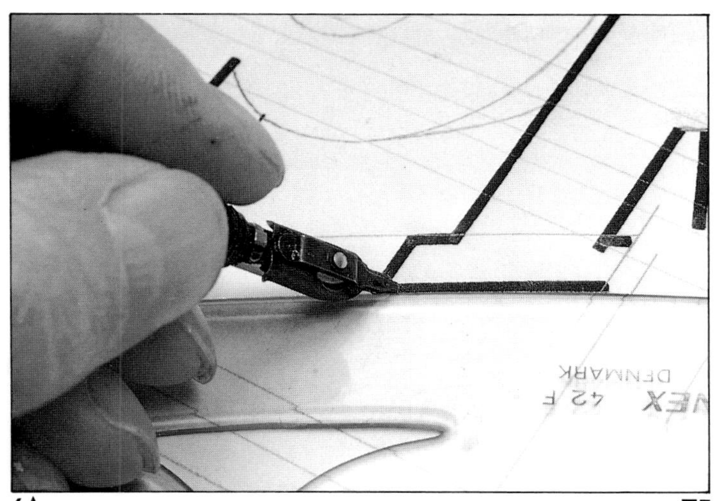

6▲

▼7

8▼

PRIORY PARK

**9**. The finished art is now ready for the printer, providing him with the keylines to indicate the two separate colors.

HEAVY OUTLINE

*To emphasize the shape of the letter forms and pull them out from the drop shadows.*

CURVES

*Achieved with the aid of French curves, since they can be moved to follow the line of any size of curve.*

CORNERS AND INTERSECTIONS

*Created by drawing slightly past the intersection in both directions to give an exact meeting point.*

## REVERSED OUT WHITE

**1.,2.,3.** Of course the ideal way to reverse lettering out of a colored background is simply to use white Letraset, but if this is not available in the chosen face black can be used. Lay the characters down and burnish them with the flat edge of a nib or any other blunt instrument. Next apply the color. If the paper has a coated background, apply a water-based paint with a wad of absorbent cotton – this will create a flat continuous tone and eliminate any brush marks. Do not use a spirit-based medium, since this will dissolve dry transfer lettering.

**4.** Use a hair dryer to speed up the drying process.

**5.,6.** When the paint is dry, remove the letters one at a time from the surface with masking tape, which will not lift the surface of the paper.

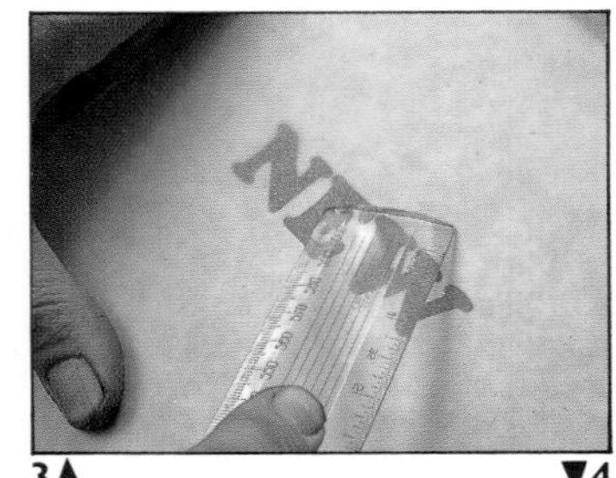

1▲ ▼2 3▲ ▼4 5▲ ▼6

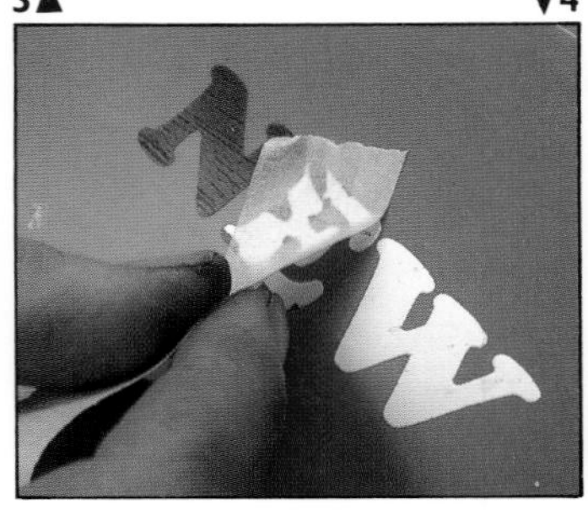

7▲ 8►

**7.,8.** Any remaining specks of lettering or background color that has seeped under the transfer and distorted the letter outline can be scratched away gently with an X-acto knife.

1▲ 2▲ 3▲ ▼4

## OUTLINE

**1.,2.,3.,4.** To produce outline lettering from a solid typeface, fill a ruling pen with process white and follow the inside of the letter forms. Then fill in with a sable brush, leaving the required outline width. It is always best to use sable brushes, since they retain their shape and springiness even when wet.

## CUSTOMIZED LETTERFORMS

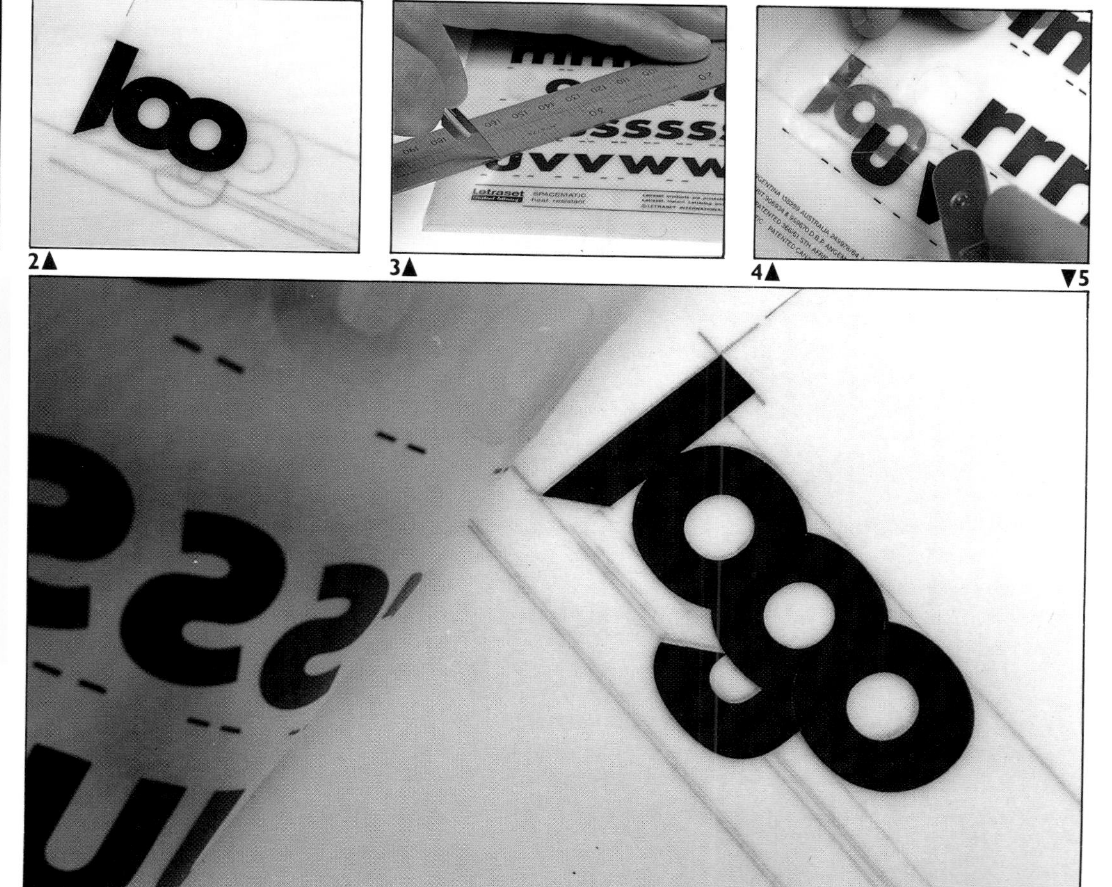

1▲ 2▲ 3▲ 4▲ ▼5

**1.,2.,3.,4.,5.** A quick way to create instant yet original letter forms is to adapt dry transfer lettering in an already existing face. Cut and shape the letters with a scalpel while they are still on the backing sheet and just rub down the required parts.

# · PHOTOGRAPHIC RETOUCHING & SPECIAL EFFECTS ·

Library transparencies and prints are often used in the graphics studio and are frequently blemished and scratched. Retouching is normally done by a specialized studio, but it is quite usual for clients to expect graphic artists to be able to retouch and combine photographs, and combine photographs with artwork. Print retouching is a common task, because unlike negative retouching, it does not entail dealing with a precious original.

One of the ground rules for retouching is to work with a print that is as large as possible, so that your handiwork is reduced in reproduction rather than enlarged. 11 × 14 inches is the largest size that you can conveniently transport.

1▲

2▲

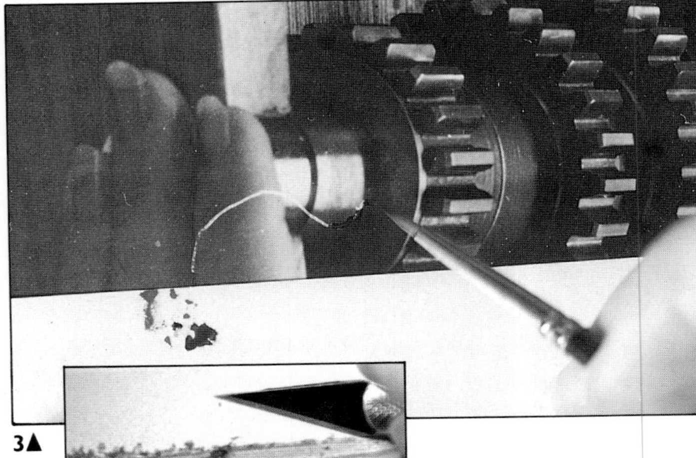

3▲

◀4

**1**. Although you can use almost any medium, a retouching paint box makes it easier to match image color as well as image tone. Protect the surface with a sheet of white paper, so that your hand does not stick to the print, and use the edge of the protective paper to match the color of the image. Use a brush that is very nearly dry for maximum control.

**2**. Pencil retouching is suitable only for unglazed, paper-based prints. Most resin-coated paper will not accept pencil retouching unless sprayed with a varnish. Also, you will be unable to re-touch any further on top of the protective fixing spray (used to prevent the retouching from rubbing off) unless you hold the print in front of the steam from a kettle to remove it.

**3**. A hairline on a negative is much more difficult to remove than a spot. The first thing to do is to match the color and tone of a given area of the hairline. Although color is unlikely to vary along the hairline, tone may – this is where the paint box comes in handy.

**4**. It is very difficult to mix a pigment that can cover a black mark. The traditional way of lightening dark areas is by knifing, as shown: either an X-acto knife or a broken piece of a razor blade held in a pin vise may be used, but it must be very sharp, and even then there is a serious risk of scratching the emulsion.

1▲

1▲

## RETOUCHING EQUIPMENT

**1**. A brush can be used for bleaching small areas and spots. Simply touch a dampened brush to a crystal or tablet of potassium ferricyanide ("pot ferri"). Reserve the brush for bleaching only.

Whether you are working on a hairline or a larger area, use a dabbing action, applying the retouching medium in tiny flecks to break up the outline of the area. With very grainy prints, you can often emulate the grain successfully.

This is an example of how an old photograph which was badly cracked and damaged has been successfully retouched.

1▲

2▲

3►

## HAND COLORING

Hand coloring is very similar to retouching. You need a fairly "weak" print to begin with, although for specific coloring you can bleach selectively.

**1.,2.** A useful short-cut in hand coloring is shown above. Apply a waterproof Stabilo Boss pen to the shiny side of acetate, or glass – anything that will not absorb the ink. Using a cotton swab, dip it into the ink and carefully apply to the print. Your can see, on this album sleeve, that the results are very effective.

**3**. The airbrush is frequently used in retouching. In this example the model has been photographed in white make-up and the cracks around her nose and mouth have been retouched. Her teeth have also been made to look much whiter.

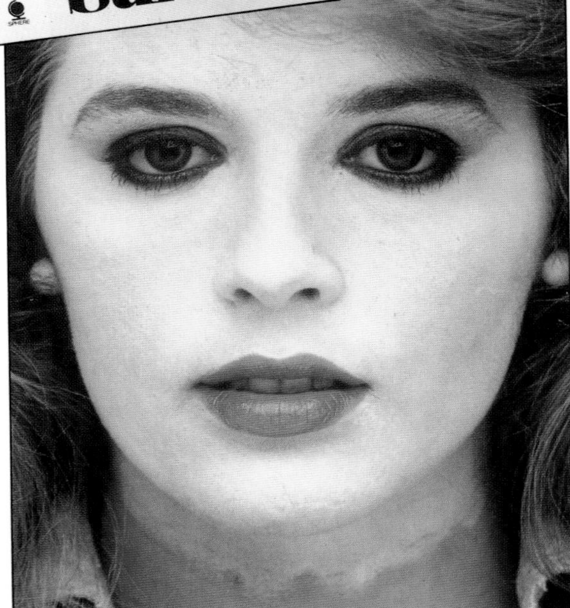

1▲

**1**. A sharp X-acto knife and a cutting mat are essential in collage work. To make the join less obvious when you are cutting follow the line of a feature in the print.

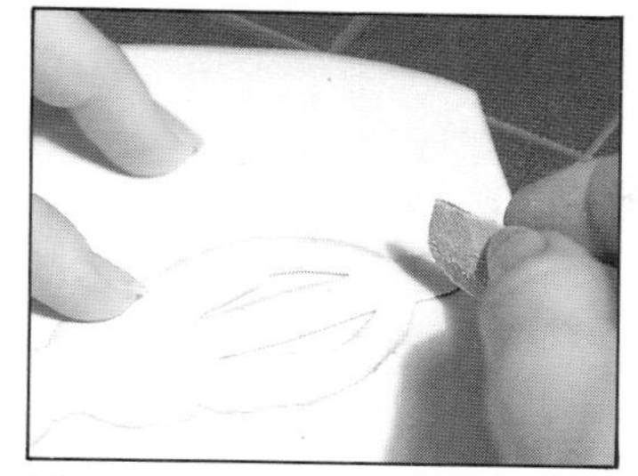

2▲

**2**. Sanding or feathering a cut print with fine sandpaper will make the joins less noticeable.

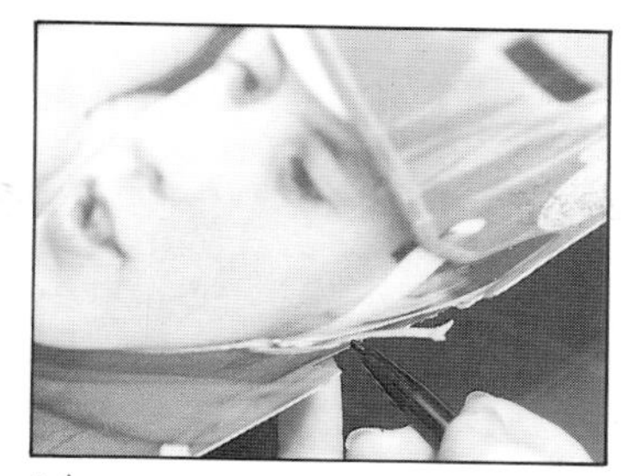

3▲

**3**. Instead of sanding you can simply blacken the cut edges with a felt tip pen, but only for fairly crude work in black and white.

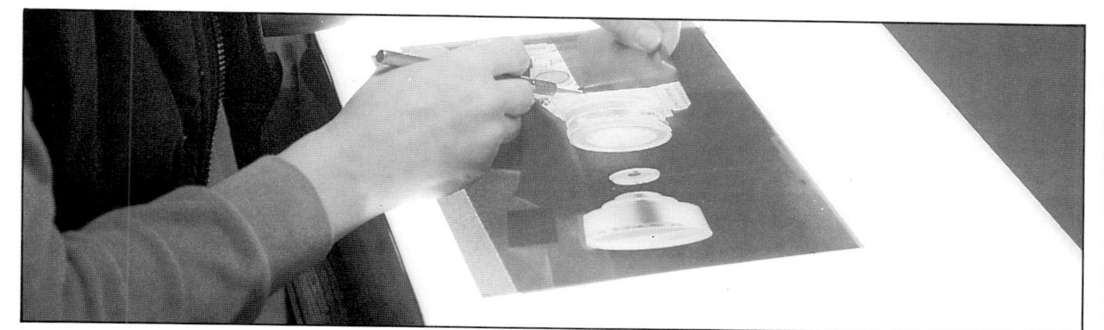

1▲

### 3. BLACK AND WHITE NEGATIVE RETOUCHING EQUIPMENT

1. A light box is the principal working surface.
2. Cotton gloves prevent finger marks on the film.
3. A magnifying glass is essential for detailed retouching.
4. A palette is used for mixing pigments and dyes.
5. Fine brushes are used for applying the dyes.
6. Cotton swabs are useful to have around and can be used for any number of purposes.

7.,8.,9. Water, opaque and dyes, respectively, are the basic materials.

10. Denatured alcohol is used for cleaning negatives prior to retouching.

11. Reducer is used for lessening density.

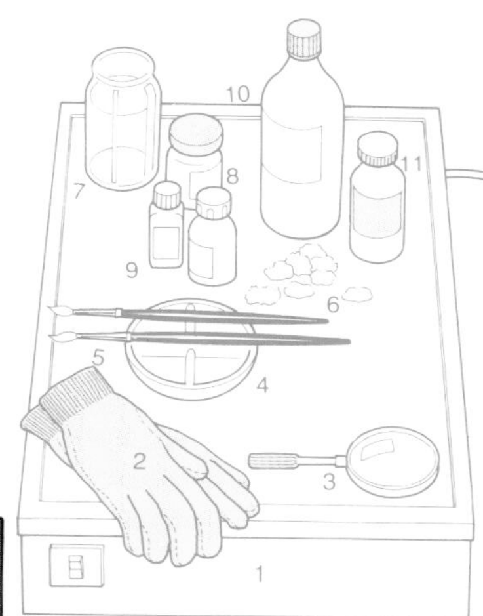


3▲

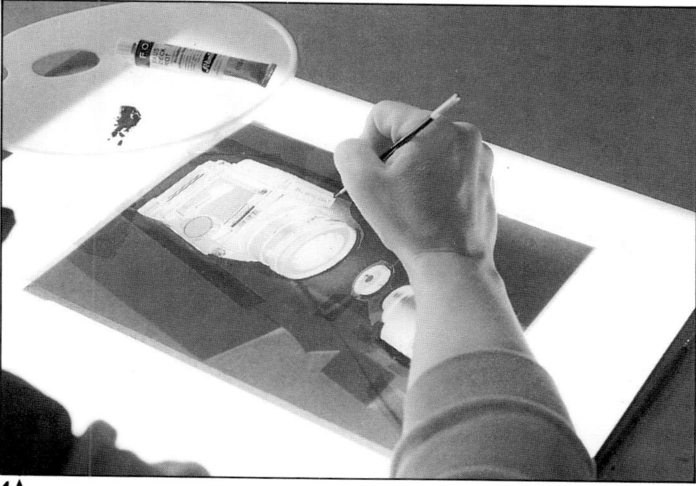

4▲

**4**. To avoid having to hand-paint large areas, a rough mask has been made up from scrap pieces of photo-opaque film. Choose your pigment carefully, since not all of them will adhere properly. Work on the emulsion side for maximum sharpness, but if coverage is a problem retouch both sides of the negative.

### RETOUCHING NEGATIVES

**1**. For safety it is best to stick the red film mask onto a sheet of acetate and work on that.

**2**. For blocking out you need a chisel-ended brush. Nip off the end hairs of a watercolor brush with an X-acto knife. This makes the brush much less sensitive to variations in pressure, which makes it easier to control line thickness.

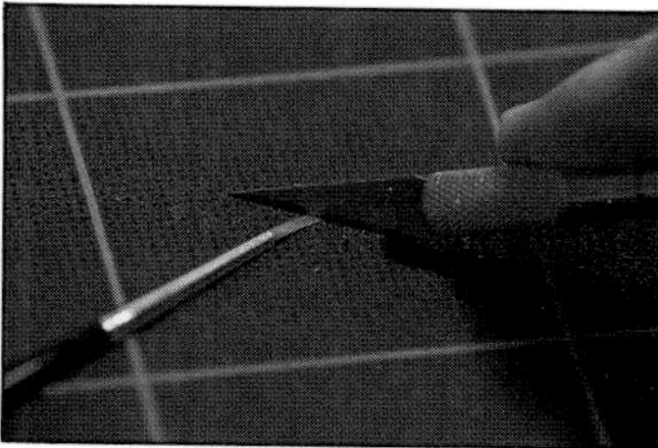

2▲

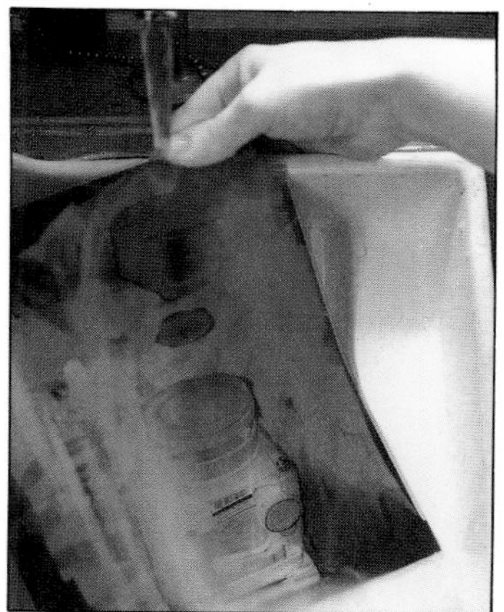

5▲

**5**. Washing off the blocking medium will be easier if it is still fresh, so do it immediately. Gentle rubbing with the fingertips will speed removal. Be careful to check when you are buying the blocking medium that it is water soluble; otherwise it will take a couple of hours to remove it.

## SLIDE SANDWICH

A slide sandwich is made by superimposing one slide on another. Both originals should be thin and light, and the patterns should be simple and dramatic or the result will be a jumbled, murky picture. Dark areas on one transparency will obscure parts of the other. This is the opposite of the approach for making a double exposure.

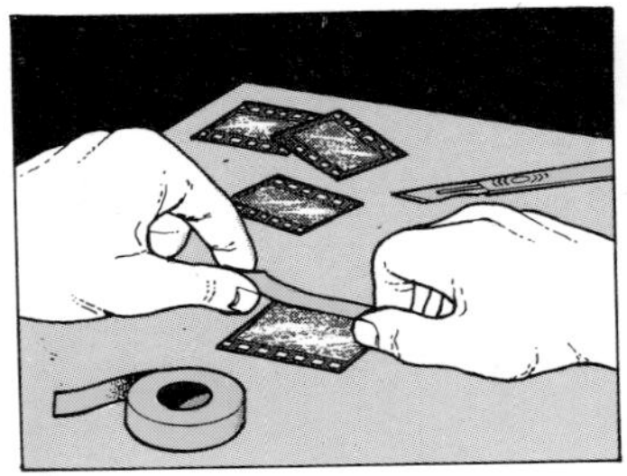

1▲

1. Try out different combinations on a light box. Remove the transparency from its mount and tape it down.

2▲

2. Position the second transparency and tape it down. Cut around the edges of the tape.

3▲

3. Use a blower and an anti-static gun to remove dust particles that are trapped in the sandwich and then mount it.

## DOUBLE EXPOSURE

In a double exposure the dark areas on one transparency must be opposite the light areas on the other. To match the two elements, either mark the ground glass of the copying camera with a grease pencil or use a screen with a grid and make a scaled-up drawing showing the main shapes.

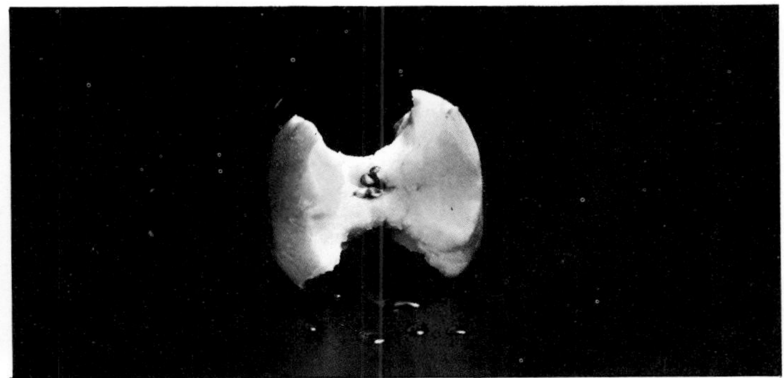

## PHOTOMONTAGE

With photomontage you can achieve effects that have only been possible by illustration in the past. This example is created by a combination of the above two pictures, using very accurate masks to block out unwanted areas on the transparencies.

Kodachrome
Kodachrome
MADE IN GT. BRITAIN REXEL CUMBERLAND Derwent Studio
MADE IN GT. BRITAIN REXEL CUMBERLAND Derwent Studio
MADE IN GT. BRITAIN REXEL CUMBERLAND Derwent Studio
MADE IN GT. BRITAIN REXEL CUMBERLAND Derwent Studio
Deep Cadmium 6
Made in Germany
T 20
rotring rapidograph ISO
UNIQUE
MADE IN ENGLAND

# STUDIO PROJECTS

# THE PROJECTS

While the first part of this handbook covered the basic skills and techniques needed by today's graphic artist, this section illustrates how they can be put into practice. The eleven projects discussed represent a cross-section of commercially applied graphic art and show the many duties the artist may have to fulfil, from initial brief onwards. As well as background information and detailed instructions – often step by step – each case study contains invaluable tips and professional shortcuts (special studio tips are highlighted in blue) gleaned from years of professional experience.

## • ARTILLERY BROCHURE •

(pp. 82-99)

Tracing an illustrated brochure from initial visuals to final artwork, this project shows a wide range of uses for the designer's skills.

- Presentation enlivened by use of "cut out" illustrations (p. 85).
- Use of Magic Marker to add shadows and soften hard lines (p. 87).
- How to make paint stick onto acetate and how to remove finger marks from it (p. 89).
- Tips for glueing small pieces of copy – eyelash curlers are surprisingly handy for this (p. 93)

## • PSION ORGANIZER •

(pp. 100-112)

Here, the emphasis is on styling and arranging the type and bringing up the rough to a highly finished state.

- Magic Marker hints and shortcuts – differing effects, covering large areas of flat color etc. (pp. 100-111).
- A new use for old paint brushes (p. 104).
- What to do when Letraset does not fit exactly to size (p. 109).

How to store Letraset without it sticking to its plastic folder (p. 111).

## • FINANCIAL TIMES INDEX •

(pp. 112-119)

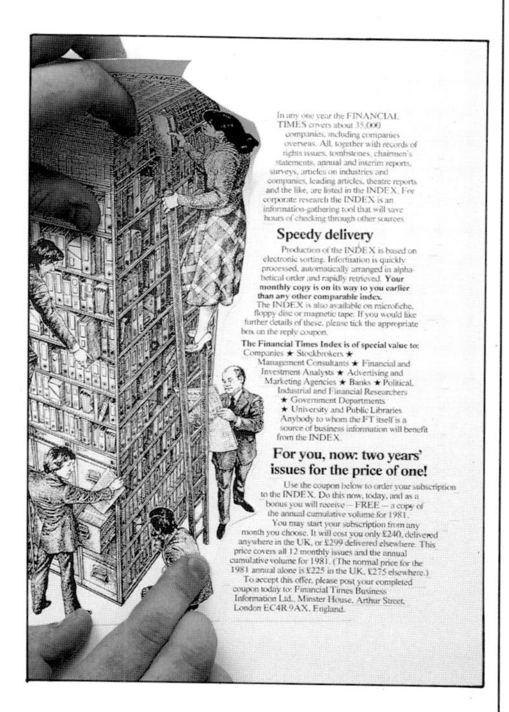



This project highlights the rôle of the paste-up artist, and also the tricks needed to create a black and white advertisement with color impact.

- How to remove stray Letraset "dots" (p. 117).
- How to achieve a "rubber stamp" effect (p. 118).
- Use of "instant art" (pp. 112-119).
- How to correct "muddy print" in PMT (p. 119).

## • TV STORYBOARD •

(pp. 120-129)

This example shows various techniques and shortcuts you can use when storyboarding, but can be applied to almost any kind of visualization.

- Magic Marker techniques – widest range of effects with minimum effort (pp. 120-129).
- Use of a cropping aid (p. 129).

## • GUERNSEY TOURIST BOARD •

(pp. 130-139)

Here, a design was needed that would incorporate a large number of simple elements, and that would be versatile enough for a wide range of reproduction techniques and merchandise.

- Use of collage (pp. 130-139).
- Transposing shapes onto colored paper to eliminate "show through" (p. 133).
- Screens for Photomechanical Transfer (p. 137).

## • FILM POSTER •
(pp. 140-145)

Like that for the Psion Organizer, this brief required a highly finished rough. It also had to be usable in both landscape and portrait formats.

- How to get "airbrushed" effect with Magic Markers (p. 142).
- Use of autotype (p. 143).
- Cropping with a border (p. 145).

## • FLY FREE •
(pp. 146-153)

This co-ordinated campaign was to revolve round a piece of original artwork, based on a very specific rough, from which elements were taken for various ads.

- Use of flat plan – importance of versatility of grid (p. 150).
- Special brochure construction for ease of handling (p. 150).

## • POINT-OF-SALE •
(pp. 154-163)

This section explores the idea of turning specially-designed flat artwork into three-dimensional packages and display units, and gives several time-saving shortcuts.

- Importance of guide lines (p. 156).
- How to get clean, accurate cuts, scores and folds (p. 156).

## • CORPORATE IDENTITY •
(pp. 164-169)

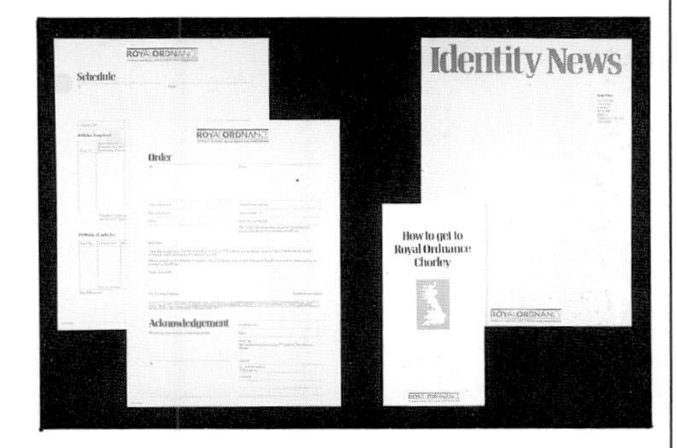


Like the Guernsey Tourist Board project, the aim was to produce images with a wide range of applications, functions and reproduction methods, but also involved updating established advertising materials.

- Step-by-step guide to blind embossing (pp. 166-167).
- Importance of color to targeted market (pp. 164-169).

## • SEALINK •
(pp. 170-179)

The images for this were based on black and white photographs supplied by the client, many of which had to be "doctored," to work in juxtaposition.

- Use of Letraset "half-tone" to define shadows (p. 173).
- Use of tape under tools to stop ink spreading (p. 174).
- "Cut outs" short cut (p. 176).

## • AIRBRUSH •
(pp. 180-185)

A step-by-step guide to an image involving a wide range of airbrush effects, and including many hints and tips on technique.

- How to enlarge type without a Grant projector (p. 180).
- Mask cutting and how to use a mask for a "soft-edged" effect (p. 182).
- Adaptation of standard letter forms (p. 184).
- Importance of protection of airbrushed work from moisture (p. 185).

# PROJECT 1

## · ARTILLERY BROCHURE ·

### THE BRIEF

This project covers the full range of the graphic artist's skills, starting with the initial visuals and following through the various procedures that lead up to the final artwork. The client – in this case the Anglo-American Historical Society – required a brochure depicting the history of artillery through the ages. The purpose of the brochure was to show the subscribers the pewter scale replicas of guns and cannon that they would be receiving monthly, courtesy of the society.

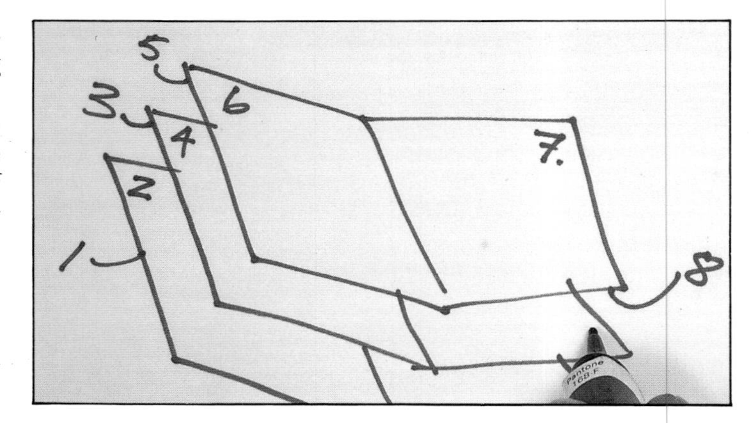


The client decided that the title of the brochure was to be "The Remarkable History of Artillery." It would feature a full-color cover (since this is the first thing prospective buyers are drawn to and often purchase on the strength of) and three colors inside to keep print costs down. The given format was twelve pages 6 by 8¼ inches, and the text and main visuals were supplied. The first stage for the artist was to arrange the text and visuals in such a way that the material was visually interesting, chronologically accurate and accessible to the subscriber. Once this was complete the specialists in the graphic studio, such as the Magic Marker visualiser, the lettering artist, the typographer and the finishing artist, made the final artwork ready for printing.

HAND LETTERING

CUT-OUT ILLUSTRATION

TRANSPARENCY STRIPPED IN

2ND COLOR OVERLAY

TYPESETTING

HALF-TONE ILLUSTRATION

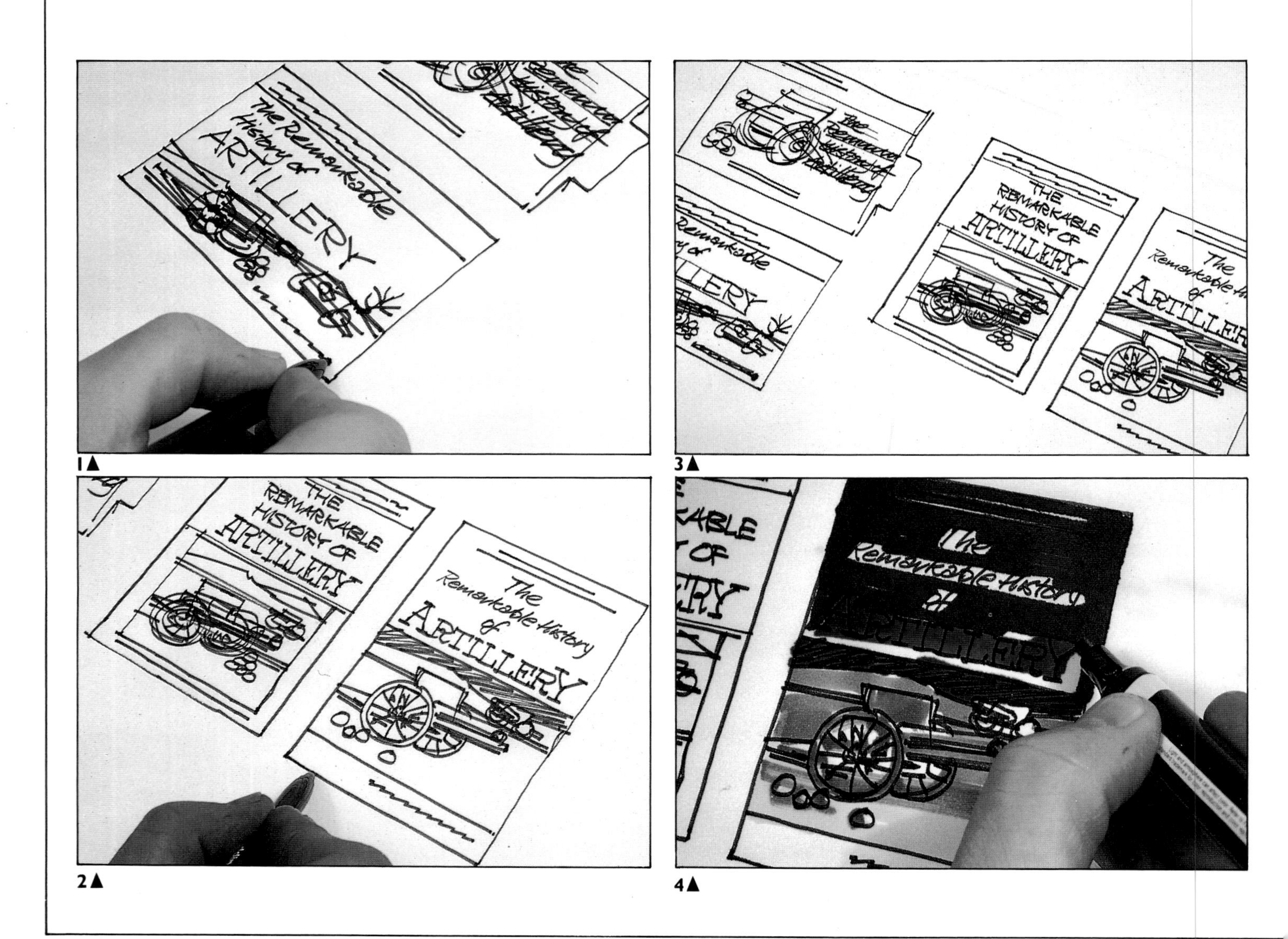


**1**. Using the photographic material supplied as reference, the artist uses thumbnail sketches to play around with his ideas on the various ways of arranging the front cover.

**2**. This method is quick, and as the artist progresses his ideas become more positive.

**3**. A final decision has been made, so it is on this sketch that the presentation visual will be based.

**4**. The artist now has to experiment with color to create an even clearer idea of what the final visual will look like.

5▲

6▲

▼7

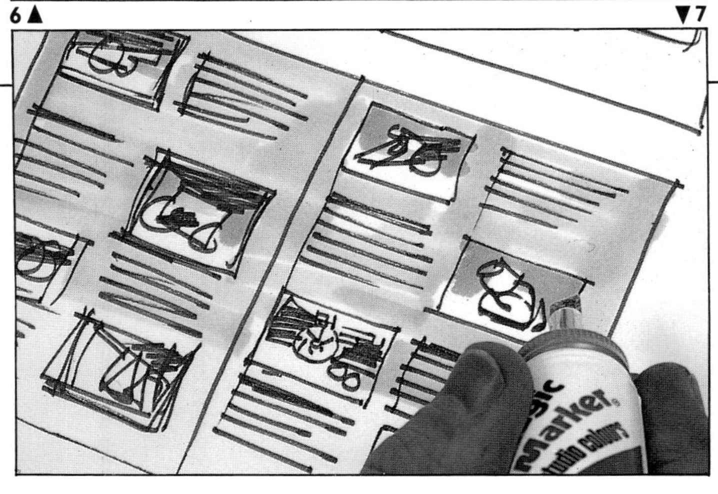

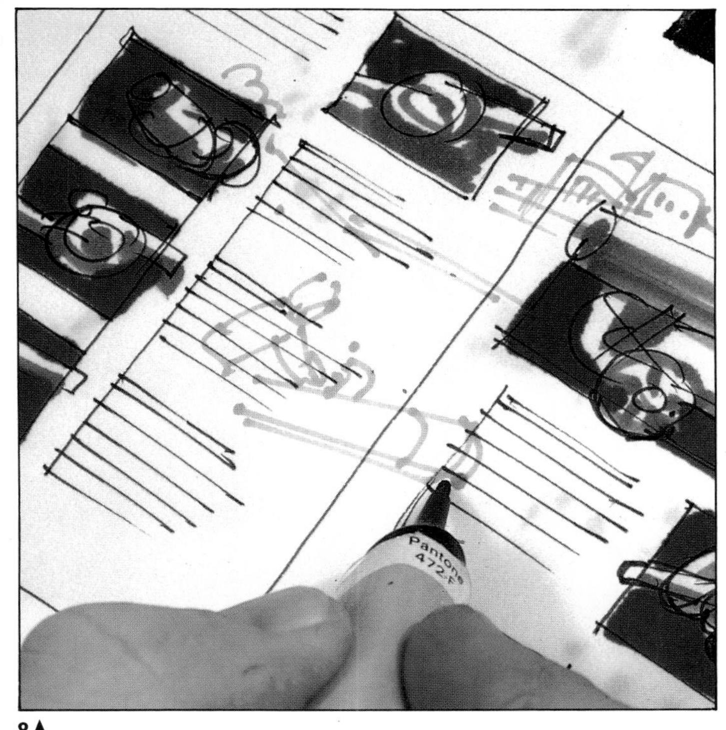


8▲

**5**. The look of the inside pages of the brochure are "worked up" in the same way as the cover, with the additional problem of where to place the type in relation to the illustrations.

**6.,7**. Remembering that there are only three colors, the artist has chosen two colors that harmonize with his choice for the front cover to form a unified publication. The light sepia serves for the all-over background and the blue for the background to lift the illustrations, with the third "color" being black.

**8**. The artist could see from the previous roughs that the pages lacked life and looked too much like an arrangement of boxes. Here we can see how, by removing the boxes and using cut-out illustrations, he makes the pages come alive.

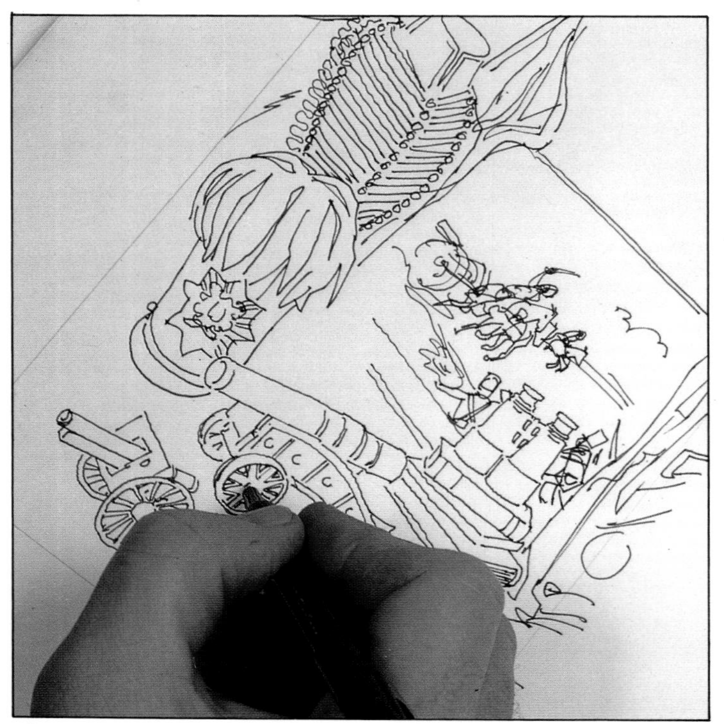

1▲

2▲

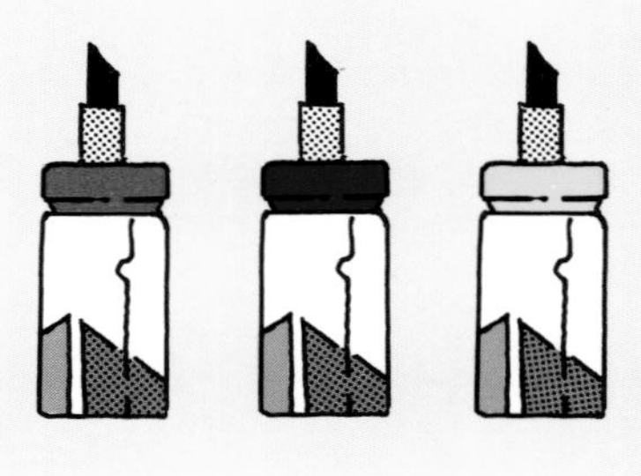

MAGIC MARKER

*This specific brand is so widely used that a lot of graphic artists refer to all felt-tipped markers as **Magic Markers**. The thick shape makes them easy to hold, giving more control. Another familiar brand is the Pantone marker. This company has standardized the color range throughout all their products including printing inks, which makes color matching far easier. However, the range is so comprehensive that most other brands can be matched to their swatches.*

**1**. Over this spread we will see the artist working through the various stages that lead to the finished client visual of the front cover. Using a camera lucida the artist traces the outline of the chosen photographic material onto layout paper.

**2**. The exact size of the front cover is ruled around the traced image with a triangle to give an accurate right angle for the corners. All the line work must be executed with a fine, bleed-proof felt tip pen.

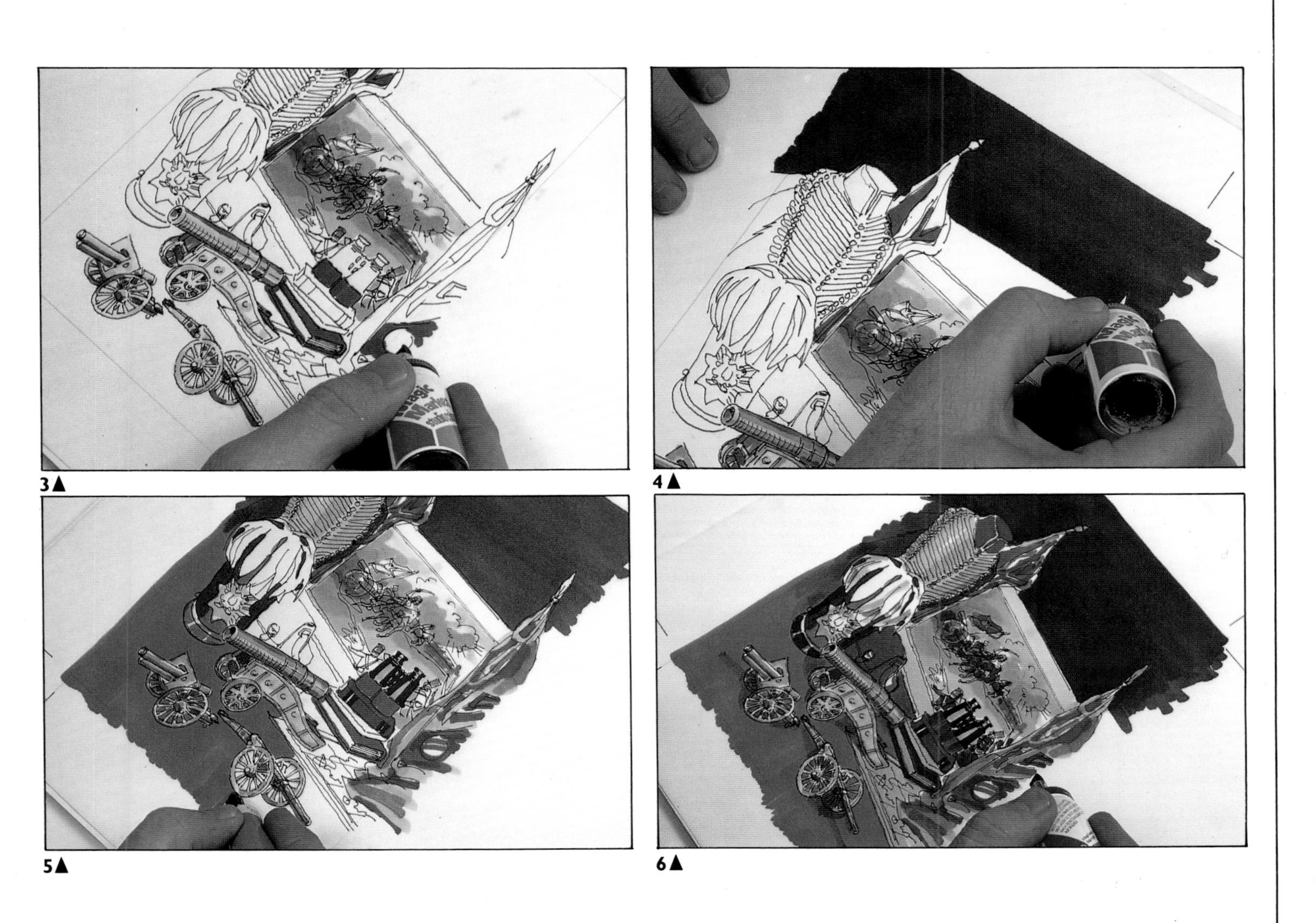


**3**. The color is now added with a Magic Marker, starting from the smaller details before proceeding to the backgrounds.

**4**. The solid background is applied with broad horizontal strokes of the same pressure to build up an even tone.

**5**. The solid background that has to fit around the more detailed illustrations is applied with shorter vertical strokes for greater control.

**6**. A light gray marker is used at the final stage to drop in shadows and soften any hard edges where colors meet, giving the finished visual far greater fluidity overall. To make colors look bolder, apply marker to the back of the paper as well.

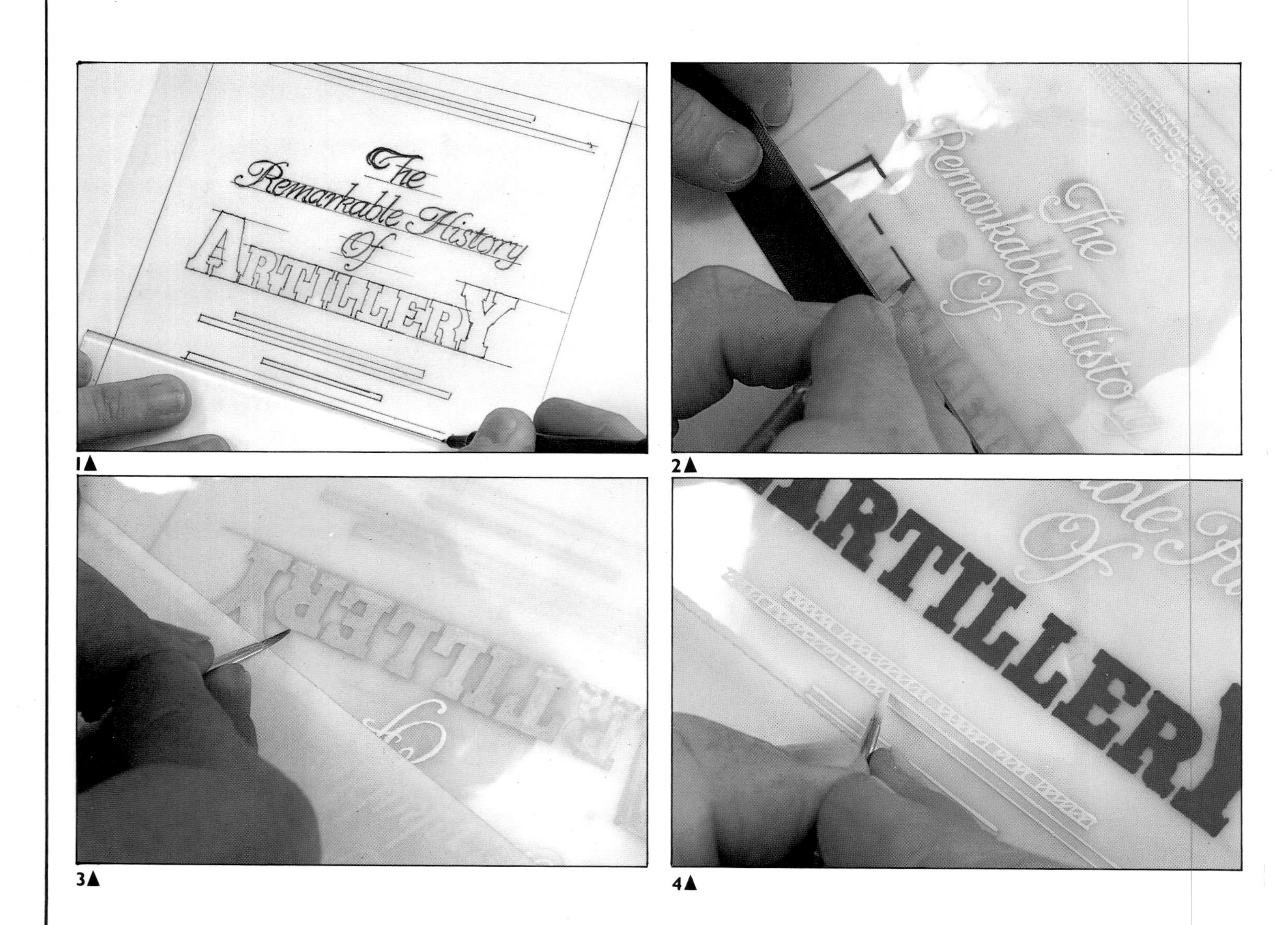


**1**. For the lettering of the front cover, the artist rules a sheet of tracing paper with the guidelines that will contain the script and show where it is to be positioned. The lettering is then drawn on the tracing paper in black.

**2.,3**. An acetate overlay is positioned securely over the tracing paper, which will act as the artist's guide. The lettering is then painted directly onto the acetate in the chosen colors – the small lettering is not painted out in full, the artist simply indicates the size and weight.

**4**. Use a mask when performing such delicate tasks; otherwise your hand will smudge the paint and spoil your work.

**5**. Once the lettering has been completed the acetate is laid over the finished visual and properly aligned.

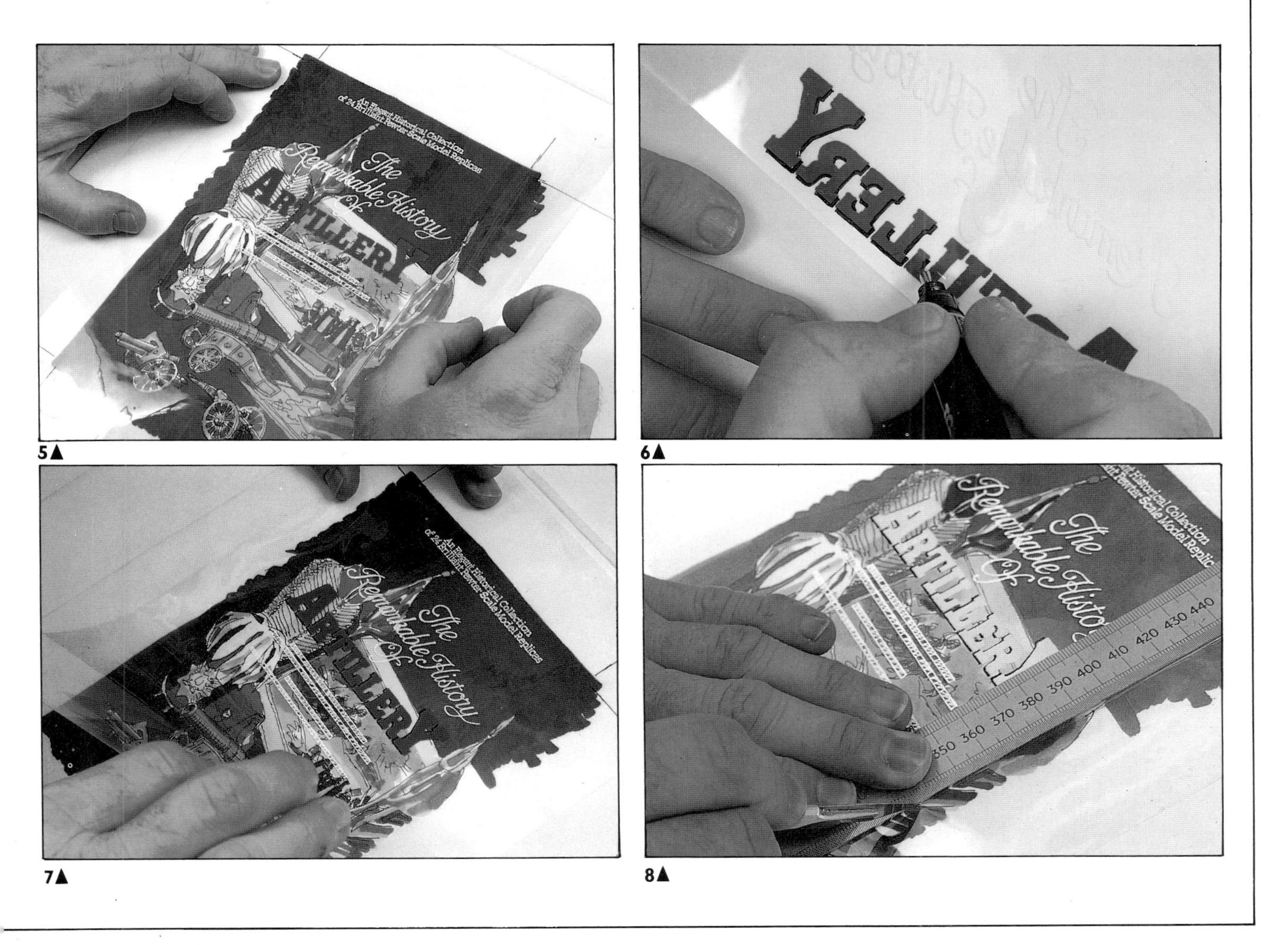


5▲ 6▲

7▲ 8▲

6. Because the word "artillery" was chosen as a focal point and will run across several colors and images, the artist decides to add a black drop shadow on the reverse of the acetate. This prevents any chance of the lettering getting lost.

7. The acetate is once again laid over the visual, and as you can see, the drop shadow has not only sharpened the word but created an almost three-dimensional effect so that it now stands out against the busy background.

8. Now satisfied, the artist aligns the acetate and trims the edges of the two layers with an X-acto knife.

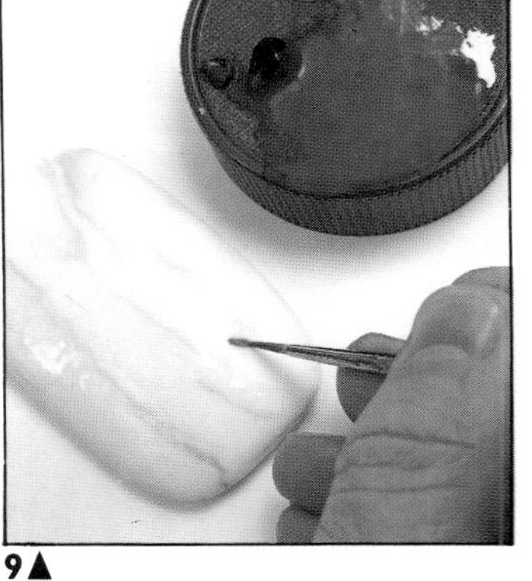

9▲

9. For water-soluble paint to adhere successfully to the smooth surface of the acetate, it must be mixed with a little cake soap or dishwashing liquid. When working on an acetate you can easily remove fingerprints or marks by wiping it over with absorbent cotton soaked in a little lighter fluid.

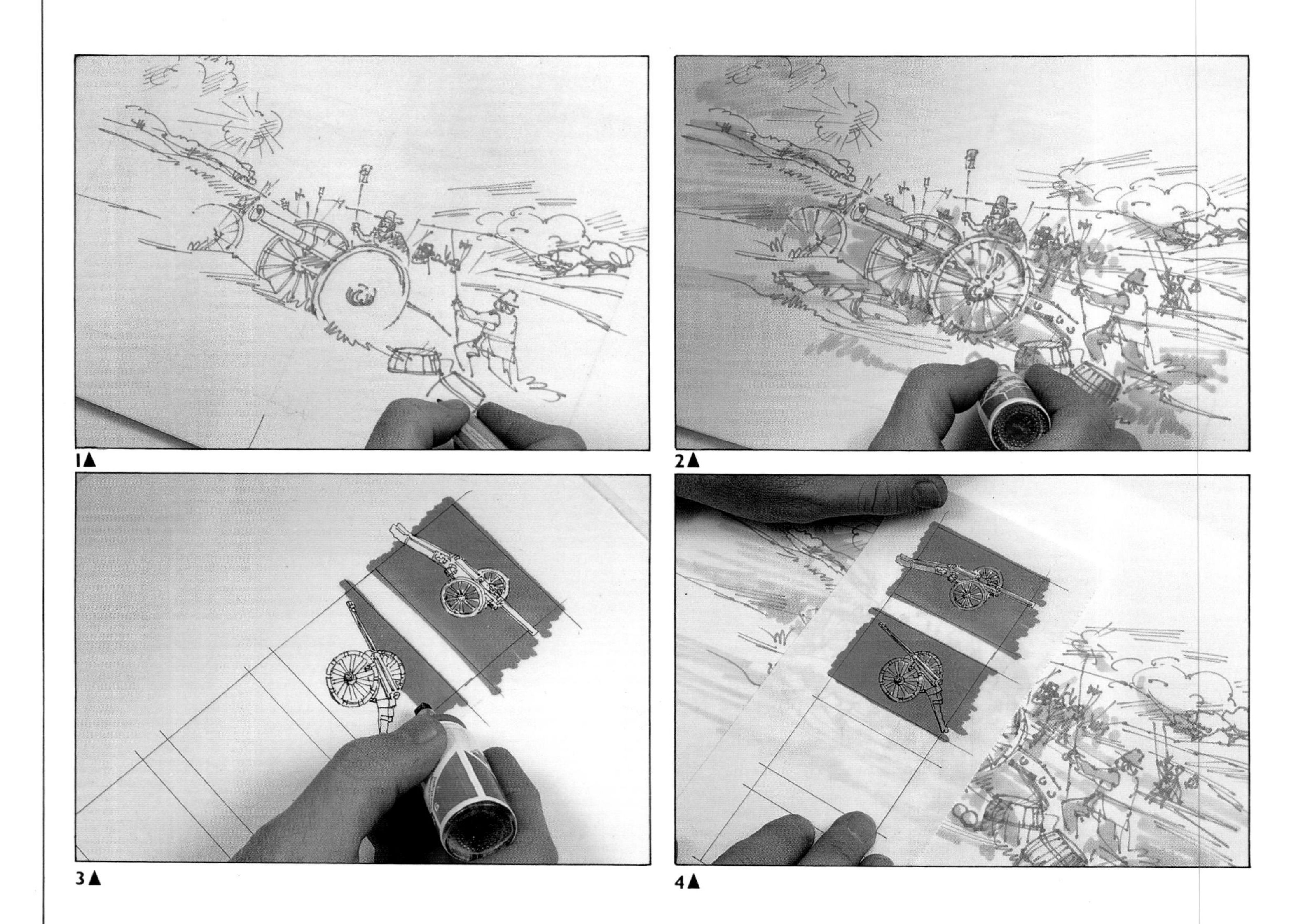

1▲ 2▲ 3▲ 4▲

**1.,2.** To represent the inside of the brochure only one spread has to be presented to the client. The artist has created atmosphere by using a background illustration, as opposed to a flat color. This was also traced onto layout paper from the photographic reference, using a camera lucida. With the limitation of one color the marker is overlaid to achieve different tones.

**3.,4.** The line illustrations and their color backgrounds are drawn on separate sheets of layout paper and placed over the background area so that the artist can experiment before deciding on the final position.

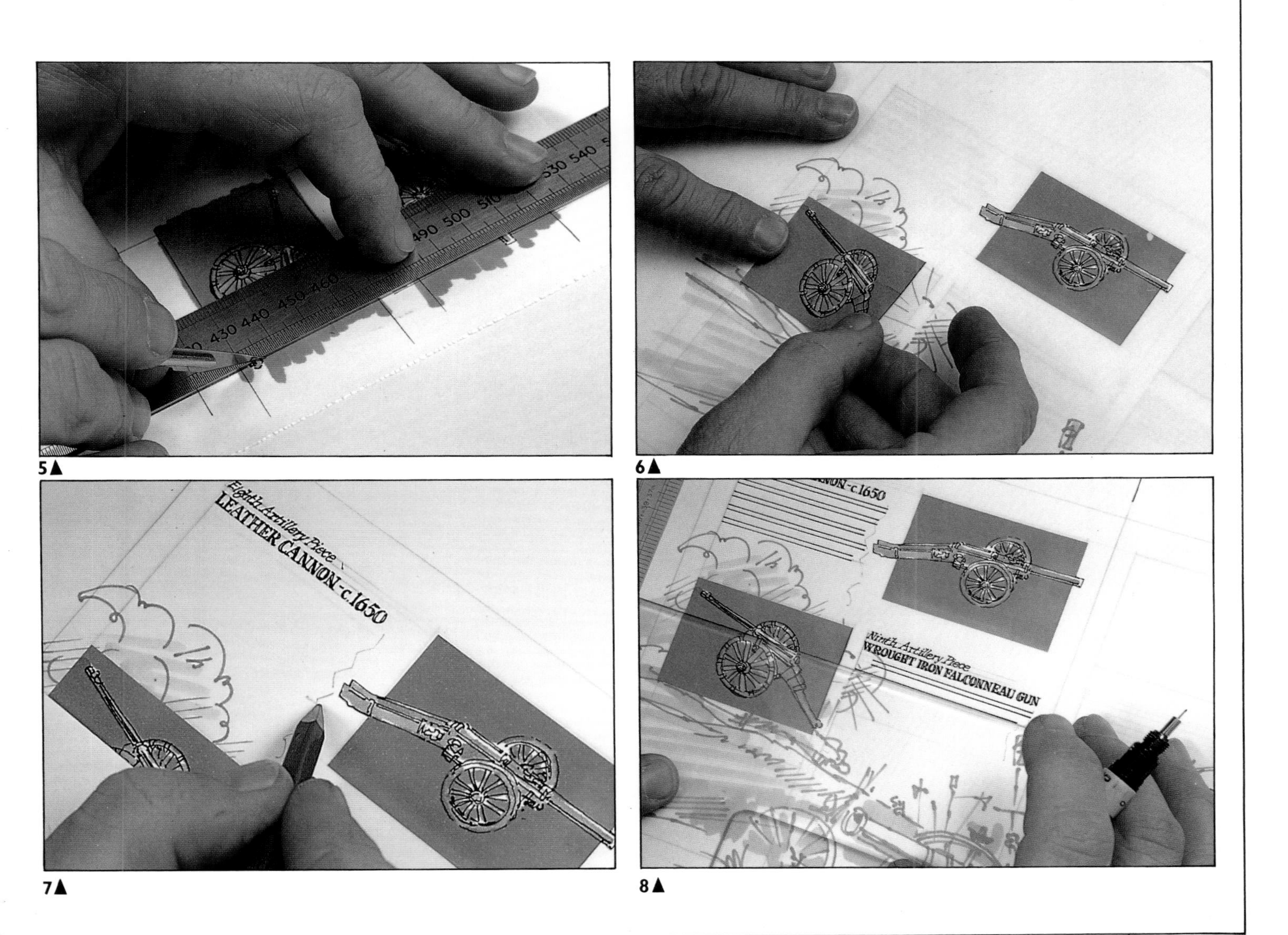


5▲ 6▲ 7▲ 8▲

**5.,6.** These illustrations are then mounted onto thin drawing paper with spray adhesive to give extra strength. They are then cut out and placed in position.

**7.** Only the main headings for the captions have to be shown – these are rendered in a fine line felt tip pen.

**8.** The text is represented by double parallel lines which are drawn accurately by placing a ruler vertically down the side of the spread, then butting a triangle against it to form a right angle. The triangle is then moved down in regular widths which can be measured accurately against the rule.

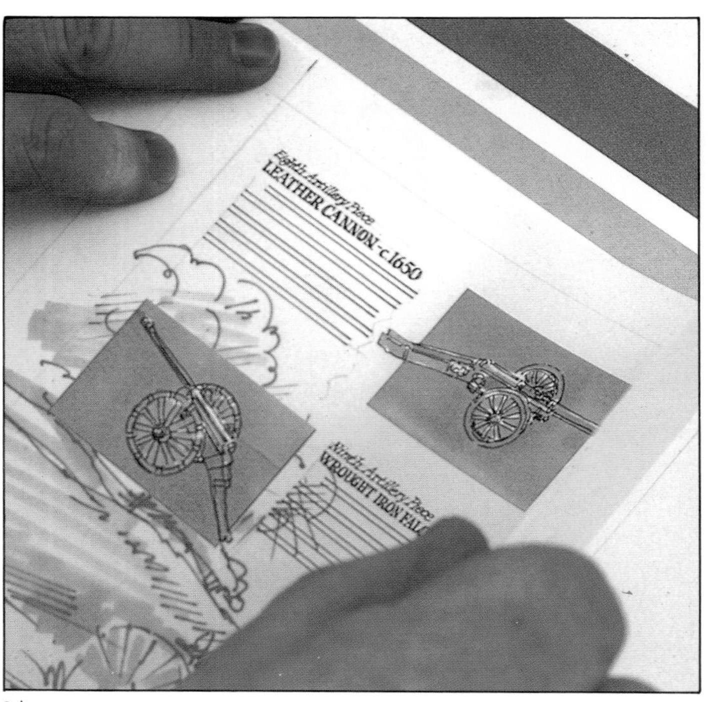


1▲

I. Now the complete spread is mounted on thin drawing paper to give it strength and support.

2▲

3▲

4▲

**2**. The point of a compass is pushed through the register marks to enable the rest of the spreads to be aligned accurately.

**3**. The artist has discovered a spelling mistake in one of the captions; at this stage corrections can easily be made.

**4**. A separate piece of layout paper is ruled and the correct lettering re-drawn.

**5**. The corrected layout sheet is then positioned exactly over the original and secured. With an X-acto knife and metal rule the artist cuts through the two layers, being careful not to pierce the drawing paper.

**6**. Once this has been done the incorrect original should peel off easily with the help of the blunt end of the knife.

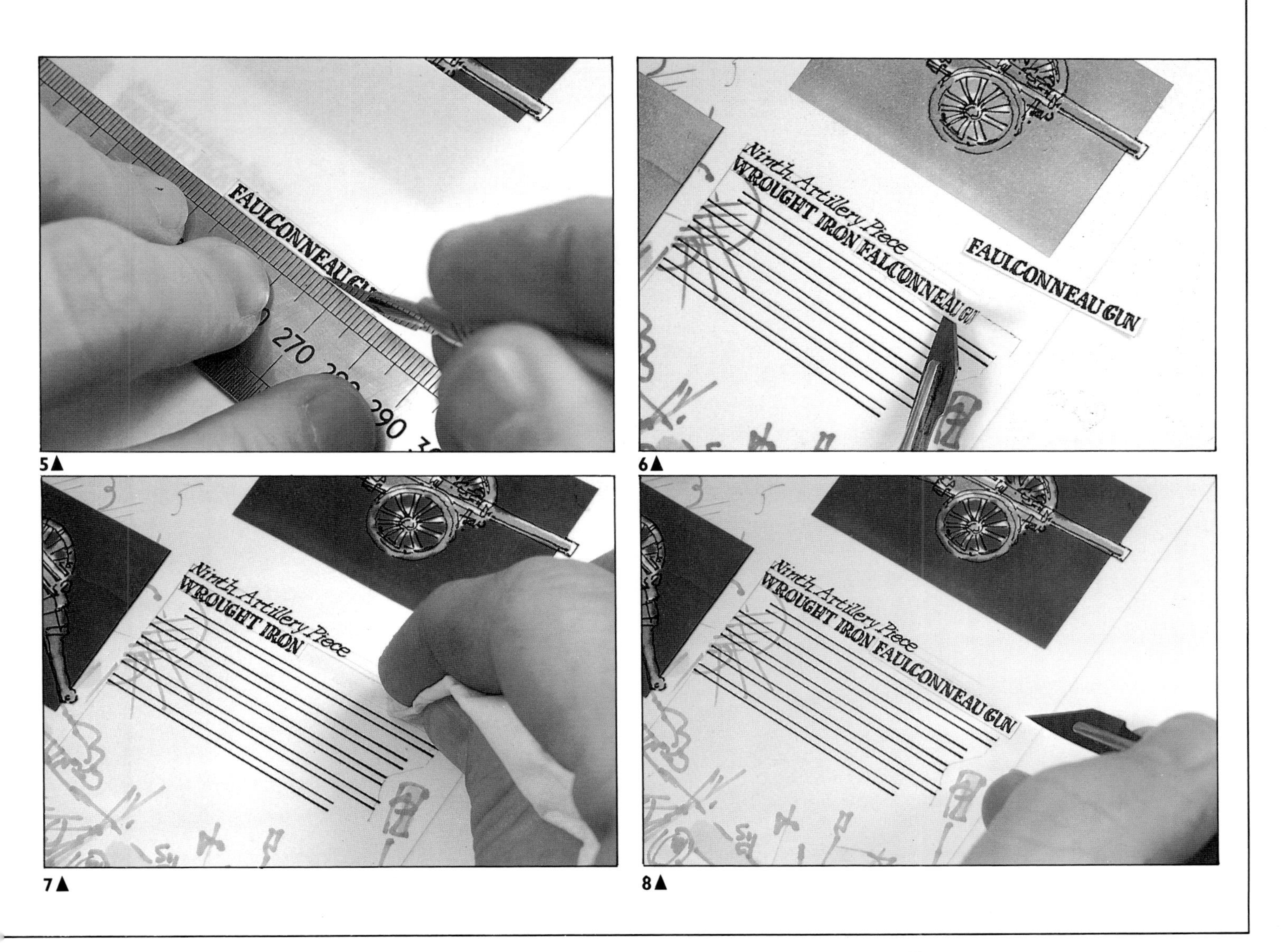


5▲ 6▲ 7▲ 8▲

**7**. The drawing paper backing will probably have traces of adhesive on it, so it is always best to remove these with a little lighter fluid.

**8**. The corrected strip is then sprayed with adhesive and carefully positioned (for it should fit exactly) before being rubbed down through a piece of layout paper.

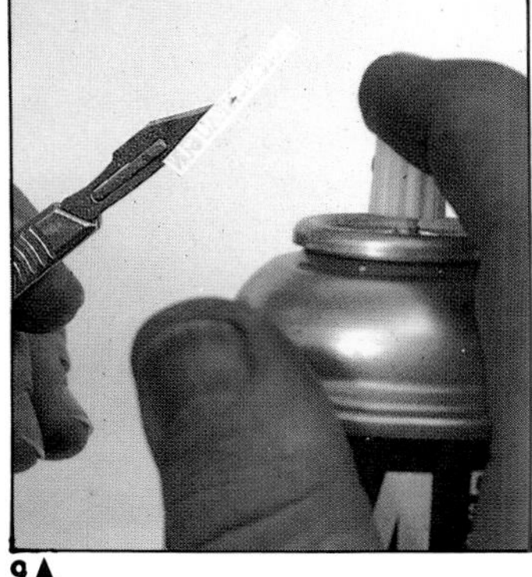

9▲

**9**. The X-acto knife is not only used for accurate cutting. When dealing with small strips, you will find if far easier to hold them on the edge of the knife, as shown, when spraying them; if you hold them with your fingers, most of the spray will land on you.

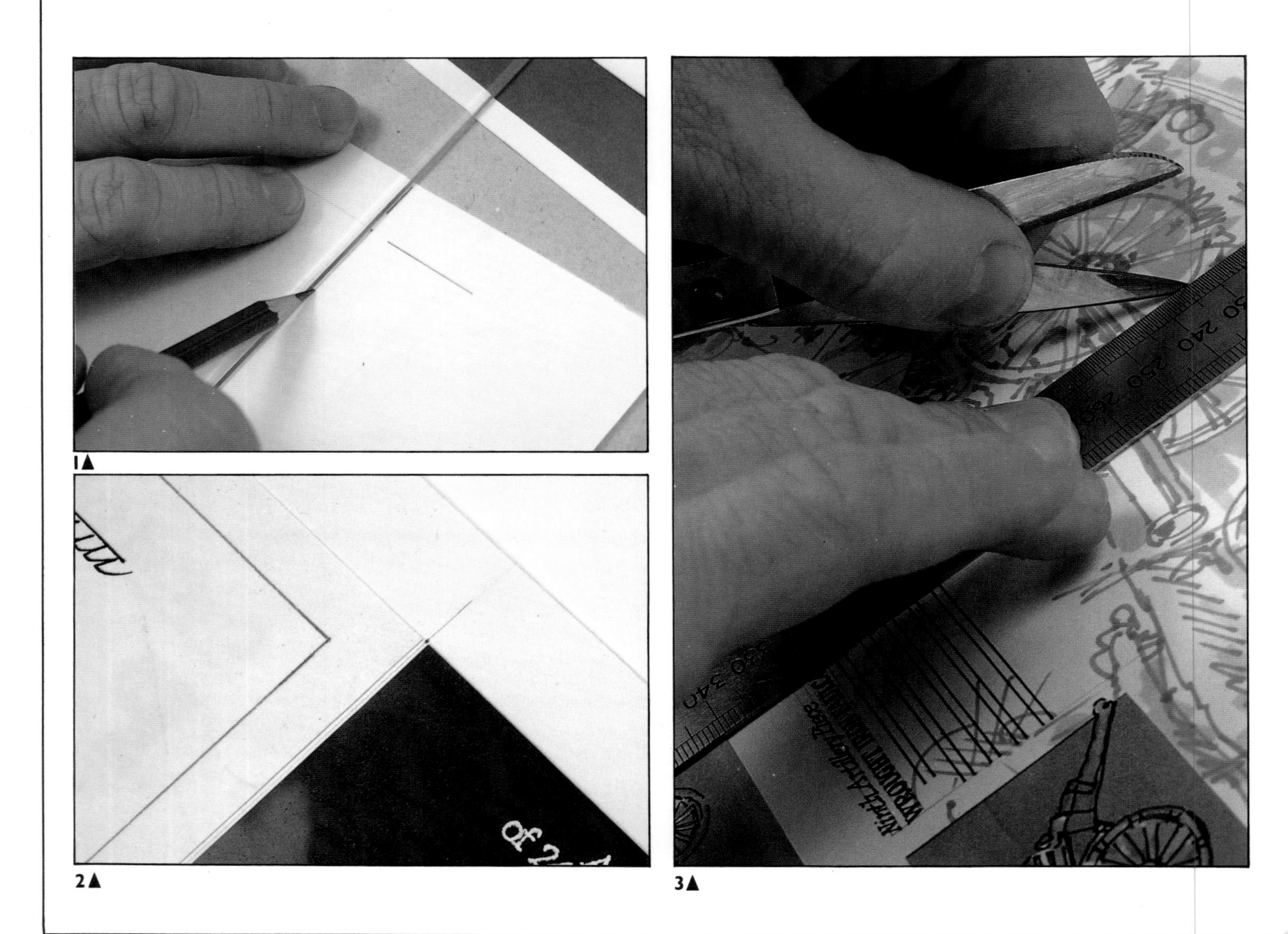

1▲

2▲

3▲

**1.,2.** The spread with the front and back covers is also mounted onto drawing paper before the dummy is made up. Then they are trimmed to size and placed in order.

**3**. Each double page has to be folded, but at this stage the spread is just scored by drawing the blunt end of a pair of scissors along a steel rule which is aligned with the register marks.

**4**. The stapler used to secure the pages is not wide enough for the spread, so it has to be used in the open position.

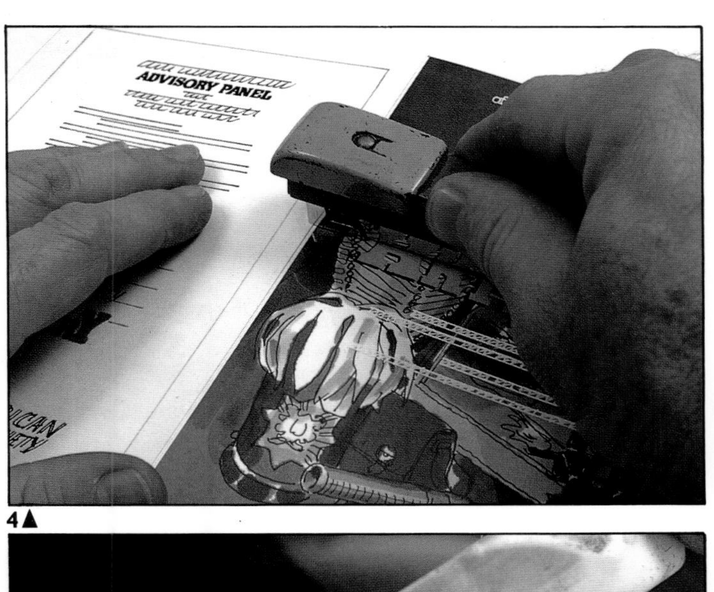


4▲

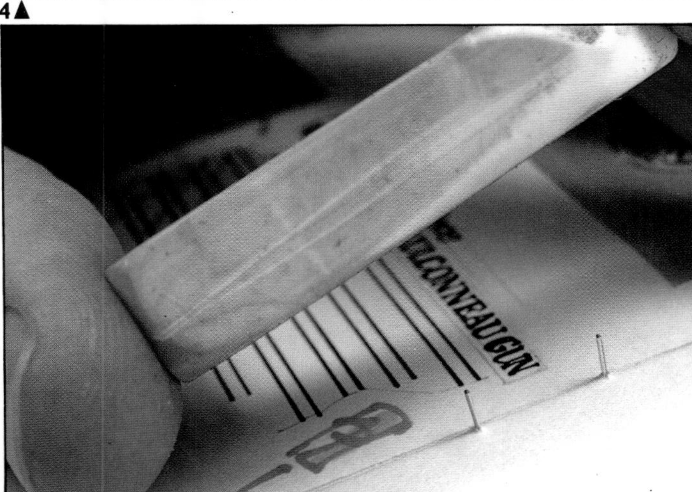

5▲

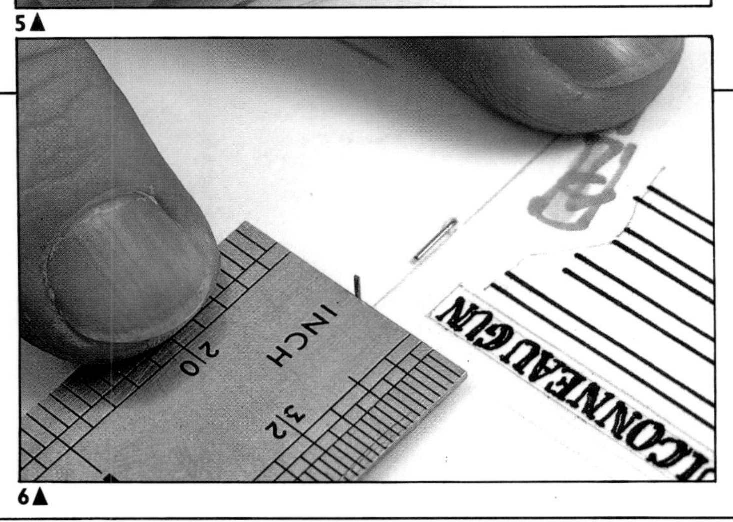


6▲

7▲

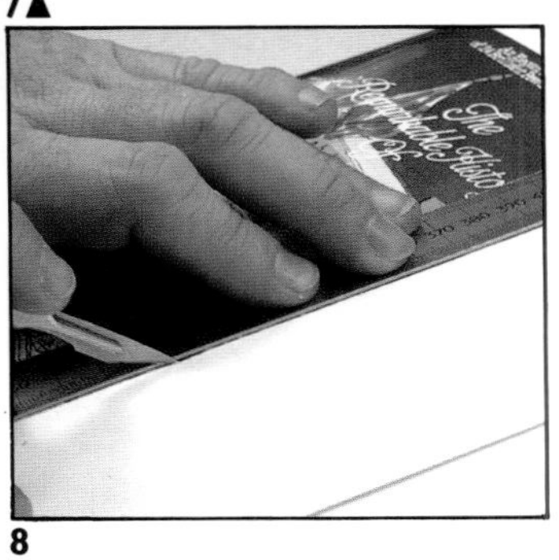

8

**5**. A soft eraser is placed underneath the brochure to receive the staple points as they pierce it.

**6**. The brochure is turned over and the staple points are folded with the end of a steel rule.

**7**.,**8**. The pages are now folded along the score marks and together given a final trim to complete the client visual.

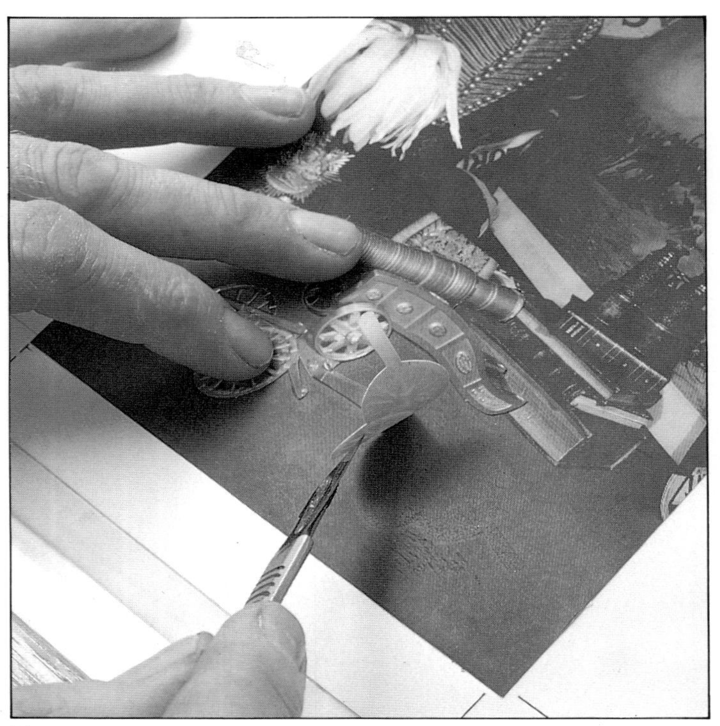

1▲

2▲

3▲

4▲

**1**. If there are any alterations, they are noted on an overlay and taken into consideration when the artwork is being produced. In this project there are no client corrections, so the artwork can go ahead as planned.

**2**. An acetate overlay is secured over the illustration on which the lettering will be drawn.

**3.,4**. The lettering is prepared in black, which will be reversed out when printed, and is positioned accurately with a parallel motion.

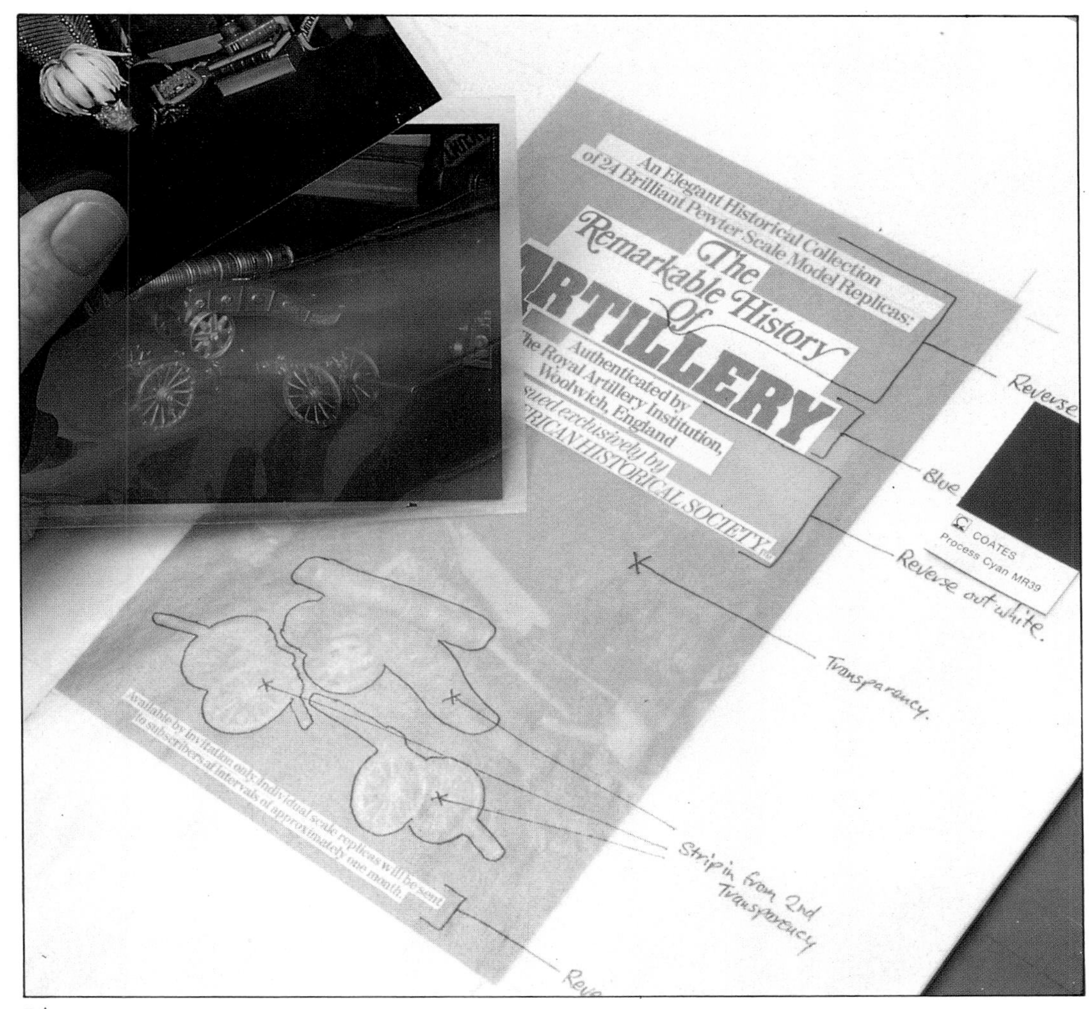


5▲

**5**. An overlay is placed over the artwork on which the instructions for the printer are written. Since the artwork was prepared in black and white, the printer must be provided with the specified colors. Here the Pantone system is put to use and swatches supplied to enable the printer to match his ink accordingly. The original transparencies are also supplied and their positions indicated.

1▲

2▲

3▲

**1**. As already stated, the inside pages are to be printed in three colors. To prepare this artwork for the printer, the artist treats colors as individual images and produces them on separate overlays. The background illustration of sepia is drawn first, on artboard.

**2**. PMTs of the text (which has been typeset) and the black line illustrations are positioned on an overlay.

**3**. On the next overlay the solid backgrounds for the line drawings are filled in. Again, all this work is carried out in black and white. From this artwork the printer will be able to produce a separate plate for each color that is to be reproduced.

A duo-tone is a two-color half-tone which is created from a black and white photograph (although it can be achieved in numerous other ways). Two plates are needed for this process, one for the black and one for the color, so the photo will have to be shot twice at different screen angles. The black plate holds the dark or shadow tones and the color plate all the middle tones. When printed together the half-tone dots from the two plates create a complete range of tones. Duotones can be particularly effective when color is important to the design but only black and white photographs are available.

# PROJECT 2

## · PSION ORGANIZER ·

**THE BRIEF**

This brief came from an advertising agency. The layout had been decided and the artist was required to arrange all the relevant information in such a way that it would draw the reader's attention to a specific point. It was decided to break the copy into separate blocks with the use of headlines, bullets and graphic symbols. The aim is an interesting and busy ad that will persuade the reader to use the response coupon.

Although the copy has not been written, "gibberish" is set in the chosen size and style for the body copy and only the headlines are "live." The client will be investing a lot of money in a campaign of this nature, so the rough produced by the studio must be almost like the finished advertisement.

MAGIC MARKER ILLUSTRATION

HEADLINE SETTING

# THE PSION ORGANISER

## THE WORLD'S FIRST PRACTICAL POCKET COMPUTER FOR LESS THAN £100

SE READY-TO-RUN PROGRAMS
STORE VITAL INFORMATION AND
RETRIEVE IT INSTANTLY

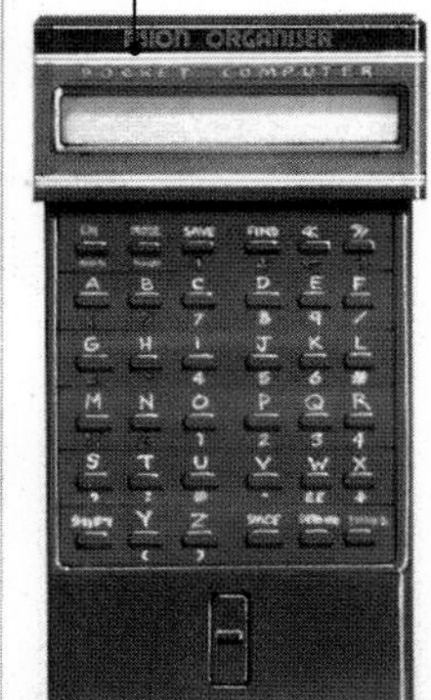


MPROVED PERSONAL PRODUCTI

IMPROVED PERSONAL PRODUCTIVITY

STORE VITAL INFORMATION AND

OLVE YOUR OWN PROBLEM
YOUR OWN SOFTW

USE READY-TO-RUN PROGRAMS
IMPROVED PERSONAL PRODUCT

READY-TO-RUN PROGRAM

Use the Organiser to store:

ORE VITAL INFORMATION AN
RETRIEVE IT INSTANTLY

FINANCE

MATHEMATICS

SCIENCE

USE READY-TO-RUN PROGRAMS FOR
IMPROVED PERSONAL PRODUCTIVITY

SLIDING CASE TO PROTECT KEYBOARD

COMPLETE RANGE OF READY WRITTEN SOFTWARE

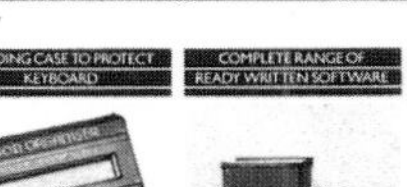

8K DATAPAK FOR PERMANENT STORAGE PROGRAM PACK

LOREM IPSUM DOLOR SIT AMET CONSECTETUER ADIPISCING

USE READY-TO-RUN PROG
IMPROVED PERSONAL PRO

ORGANISER

DATAPAKS

PROGRAM PACKS

FORMATTER

THE PSION ORGANISER IS A PRACTICAL COMPUTING OPPORTUNITY NO SERIOUS ENTHUSIAST CAN AFFORD TO IGNORE. FILL AND RETURN THE ORDER COUPON TODAY AND GET THE POWER OF A DESK-TOP MICRO IN YOUR POCKET

PSION

DUMMY "BULLETED" TYPE

SYMBOLS

RESPONSE COUPON

"LIVE" SIDE HEADS

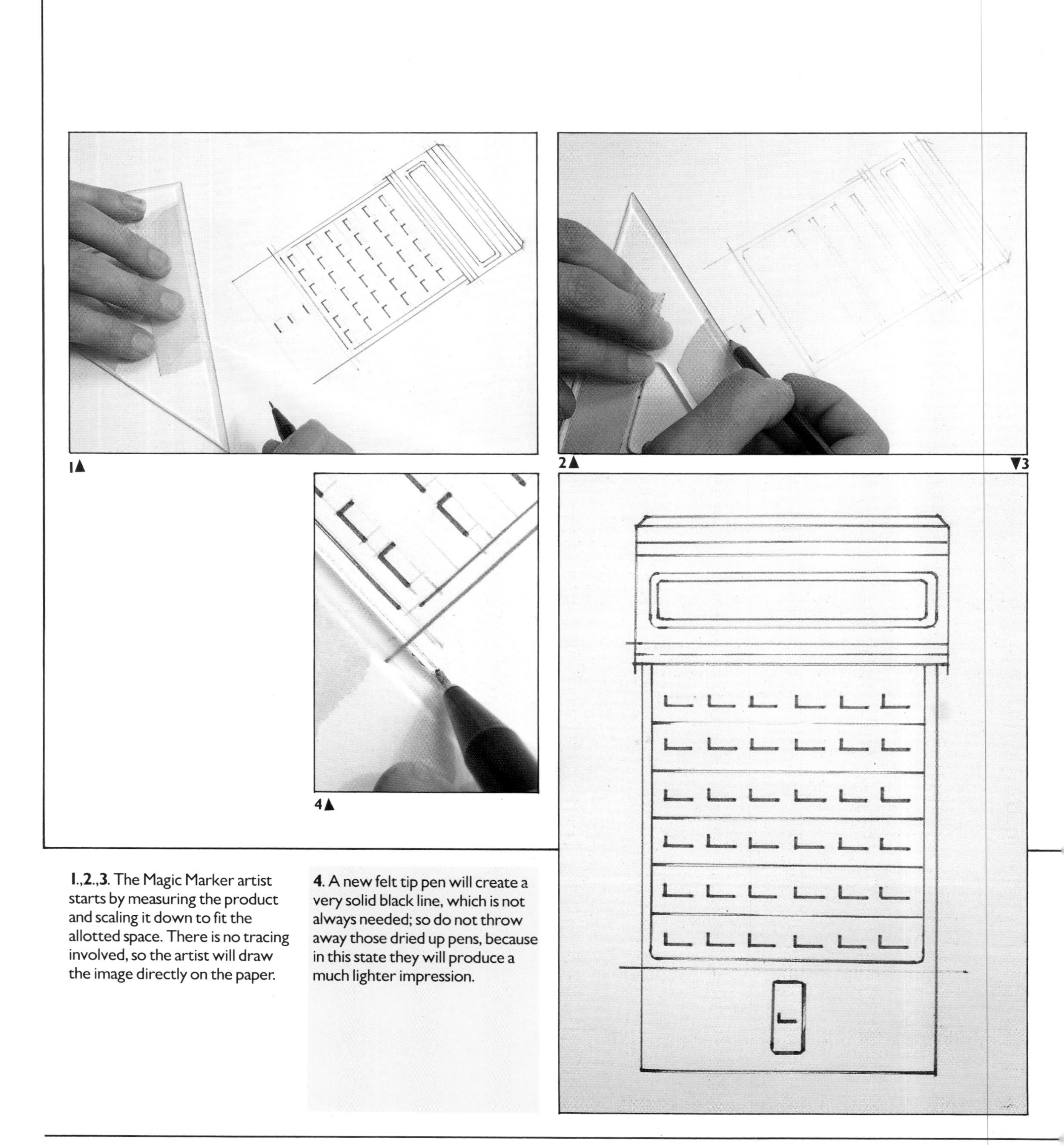

1.,2.,3. The Magic Marker artist starts by measuring the product and scaling it down to fit the allotted space. There is no tracing involved, so the artist will draw the image directly on the paper.

4. A new felt tip pen will create a very solid black line, which is not always needed; so do not throw away those dried up pens, because in this state they will produce a much lighter impression.

**5.,6.** Although working within a given space, the Magic Marker artist needs to make long strokes. When the color work begins, the artist extends the strokes beyond the outlines and cuts out the image.

**7.,8.** The artist lays down the background color and gradually fills in the various sections.

1▲

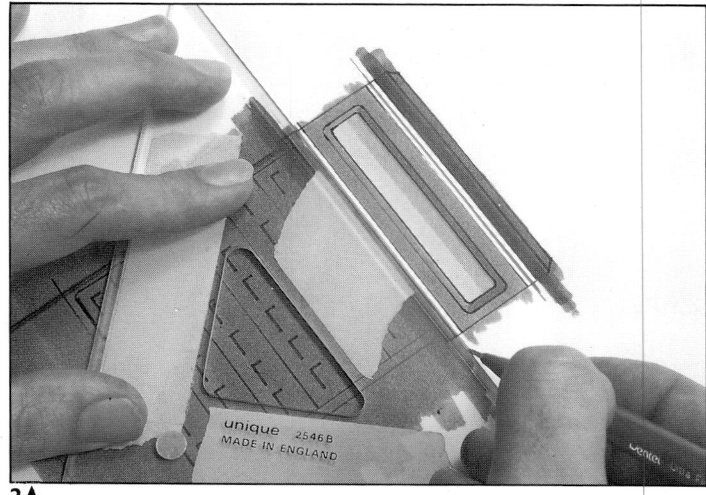


2▲

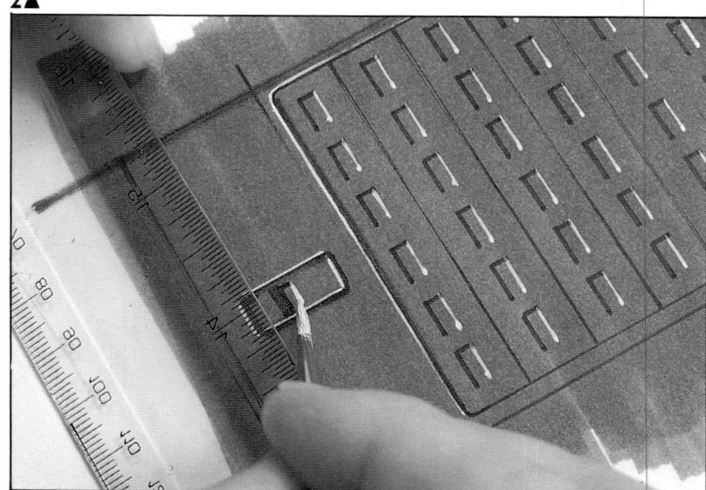

3▲

**1.,2.** The artist will now complete the drawing by putting in all the fine details and highlights.

**3.,4.** Felt tip pens are more versatile than one imagines; a wide variety of different effects can be achieved simply by cutting the nibs at various angles. Also, think twice before throwing out old brushes that have lost some of their bristles, for they are perfect for producing thin lines.

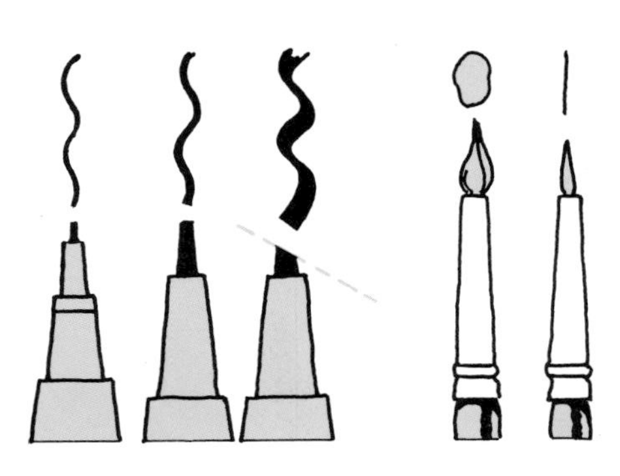

4▲

5▲

6▲

**5.,6.** Here the artist has cut the nib of his Magic Marker like a chisel to match the width of the computer keys. By doing this he is able to draw them in one stroke. To complete the illustration he hand letters the keys in white paint, leaving just the trimming to be done.

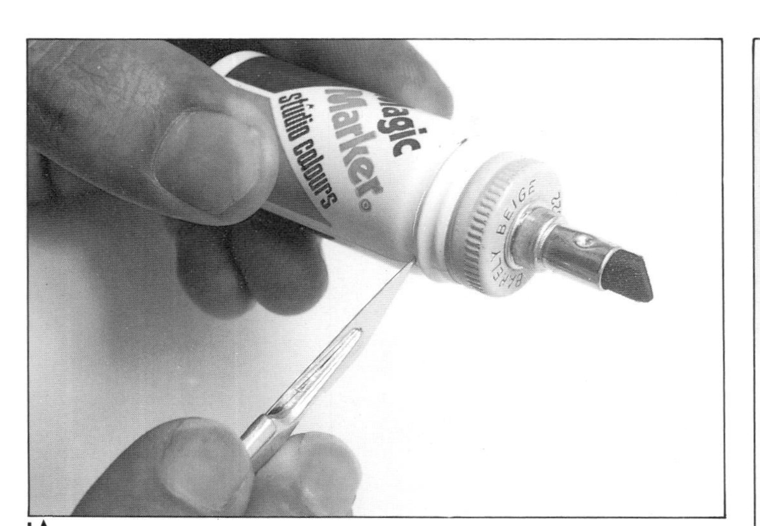


1▲

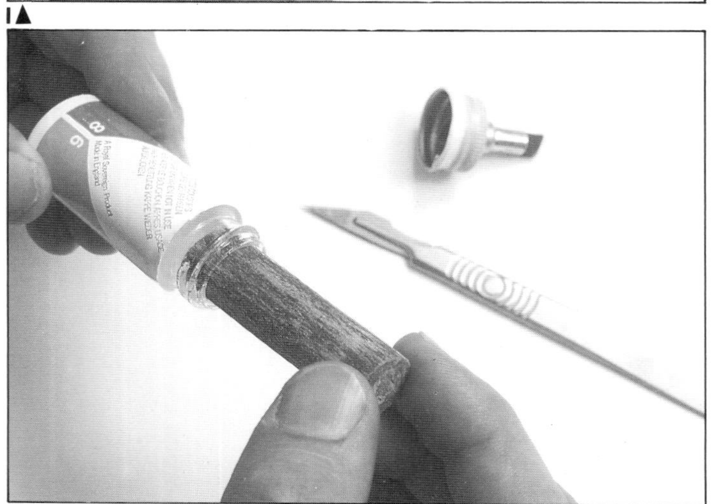

2▲

3▲

**1.,2.** Here we reveal the inside story of a Magic Marker! Cut the top off the marker with an X-acto knife (this is the only occasion when you do not have to use a fresh blade) and extract the piece of filling, which is soaked with the ink.

**3.** You can now use it to cover large solid background areas at a much faster pace. It is not just speed that is gained from this technique: a more even tone can be built up as the artist uses wider sweeping strokes without the restriction of a narrow nib.

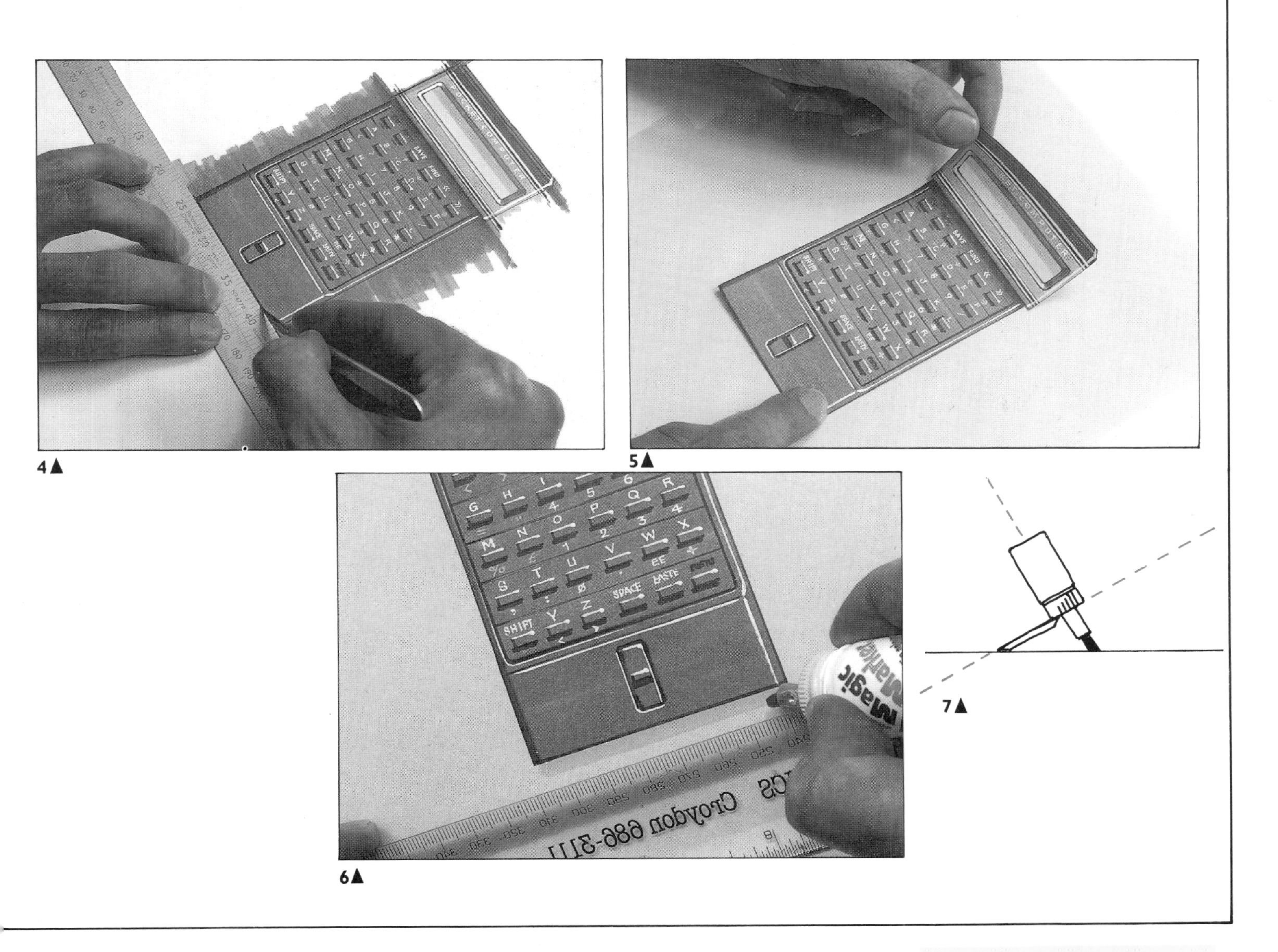

4▲ 5▲ 6▲ 7▲

**4.**,**5.**,**6.** To continue with the Magic Marker illustration: the waste area is trimmed away and the image laid onto the background on a separate sheet. To achieve the feeling of a three-dimensional image the artist adds the final shadows.

**7.** When using the ruler upside down, as required for Magic Marker work, you can place it at an angle, which will give extra support to the marker when drawing straight edges.

1▲ 2▲ 3▲ 4▲

**1.,2.** The actual name of the computer had to be shown, so a PMT of the chosen typeface was taken and reversed out. After the PMT is cut to size, to prevent any white edges from showing, a black felt tip pen is run along the edges before the word is placed in position.

**3.,4.** A tracing is made of the exact space into which the illustration will be dropped, and placed over the image. A pair of dividers are pushed through the two layers at the corners, creating instant crop marks. It is then cut to size and placed in its final position on the finished rough.

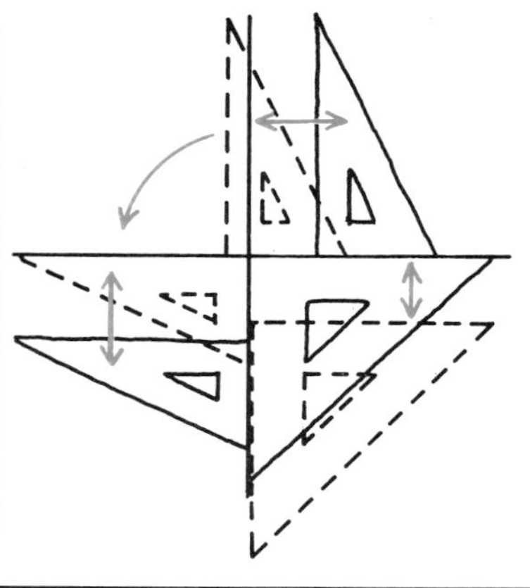

*This diagram shows how parallel lines can be constructed accurately within one area using two triangles. Draw a right-angled cross and place the triangles on a line, as shown. By moving them around together you can make sure your parallel lines are always equidistant.*

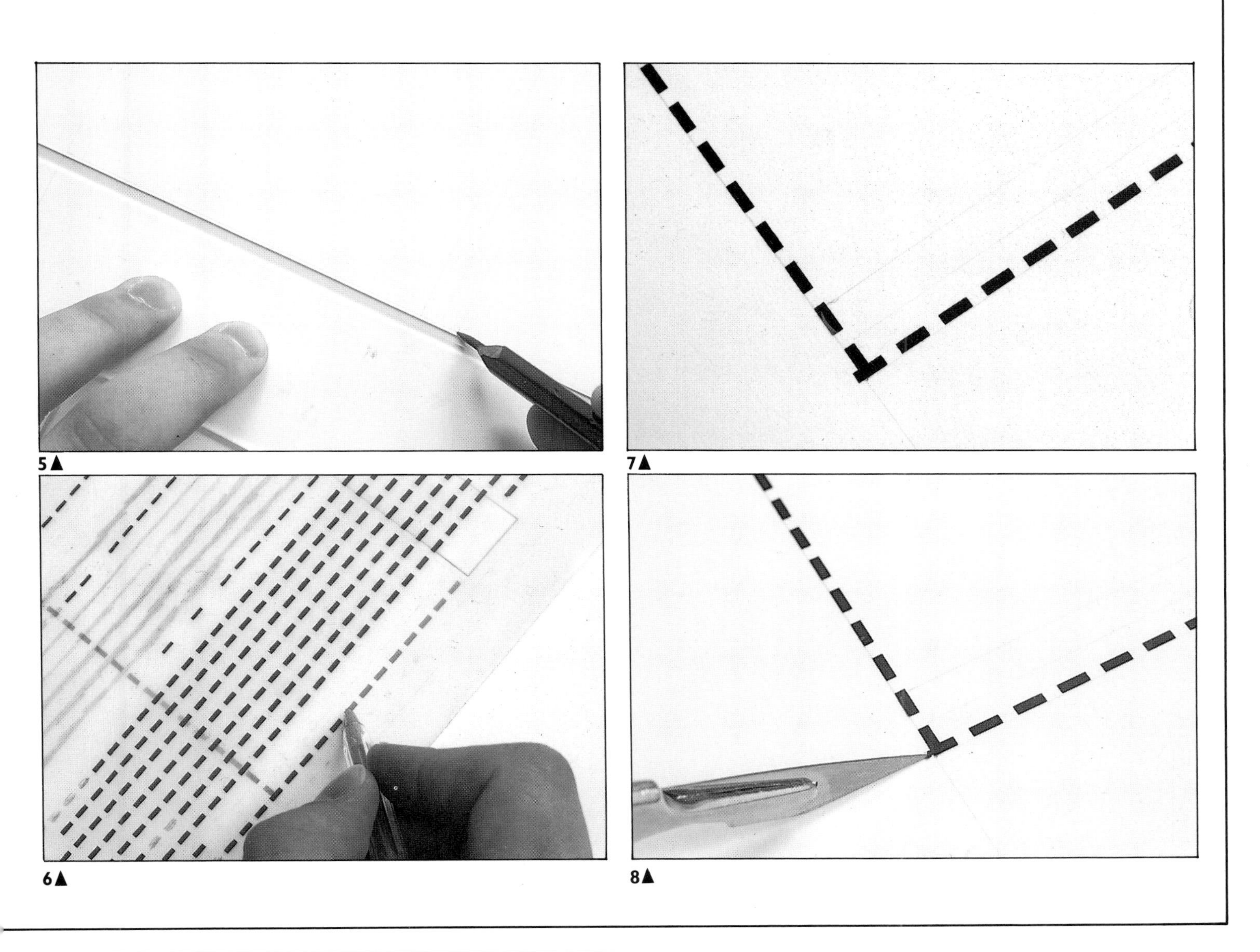

5▲ 7▲ 6▲ 8▲

**5.,6.,7.,8.** The ad is completed by the layout artist. The coupon is constructed by drawing the outline of its allotted size in pencil. This will provide the guidelines along which the Letraset will be burnished. In this case the artist chooses a ballpoint pen to rub down the dash lines, since they are relatively small and tricky to handle. The advantage of dry transfer sheets for this type of work is that the letters are already evenly spaced. However it is only rarely that they fit the size exactly, so any overlap at the corners is scraped back gently with the point of an X-acto knife.

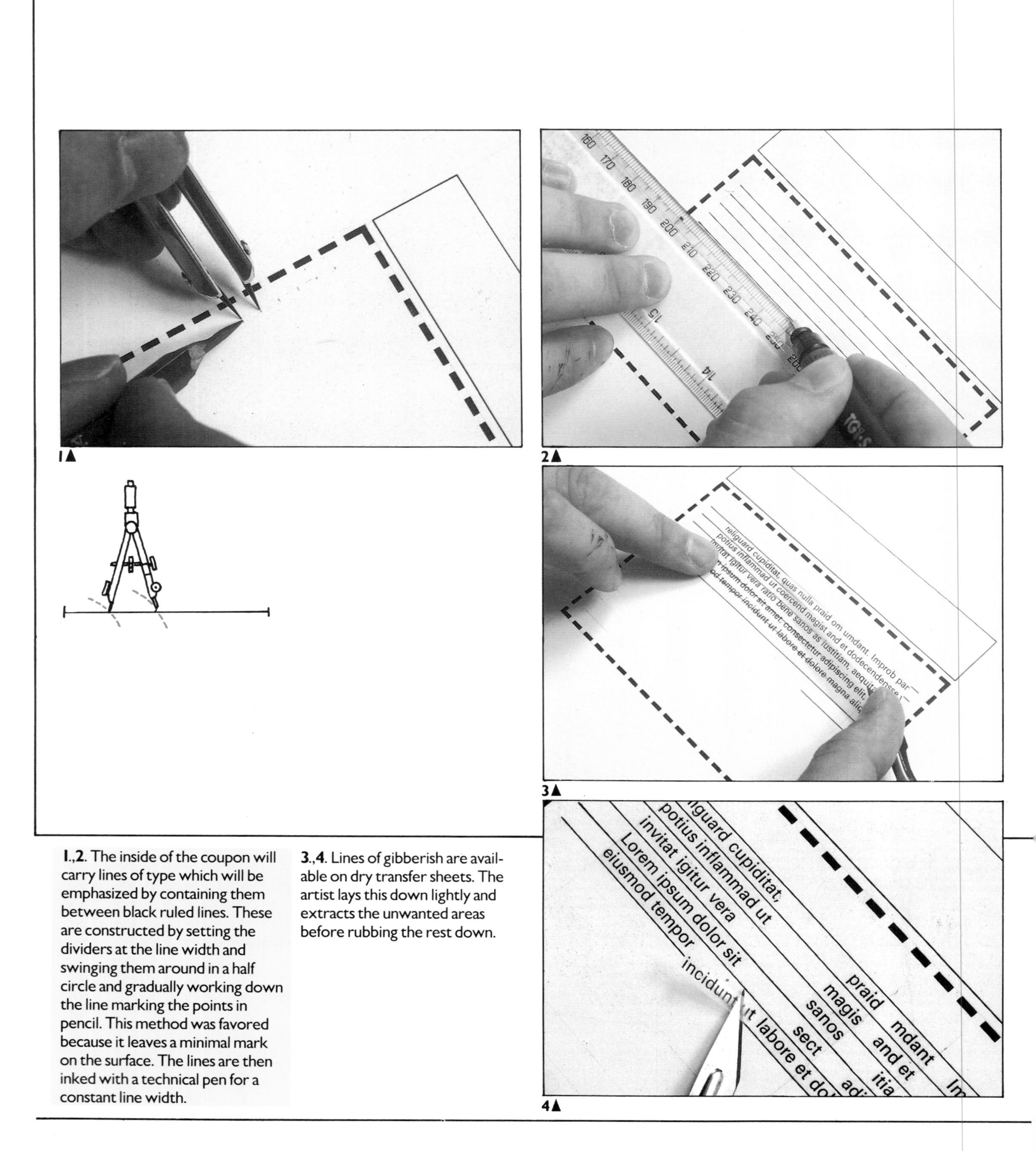


**1.,2.** The inside of the coupon will carry lines of type which will be emphasized by containing them between black ruled lines. These are constructed by setting the dividers at the line width and swinging them around in a half circle and gradually working down the line marking the points in pencil. This method was favored because it leaves a minimal mark on the surface. The lines are then inked with a technical pen for a constant line width.

**3.,4.** Lines of gibberish are available on dry transfer sheets. The artist lays this down lightly and extracts the unwanted areas before rubbing the rest down.

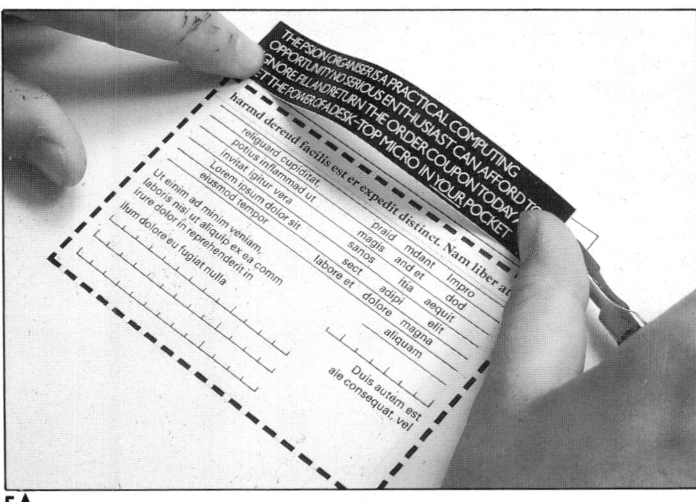

5▲

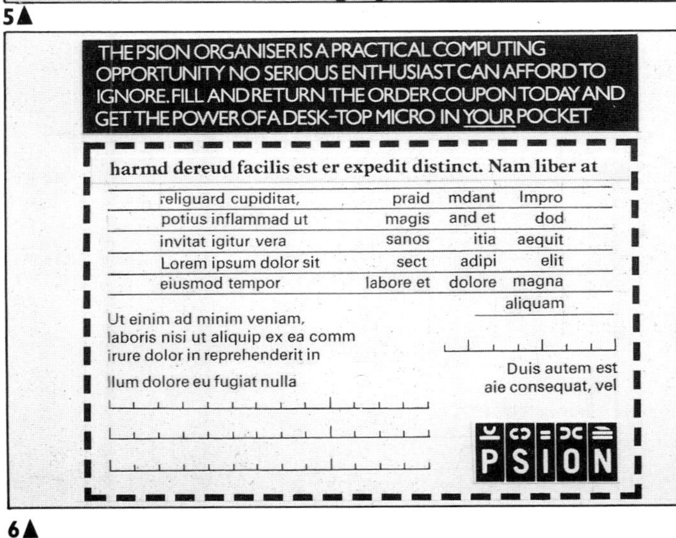

THE PSION ORGANISER IS A PRACTICAL COMPUTING OPPORTUNITY NO SERIOUS ENTHUSIAST CAN AFFORD TO IGNORE. FILL AND RETURN THE ORDER COUPON TODAY AND GET THE POWER OF A DESK-TOP MICRO IN YOUR POCKET

**harmd dereud facilis est er expedit distinct. Nam liber at**

| | | | |
|---|---|---|---|
| religuard cupiditat, | praid | mdant | Impro |
| potius inflammad ut | magis | and et | dod |
| invitat igitur vera | sanos | itia | aequit |
| Lorem ipsum dolor sit | sect | adipi | elit |
| eiusmod tempor | labore et | dolore | magna |
| | | | aliquam |

Ut einim ad minim veniam,
laboris nisi ut aliquip ex ea comm
irure dolor in reprehenderit in
Illum dolore eu fugiat nulla

Duis autem est
aie consequat, vel

PSION

6▲

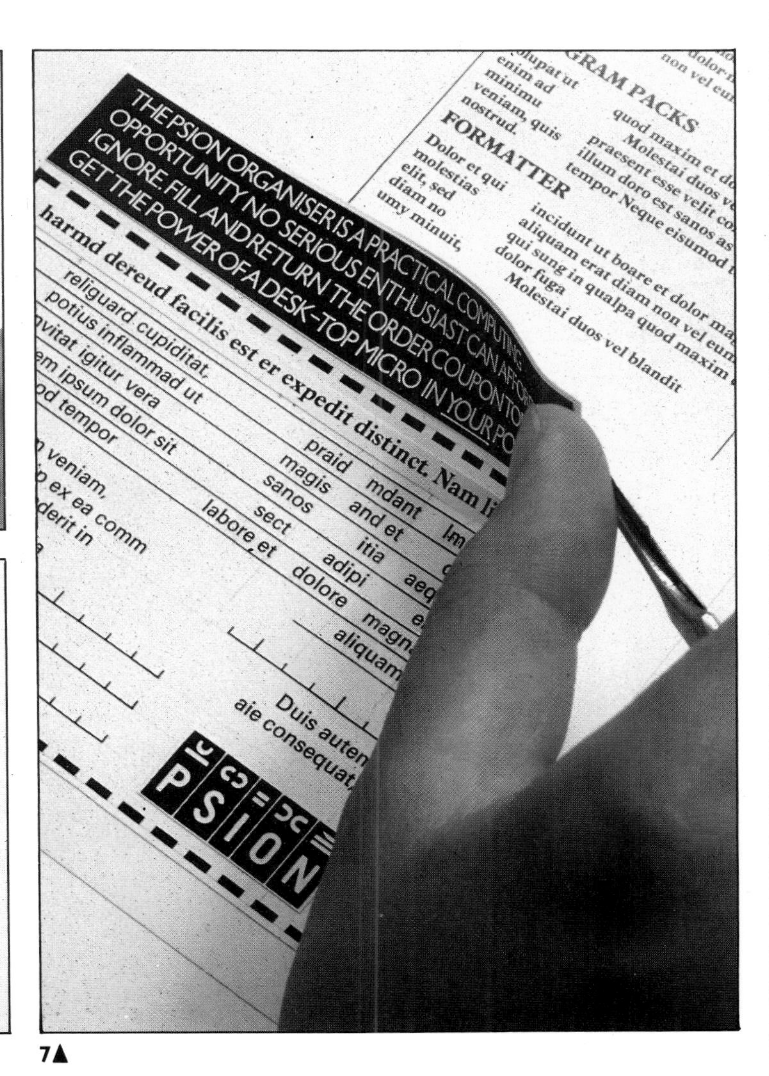


7▲

**5**. The blank areas, which the customer will, hopefully, fill in, are put down in Letraset.

**6**. The copy at the head of the coupon had actually been written, so it was typeset, and a reversed PMT was made to size.

**7**. With all the components now in place, a PMT is taken of the whole before it is pasted onto the final board. PMTs are always used, since Letraset is not permanent and will lift off a surface after constant handling.

**8**. When storing an original containing Letraset in a portfolio with plastic sleeves, always remember to cover it with a sheet of tracing paper, since the lettering will attach itself to this type of surface.

# PROJECT 3

## · FINANCIAL TIMES INDEX ·

### THE BRIEF

This type of project will usually come to the graphic studio via an ad agency, so the majority of the groundwork has already been carried out and in some cases the illustration itself commissioned. The agency will have discussed the client's needs in full and presented the initial roughs, so by the time it reaches the studio there will be a very tight brief and specific instructions.

The skills involved in a project of this nature are those of a paste-up artist. The artist involved will not be creating an original drawing but laying down all the components supplied to him in such a way as to create a well-balanced ad that will draw the attention of the reader to the vital information immediately. The advertisement is specifically for reproduction in a newspaper and therefore in black and white only. To create the impact that is necessary without the use of color and to accommodate the amount of information in a clear manner, various tricks and techniques, such as breaking up the type, will have to be employed.

*The black line illustration will be the central focal point around which all the copy will be fitted. It was obviously drawn in a horizontal format for the newspaper page. The aim is to show the amount of staff time it takes to search for specific information in an old-fashioned filing system, which also relies on the information having been replaced in its correct slot when previously used. This reminds the reader of all these points instantly in visual terms, thereby avoiding the monotony of constant comparisons in the text.*

*On the following page we have shown the finished artwork for the ad.*

CONCEPT ILLUSTRATION
HEADLINE SETTING
SPECIAL ARTWORK EFFECTS
Use this new, comprehensive
INDEX TO THE FINANCIAL TIMES
to save hours of checking through other sources.
Now you can use your FINANCIAL TIMES not only as your daily source of business news but also as a valuable historical record.
With this new monthly INDEX you can immediately trace anything published from January 1981 to the issue and the page.
Use it to go back over the various stages in a bid or merger, for example; to monitor significant developments in a particular company or industry; to refer to any event or personality whenever there is anything you wish to clarify.
Instant reference
The INDEX gives you instant reference. Information is grouped under three headings – Corporate, General, and Personalities – giving you sufficiently detailed and comprehensive coverage of every news item. And as the illustrations show you, it is easy for you to cross-reference a particular story under each heading.
THE INDEX GIVES YOU THE MAIN POINT OF EACH STORY. THE DATA BASE IS COMPREHENSIVE, ACCURATE AND UP TO DATE. THIS EXTRACT FROM THE Corporate SECTION COVERS SHELL.
THE PRICE RISE NOTED IS ALSO COVERED IN THE General SECTION, UNDER PETROL.
THE UK SHELL AND UK PETROL ENTRIES BOTH REFER TO MR. BOOTH, WHO HAS HIS OWN ENTRY IN THE Personalities SECTION.
EACH ENTRY CONCLUDES WITH DATE, PAGE AND COLUMN REFERENCE. THE FT'S EIGHT COLUMNS ARE LISTED A-H. THUS Aug 19-6c MEANS THAT THE ITEM APPEARED IN THE ISSUE OF 19TH AUGUST, ON PAGE 6, IN COLUMN 3.
What users say about this Index
"Used as first service when trying to trace obscure articles."
"A very thorough index to the best source of business information."
"Excellent in all respects. A great time-saver."
FINANCIAL TIMES
ORDER TODAY TO GET TWO YEARS' ISSUES FOR THE PRICE OF ONE.
In any one year the FINANCIAL TIMES covers about 35,000 companies, including companies overseas. All, together with records of rights issues, tombstones, chairmen's statements, annual and interim reports, surveys, articles on industries and companies, leading articles, theatre reports and the like, are listed in the INDEX. For corporate research the INDEX is an information-gathering tool that will save hours of checking through other sources.
Speedy delivery
Production of the INDEX is based on electronic sorting. Information is quickly processed, automatically arranged in alphabetical order and rapidly retrieved. Your monthly copy is on its way to you earlier than any other comparable index.
The INDEX is also available on microfiche, floppy disc or magnetic tape. If you would like further details of these, please tick the appropriate box on the reply coupon.
The Financial Times Index is of special value to:
Companies ★ Stockbrokers ★ Management Consultants ★ Financial and Investment Analysts ★ Advertising and Marketing Agencies ★ Banks ★ Political, Industrial and Financial Researchers ★ Government Departments ★ University and Public Libraries
Anybody to whom the FT itself is a source of business information will benefit from the INDEX.
For you, now: two years' issues for the price of one!
Use the coupon below to order your subscription to the INDEX. Do this now, today, and as a bonus you will receive – FREE – a copy of the annual cumulative volume for 1981.
You may start your subscription from any month you choose. It will cost you only £240, delivered anywhere in the UK, or £299 delivered elsewhere. This price covers all 12 monthly issues and the annual cumulative volume for 1981. (The normal price for the 1981 annual alone is £225 in the UK, £275 elsewhere.)
To accept this offer, please post your completed coupon today to: Financial Times Business Information Ltd., Minster House, Arthur Street, London EC4R 9AX, England.
MONTHLY INDEX to the FINANCIAL TIMES
December 1981
TO EVERY ORGANIZATION THAT USES THE FT AS A REFERENCE TOOL THIS INDEX IS WORTH MANY TIMES ITS PRICE IN MAN-HOURS SAVED THAT WOULD OTHERWISE BE SPENT IN SEARCHES.
HALF-TONE PHOTO
INSTANT ART
ARTWORK ILLUSTRATION
RUN-AROUND TEXT

1▲

2▲

3▲

▼4

1. A PMT is made from the artwork and placed in position on the board. The type has been set ranged left to keep things simple, and the artist will re-position it himself.

2. Remember that when moving lines of type to run around an outline shape you must cut straight lines between every line, so that when they are moved the lines will still run parallel. Always cut toward yourself, since this makes it easier to apply even pressure and does less damage if the knife slips. (See p. 00.)

3.,4. A sheet of tracing paper is placed over the illustration and the outline traced in black. The artist decides on the distance from the edge of the illustration to which the type will be fitted and draws this freehand on the sheet.

5▲

6▲

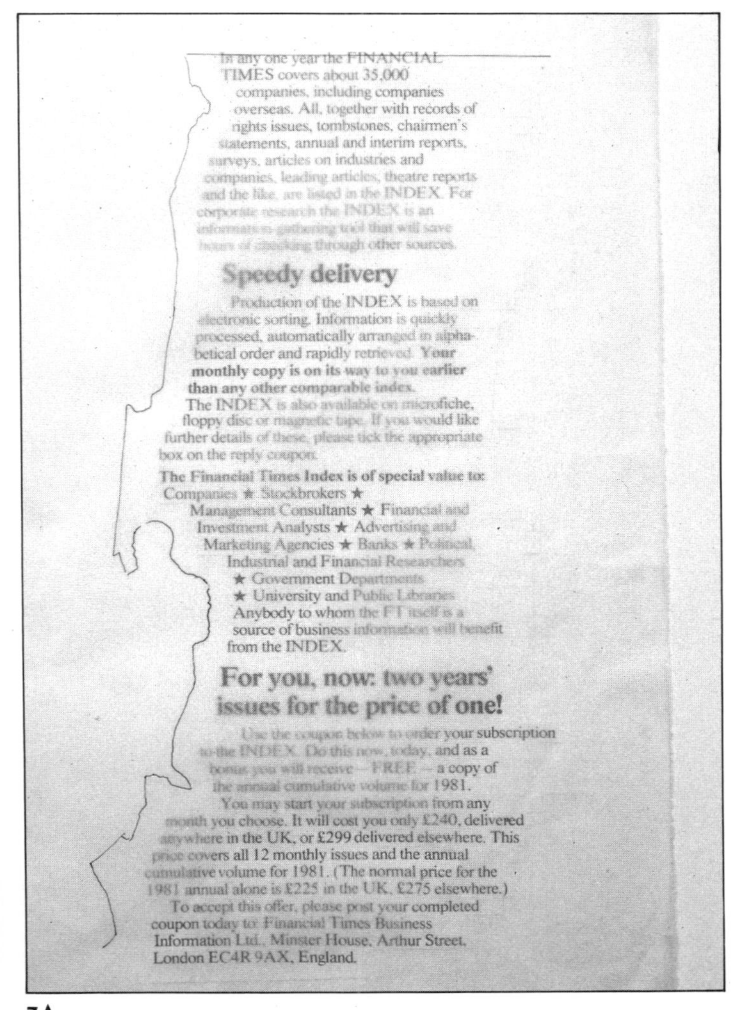

In any one year the FINANCIAL TIMES covers about 35,000 companies, including companies overseas. All, together with records of rights issues, tombstones, chairmen's statements, annual and interim reports, surveys, articles on industries and companies, leading articles, theatre reports and the like, are listed in the INDEX. For corporate research the INDEX is an information-gathering tool that will save hours of checking through other sources.

## Speedy delivery

Production of the INDEX is based on electronic sorting. Information is quickly processed, automatically arranged in alphabetical order and rapidly retrieved. **Your monthly copy is on its way to you earlier than any other comparable index.**

The INDEX is also available on microfiche, floppy disc or magnetic tape. If you would like further details of these, please tick the appropriate box on the reply coupon.

**The Financial Times Index is of special value to:**
Companies ★ Stockbrokers ★ Management Consultants ★ Financial and Investment Analysts ★ Advertising and Marketing Agencies ★ Banks ★ Political, Industrial and Financial Researchers ★ Government Departments ★ University and Public Libraries

Anybody to whom the FT itself is a source of business information will benefit from the INDEX.

## For you, now: two years' issues for the price of one!

Use the coupon below to order your subscription to the INDEX. Do this now, today, and as a bonus you will receive — FREE — a copy of the annual cumulative volume for 1981.

You may start your subscription from any month you choose. It will cost you only £240, delivered anywhere in the UK, or £299 delivered elsewhere. This price covers all 12 monthly issues and the annual cumulative volume for 1981. (The normal price for the 1981 annual alone is £225 in the UK, £275 elsewhere.)

To accept this offer, please post your completed coupon today to: Financial Times Business Information Ltd., Minster House, Arthur Street, London EC4R 9AX, England.

7▲

**5.,6.** The traced sheet is secured along one side over the type, and each line is lifted individually under the sheet and butted up to the drawn edge.

**7.** Even without the illustration it is easy to see how the run-around type has given more unity to the text and illustrations.

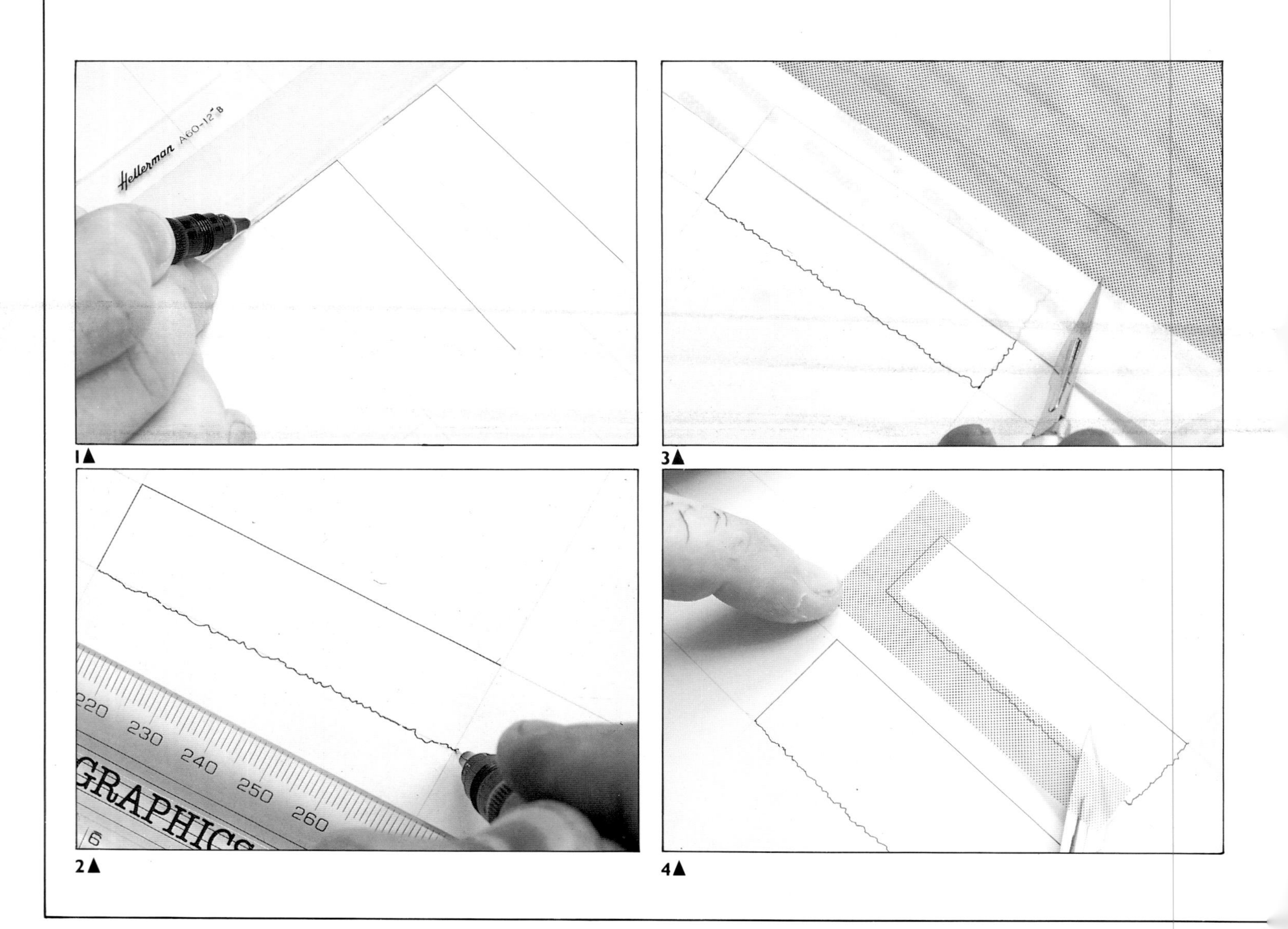


**1**. The ad incorporated quotations from various large companies who had actually invested in the system. Rather than use straight boxes, the agency decided to make it look as if the comments had been torn straight from the page of a publication in which they had been printed. This procedure is started by drawing and plotting the box areas on the page in pencil. The boxes are then drawn over with a technical pen, since this will give an accurate fine line and constant width.

**2**. The bottom line of the box will be the torn edge, so using the straight pencil edge as a guide, the artist draws the "wiggly" line freehand.

**3**. To pull them out of the page and draw attention to the boxes he creates a 3-D effect by using a shadow. Luckily for the artist, the dots are available on a sheet of Letraset, so he won't have to draw them himself. The dry transfer dots are placed over the box and the amount needed cut out with an X-acto knife.

**4**. At this stage the protective backing sheet for the Letraset must be kept in place, since this will prevent any of the dots from sticking to the artwork where they are not wanted. The piece is then positioned but not rubbed down with any pressure, since some areas will have to be removed.

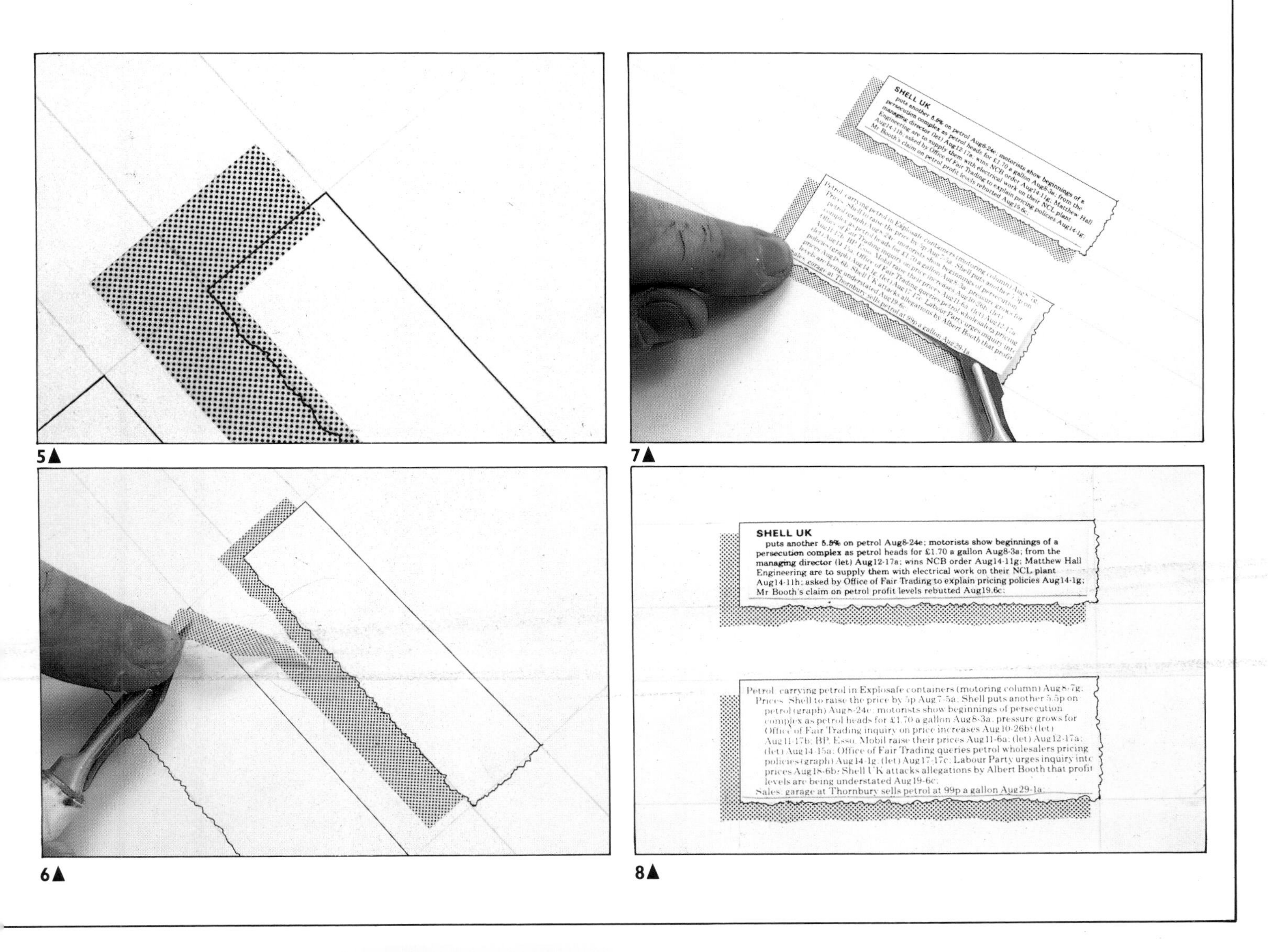


**5**. The artist now has to do all the trimming. The black lines are followed with the knife and the underneath trimmed freehand. The excess is lifted off with the help of the knife point.

**6**. If any dots have stuck to the artwork they can be cleaned off by dabbing them with the sticky side of a piece of tape. Do not press hard, for this could damage the surface of the board – just keep applying a clean area of tape until they eventually come away.

**7.,8**. A piece of layout paper is then placed over the shadow and given a final rub down. The copy is trimmed, positioned and finally stuck down into the box. Note how each box contains a different style of typesetting to indicate that the cuttings were taken from more than one publication.

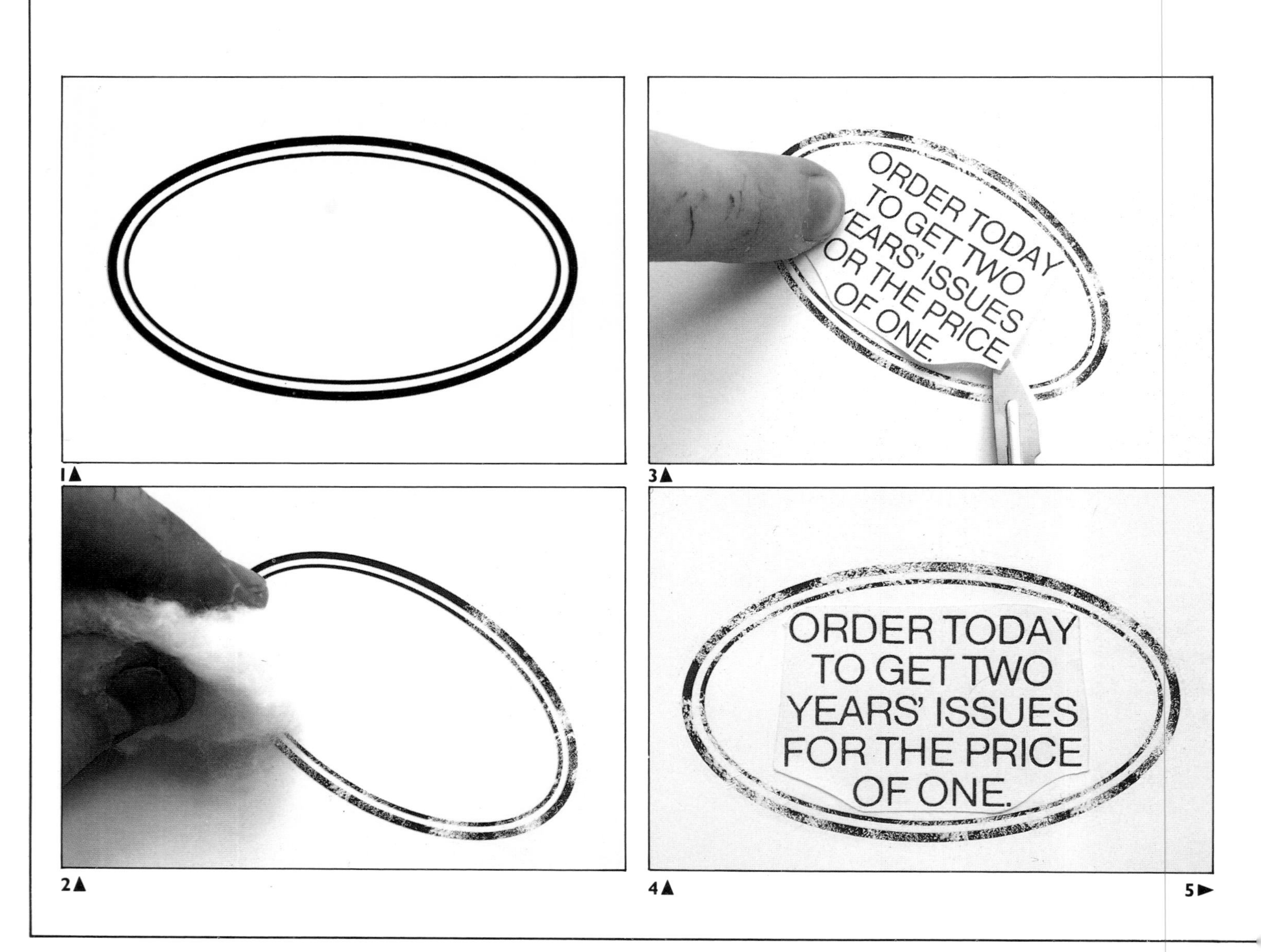


1▲ 3▲ 2▲ 4▲ 5►

**1**. To separate and draw attention to the special offer it was decided to use a rubber stamp effect. This adds to the feeling that the offer has been stamped on for that day only and must be taken up immediately.

**2**. A quick, simple way of achieving a rubber stamp effect is to adapt a Letraset oval. Most people know that a rubber stamp very rarely produces a perfect image, so a piece of absorbent cotton with white paint is dabbed at irregular intervals to break up the solidity of the line.

**3**.,**4**. The copy is cut out and positioned before finally being fixed.

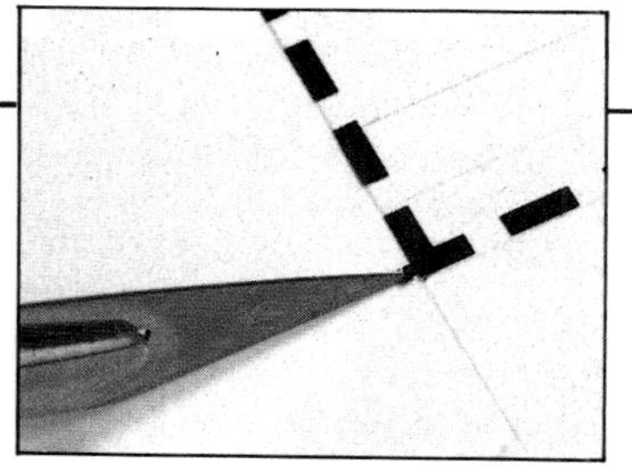

**5.** The illustration is now cut out and positioned, this time using the type as a guide. The original photograph of the reference book will have been converted into a half-tone. If, once the PMT has reduced to the required size, the print apears muddy, then you have chosen the wrong size of dots i.e. the screen ruling is incorrect. It is possible to change the screen at this stage.

The final component is the coupon to cut out and use to order the system. Both the broken lines and scissors are taken from Letraset and rubbed down into position. This time as the corners coupon have to be exact, the excess Letraset is gently scraped away with the tip of an X-acto knife. After protecting the finished artwork with a secure overlay, the artist can now send it to the printer.

# PROJECT 4

## · TELEVISION STORYBOARD ·

### THE BRIEF

Television storyboards are presented as a series of "still" separate images in individual frames (rather like a comic strip) which represent a sequence for moving pictures or film. Although only roughs, they are taken to a very high standard, since they will be used both to talk the client through the idea and for market research at a later stage. Because of the high costs involved in producing an ad, the storyboards, rather than the finished film, are shown to a sample of the viewing public.

Over the next pages we will show how one frame is worked up. There was no brief, since the illustration we have used was purely an exercise to demonstrate Magic Marker techniques; however, this type of brief would usually come from an advertising agency who would supply the products and any ideas they have already discussed with the client in the form of crude stick figure sketches, accompanied with a few "gags" or copy. Most storyboards are executed in color, and every individual artist will have his or her own style which the ad agency takes into consideration when making their choice of studio. On some occasions the client might want to see up to six different ideas – in which case they will be done in black and white.

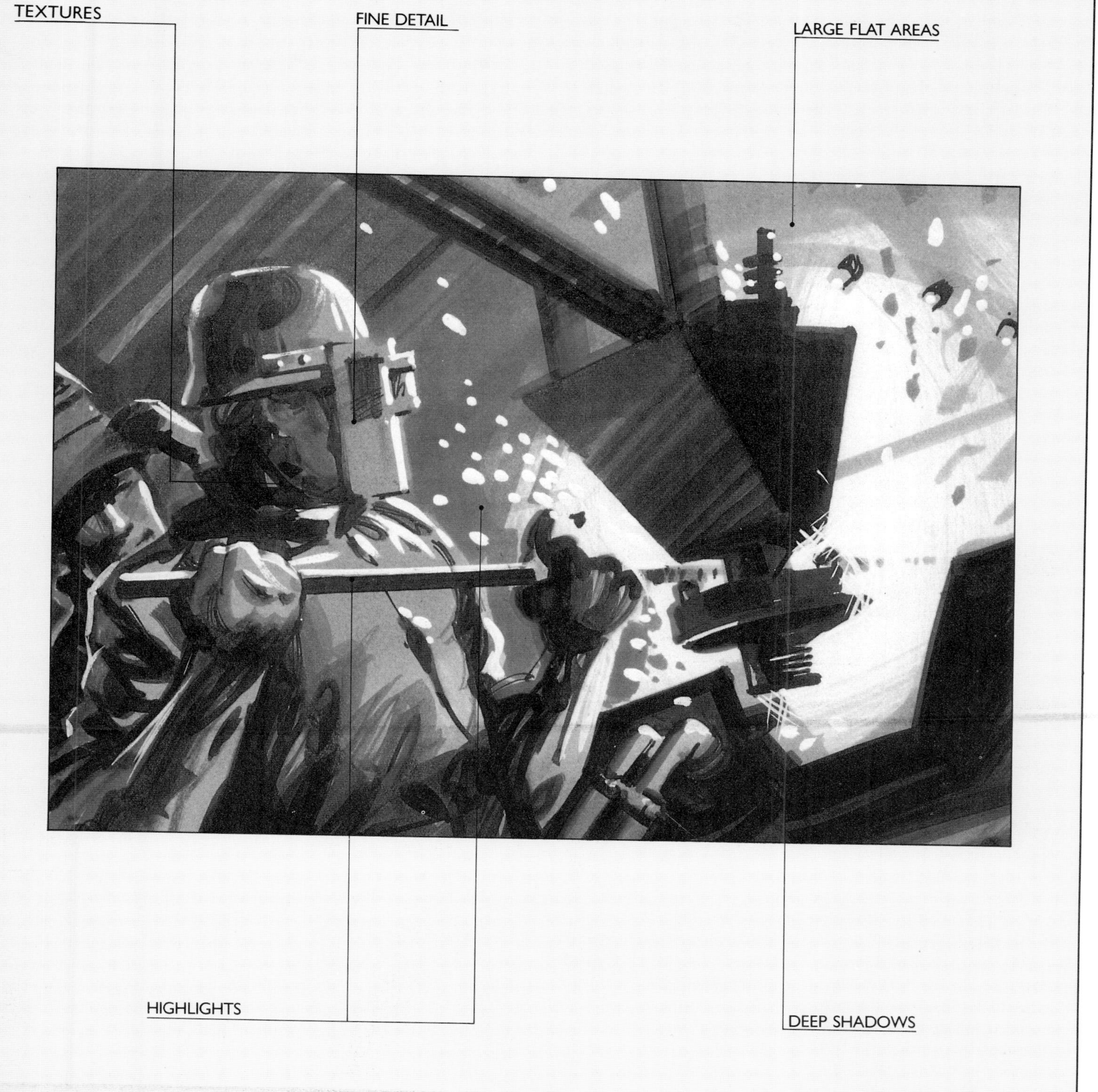

TEXTURES

FINE DETAIL

LARGE FLAT AREAS

HIGHLIGHTS

DEEP SHADOWS

1▲

2▲

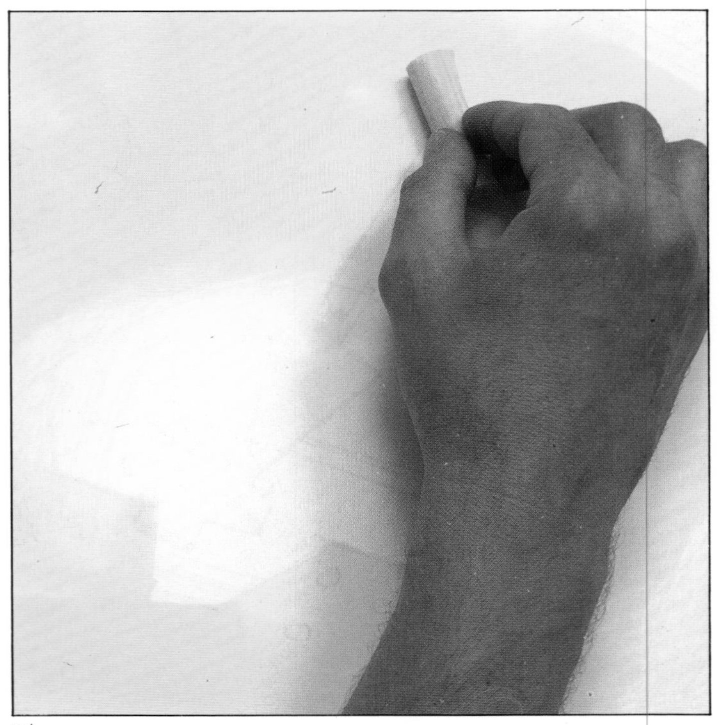

3▲

**1**. The artist begins by making a very rough pencil sketch. A sheet of tracing paper is then placed over the top, and using the initial sketch as a guide the artist makes the image more positive and rubs out the superfluous lines. This might be done several times.

**2**. An overlay is placed over the final pencil sketch and the background laid down.

**3**. The quickest way to cover large areas of background with Magic Marker is to cut off the top and extract the piece of fiber which is soaked in the color. This way a far more even tone is achieved. (See p. 106.)

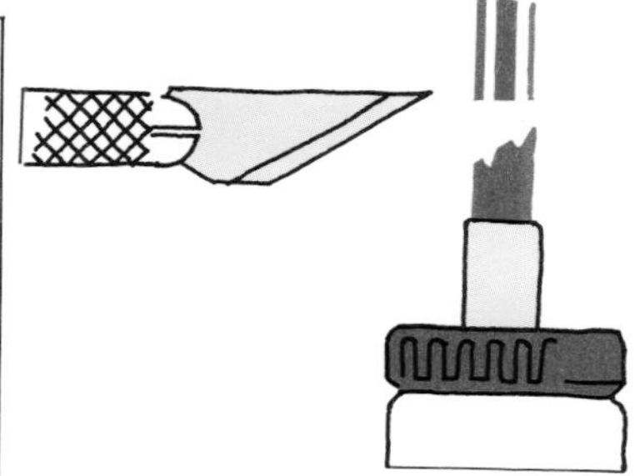

5. By splitting a marker nib into three the artist can achieve a series of lines that are the same but of varying width – very useful for producing images of things such as hair and water.

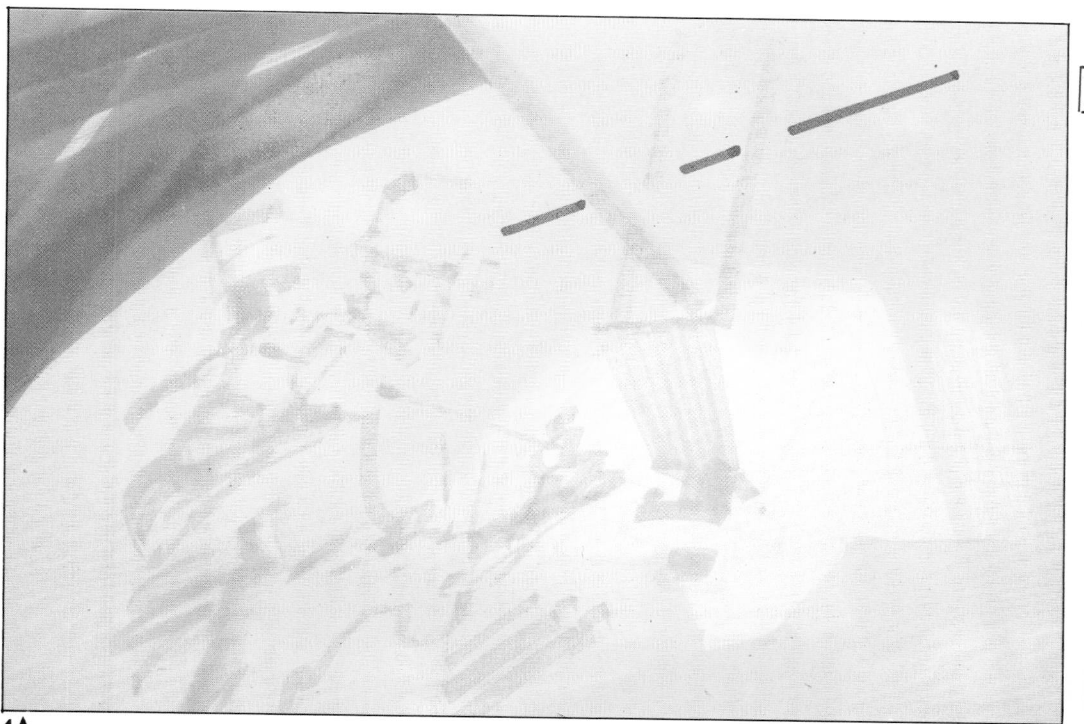

4▲

▼5

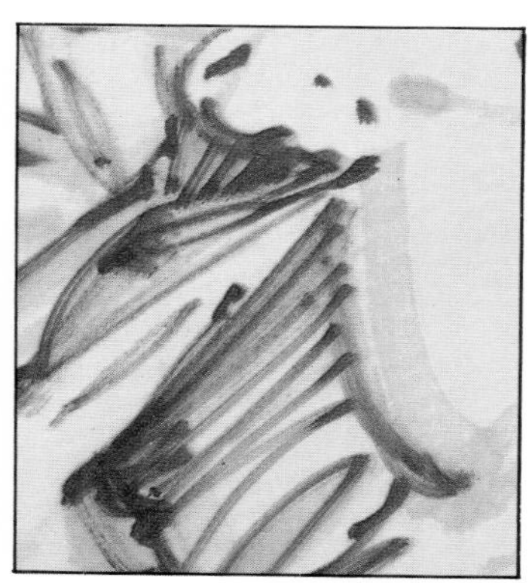

4. The artist is now following the pencil rough underneath and adding the figures and various components, always working in stages and constantly building up to darker, more positive, strokes.

1 ▲

▼ 2

**1.,2.** The artist is gradually introducing different colors, and as the illustration builds up so does the artist's confidence. When working with markers, speed of line is vital, and the artist must always be bold and brutal.

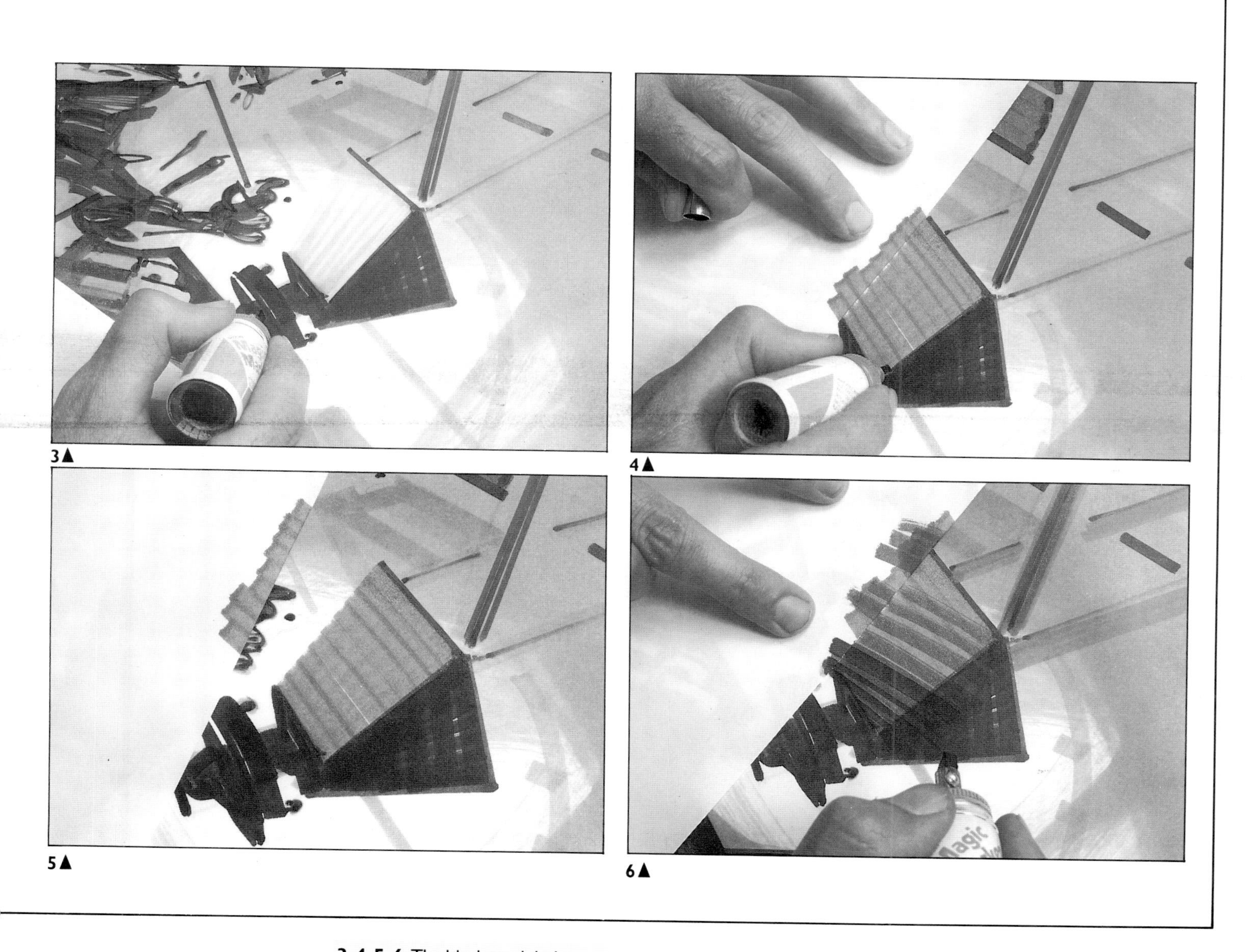

3▲ 4▲ 5▲ 6▲

**3.,4.,5.,6.** The blacks and darker shades are now being laid down. When a straight edge is required a sheet of paper is placed along the edge as a mask so that the artist's bold strokes are not suddenly interrupted and a constant weight of color is achieved.

1▲

2▲

3▲

**1**. Since the overall aim is to create the impression of heat, orange shades are added to produce a glow.

**2.,3**. Any fine details are added with a black felt tip pen at this stage. The artist keeps these details to a minimum.

4▲

▼5

**4.,5.** By standing back and viewing the illustration as a whole, one can see that the artist has succeeded in creating the illusion of a detailed image using sketchy lines and simple squiggles. This is the advantage and attraction of Magic Marker work.

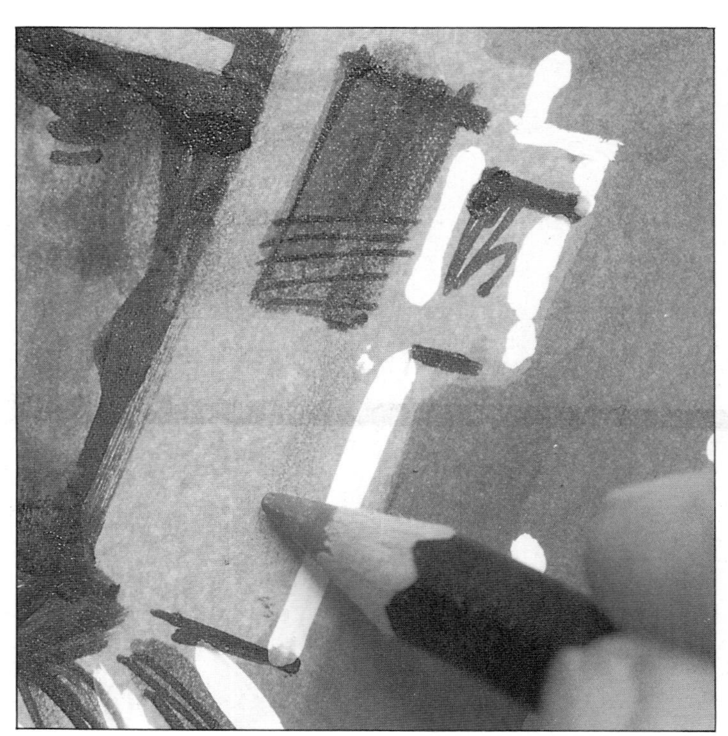

1▲

2▲

3▲

**1.**,**2.**,**3.** Highlights are added at the final stage. White paint is used, except for the softer highlights, where colored pencils are much more effective.

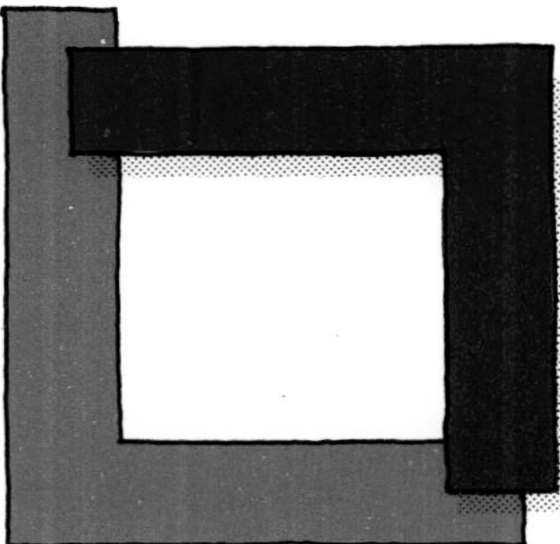

4. The artist is not sure at which angle the image will create more impact, so he makes use of a simple cropping aid. This consists of two large L-shapes cut from cardboard. They are placed over the illustration and can be moved around to any position.

4▲ ▼5

5. These two pictures show the finished illustration cropped at different angles and how this changes the whole movement of an image.

# PROJECT 5

## · GUERNSEY TOURIST BOARD ·

**THE BRIEF**

The Guernsey Tourist Board had no previous ideas, except that the butterfly was used as a symbol of the island and, since it already appeared on postage stamps, would form a good basis for the first steps of creating a continuous theme. The other information supplied from the client was a list of the island's main attractions – country walks, beaches for sunbathers, sailing, food and wine and an abundance of flowers and tropical plants.

The designs would not only be used for brochures, advertising and posters, but would have to be easily adaptable for various methods of reproduction, as the promotional products would range from stickers and calendars to t-shirts, towels and even stockings! The artist's solution was to employ a technique that creates cut-out solid shapes – collage. This is simple and versatile but also bold and visually stunning.

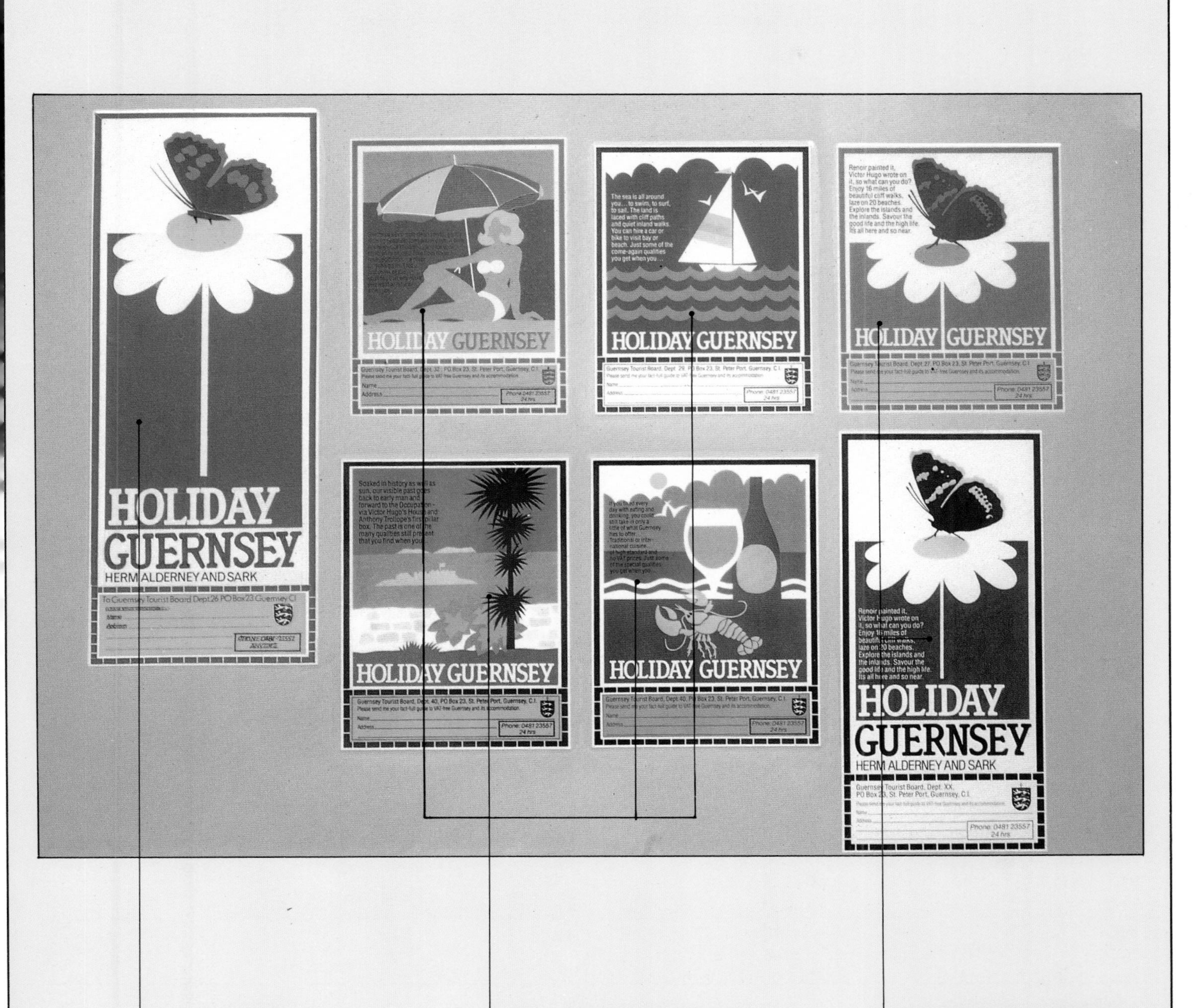


CLIENT ROUGH

FULL COLOR ILLUSTRATIONS

COLOR/MONO ADAPTATIONS

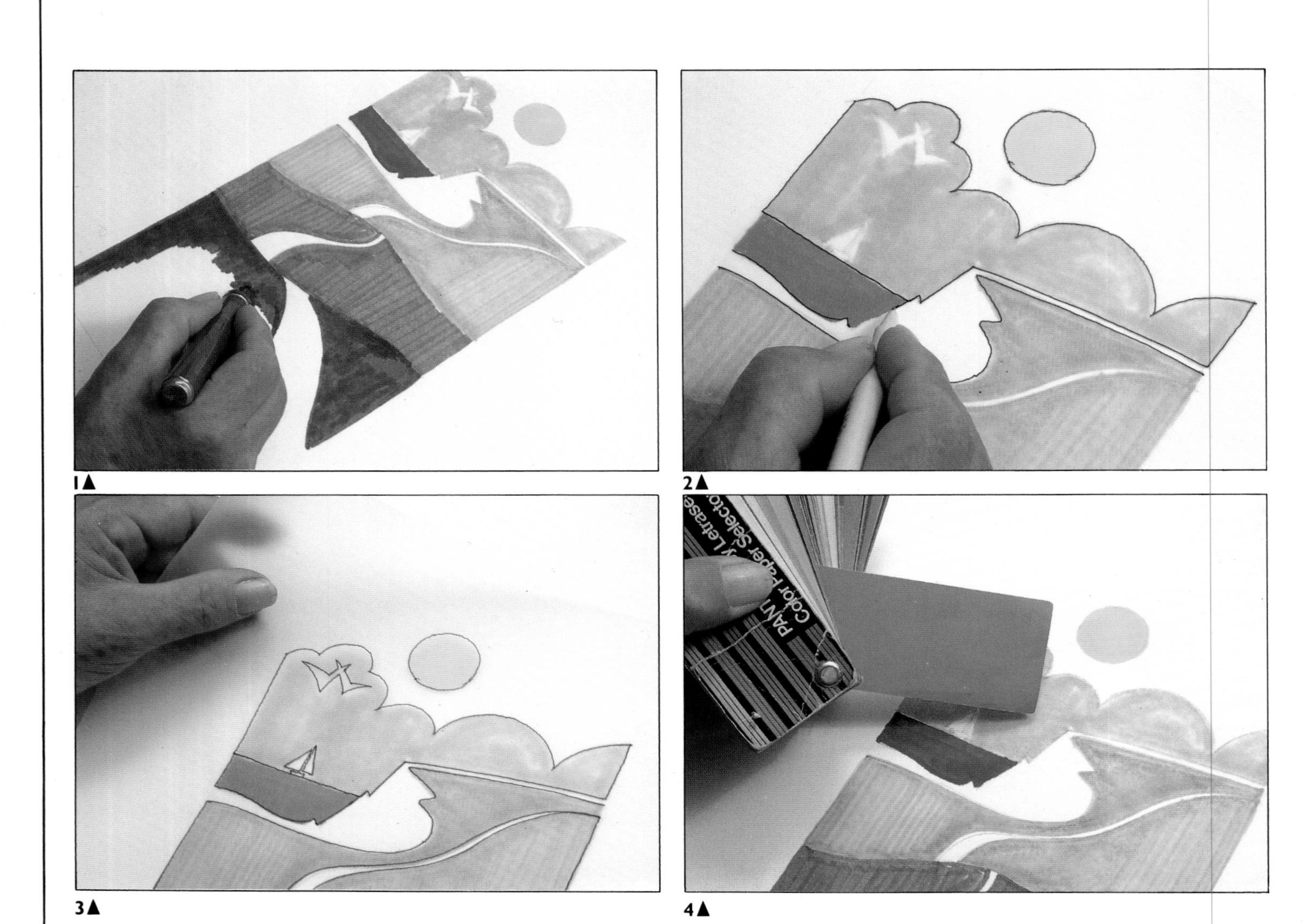

**1**. Here we follow the artist through the country walks illustration – starting off by laying down the solid areas of color with a Pantone marker, since these can be matched exactly with the Pantone colored paper range.

**2.,3**. On a separate overlay the solid areas are outlined in black, since this will eventually become the artist's cutting guide.

**4**. The artist is using the Pantone swatch system to match the chosen marker colors to their colored paper range.

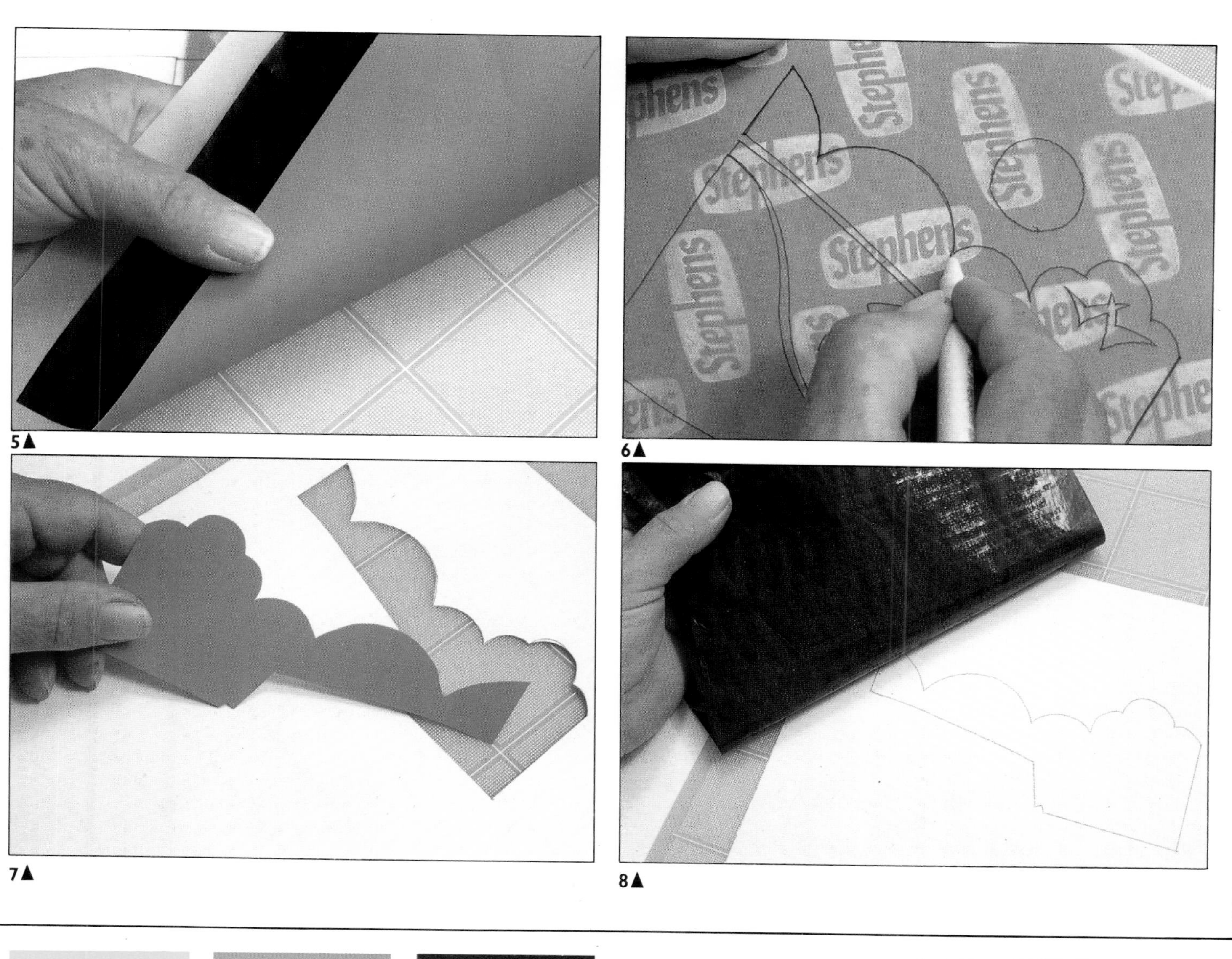


5▲ 6▲ 7▲ 8▲

**5.,6.,7.,8.** To prevent any trace of the outlines from showing, the artist reverses the shapes and transposes them onto the back of the colored paper. The best way of doing this is to "push through" the outlines with a hard pencil by placing a sheet of carbon paper between the traced overlay and colored sheet. Remembering to fit a new blade to the X-acto knife, cut out the outline.

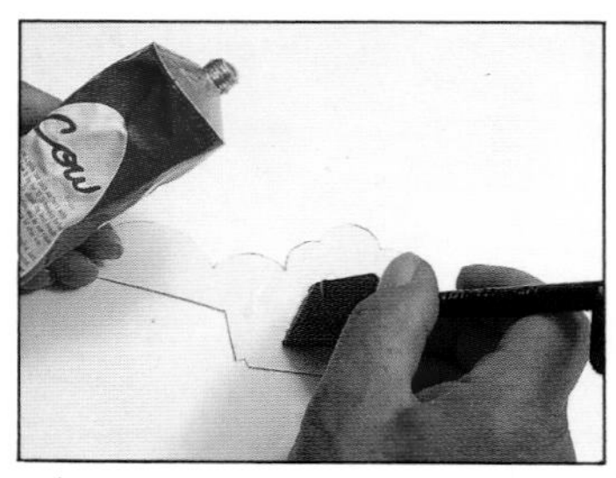


2▲

3▲

**1**. Once all the colored shapes have been cut out, the artist pieces them together rather like a jigsaw.

**2**. A rubber adhesive is applied to the back of the forms. It will not form an instant bond on contact, allowing the artist to maneuver the pieces on the board.

**3.,4**. The white background areas are automatically created by the surface of the white board, but the smaller white details are produced from white paper in the same way as the colored areas.

4▲

5▲

**5**. Using a composite of the cut-out shapes, a half page ad is created. The four main attractions of the island have been translated into simple shapes, showing that nothing is lost by omitting fine detail. In fact the versatility of these shapes means that they can easily be adapted to any size of advertisement for any publication. The shapes can also be mixed and matched, or stacked on top of each other.

1▲

**1.** It has been decided to place a two-color ad in various newspapers and magazines around Europe. Using a print of British base artwork, the artist uses an overlay to show the positioning of the foreign language copy. In this case the type is being reversed out of the illustration, so it will also be on an overlay on the original artwork. It is worthwhile remembering – if your copy is likely to be translated into a foreign language at a later stage – that the number of words will vary from one language to another. English tends to take less space than French or German, for example, so leave a little extra space.

2▲

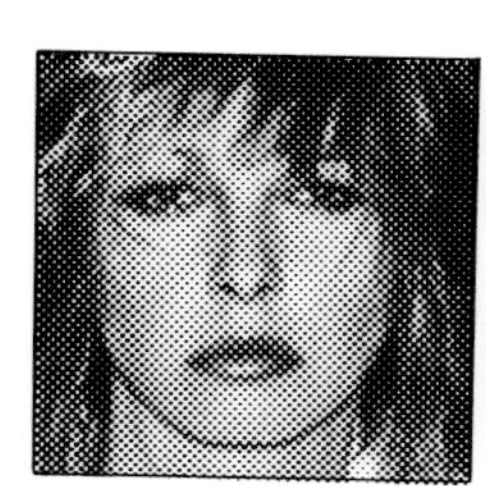

55 lines per inch
20 lines per centimetre

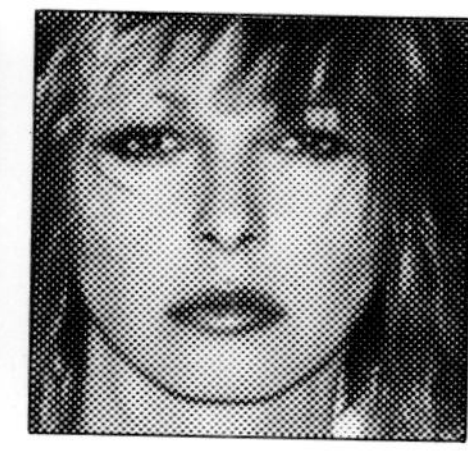

65 lines per inch
26 lines per centimetre

85 lines per inch
35 lines per centimetre

100 lines per inch
40 lines per centimetre

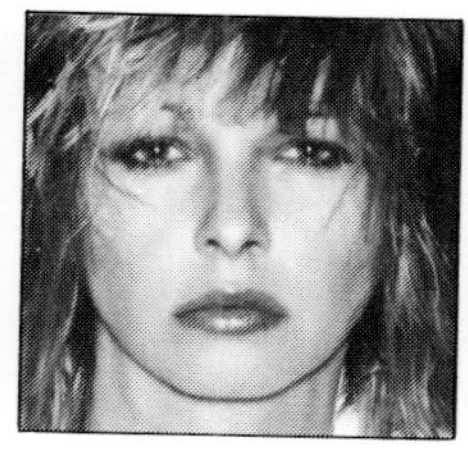

120 lines per inch
48 lines per centimetre

133 lines per inch
54 lines per centimetre

150 lines per inch
60 lines per centimetre

175 lines per inch
70 lines per centimetre

200 lines per inch
80 lines per centimetre

These pictures show a whole range of screens that are available, from coarse to fine.

**2.** This is the final artwork for a black and white ad, ready to be made into a printing plate. Instead of presenting the printer with separate pieces of artwork for origination, the studio has already screened the illustration and supplied a film overlay. This saves time, since everything is done in the studio.

These black and white ads will be printed by the offset process, and so half-tones will have to be made from the black and white photographs (known as continuous tone originals).

A photograph does not consist only of black and white areas but is made up of infinite shades of gray. These cannot be printed as such by the offset process, and so the grays have to be simulated by breaking up the picture into small dots: the dots are largest in the dark areas and very small in the pale areas, so that the printed effect is shades of gray, although only black ink has been used. The half-tone effect is obtained by placing a "screen," in the back of the camera between the lens and film, thereby breaking the image up into dots. In black and white reproduction the screen is usually placed at an angle of 45° to the hori zontal this makes the rows of dots less obvious to the eye.

Screens can be coarse or fine, depending on the paper that is to be used – the rougher the paper, the coarser the screen required. The numbers used to describe the screens represent the number of lines per inch or lines per centimeter on the screen. Most commercial magazine and book printing on typical papers uses 133 or 150 (per inch), but newspapers can go as low as a 65 screen.

# GUERNSEY HOLIDAY NEWS

HOLIDAY GUERNSEY

PUBLISHED BY THE GUERNSEY TOURIST BOARD EDITED BY EDWARD OWEN VOL 1 ISSUE 2

## BEST-EVER AIR LINKS

After a record year for air travel, with over 650,000 passengers handled at the airport, Guernsey is set to have its best-ever air links this season.

Direct flights from 28 airports in the UK and Eire are scheduled with extra capacity planned on several routes.

From April 1 Air UK is to operate daily flights with Shorts 360 aircraft from Stansted instead of last season's weekend-only departures.

In a bid to build up Stansted as an alternative London airport for Guernsey holiday traffic, the normal fare has been reduced to £92 return (against £104 from Heathrow) and the APEX fare held at £80 all week (against £94 from Heathrow).

Senior citizens' fares, being dropped at Heathrow, will still be available from Stansted. A further inducement is seen as the cheap parking at Stansted.

Air UK is offering more capacity from Exeter with Guernsey-only flights using 35-seat Shorts 360 aircraft instead of last year's 44-seat F27 flights shared with Jersey.

From Southampton, Air UK is planning for a 10% growth in traffic using F27 and Shorts 360 aircraft.

However, a battle is pending for Southampton traffic because Guernsey Airlines has applied to move on to this route and undercut Air UK with a £29 single "Walk-on" fare.

Meanwhile Guernsey Airlines is anticipating an overall increase in capacity of about 10% on its existing routes to the island from 12 mainland airports, which include Gatwick and Manchester.

British Midland is to operate two flights daily between East Midlands and Guernsey instead of last season's one flight, using F27 aircraft.

This will enable passengers from Belfast and Glasgow, who previously had to travel via Jersey, to fly direct to Guernsey over East Midlands.

This airline has cut its prices for 1986 by introducing Superkey fares, payable four months in advance, which give a £15 saving over standard excursion rates.

From Birmingham and East Midlands, Superkey fares range from £90 return midweek in June to £105 at weekends in July and August.

Also offering a reduction on last year are British Midland's Spring excursion fares (no advance purchase) at £90 return midweek and £95 at weekends in April and May from Birmingham and East Midlands.

Dan-Air is to operate separate flights to Guernsey from Bristol and Cardiff instead of a combined service.

The airline has been forced to withdraw the BAe 146 jet aircraft from Channel Island routes despite traffic figures "exceeding expectations;" this is because the associated Amsterdam sector proved unprofitable. But capacity will be maintained with 44- and 48-seat 748 aircraft.

Dan-Air is holding its APEX fares at the 1985 level (e.g. £62 midweek and £68 weekends from Bournemouth), and has introduced a "midway" one-month excursion with no advance purchase requirement (£66 midweek and £72 weekends from Bournemouth).

Brymon Airways will be operating daily Plymouth-Guernsey flights with 20-seat Twin Otters, and Aer Lingus Commuter is introducing Dublin-Guernsey flights on Saturdays from June 7 to September 30 with Shorts 360 aircraft.

### Guernsey Makes a Colourful Splash

***Shown here are the new colourful point of sale units that will be carrying the Guernsey message throughout the UK during the coming year.***

***Specially designed for either large or small outlets, the design complements the well known daisy and butterfly theme which has proved to be so popular.***

### CI Ferries extends family offers

**Channel Island Ferries is providing more midweek money-saving options for families on its service from Portsmouth this year.**

The scheme has been extended to cover three adults or two adults and two children (aged 4-13), travelling with or without car — and Friday is now counted as midweek.

These family rates run from £100 to £120 return without car and £150 to £190 with car, according to season.

Special four-day returns have also been introduced with both fares and car rates starting at £35.

Channel Island Ferries, which is associated with Brittany Ferries, is operating its 4,250-tonne *Corbière* to much the same schedules as last season.

There will be Tuesday to Saturday departures at 1000 hrs to Guernsey via Jersey until May 3, and then daily sailings from May 6 to October 4, with crossings direct back from Guernsey to Portsmouth at 2245 hrs.

*Note:* Until May 4 there is an overnight direct sailing from Portsmouth to Guernsey at 2300 hrs on Sundays, arriving at 0630 hrs.

'IN HOUSE' MAGAZINE

Here we can see how the artist's original idea of simplicity paid off. The message is conveyed clearly and converts easily for all the products. A standard typeface was chosen to complement the style and again will be used throughout to maintain the continuity. Some of the products will be given free in a promotional pack when a trip is arranged, others may be purchased from the tourist office.

Even though the brief for this project has been completed, in a campaign of this nature it will not necessarily mean that the job has come to an end. In situations like this, it is vital that the artwork be stored and filed, since the campaign will usually involve reprints and updates. It is always possible that the client will return to the idea for a new promotion, so always stamp the back of the artwork with the client's name and a job number to correspond with the client's file.

DISPLAY CARD

CALENDAR

BROCHURE

CAR STICKER

PROMOTIONAL GIFTS

# PROJECT 6

## · FILM PROMOTION POSTER ·

### THE BRIEF

The art of creating a successful film poster is highly specialized. The "story" has to be captured in one illustration which will make the public want to go and see it and which will adapt to different formats of promotion – like any other form of advertising. The first step is to talk to the distributors and hear how they see the film, the second is for the graphic artist to see the film. The "art" is in marrying the two views successfully.

In this case the brief was fairly loose. The artist was told what the client did *not* want, but the choice of an image was left up to him. Magic Markers were used – the difference in this project is that in such a highly finished rough the artist will pay more attention to detail. The "airbrushed look" was achieved by mixing pastel crayons with the markers.

COMMISSIONED ILLUSTRATION

REVERSED OUT TYPE

JOHN BOORMAN'S

THE EMERALD FOREST

15

HAND LETTERING

Based on a true story.

SYMBOLS AND LOGOS

JOHN BOORMAN'S "THE EMERALD FOREST" PRODUCED AND DIRECTED BY JOHN BOORMAN
WRITTEN BY ROSPO PALLENBERG EXECUTIVE PRODUCER EDGAR F. GROSS CO-PRODUCED BY MICHAEL DRYHURST
STARRING POWERS BOOTHE · MEG FOSTER · CHARLEY BOORMAN

READ THE PENGUIN PAPERBACK

READ 'MONEY INTO LIGHT', JOHN BOORMAN'S DIARY OF THE MAKING OF 'THE EMERALD FOREST'. NOW IN FABER PAPERBACK.

ORIGINAL SOUNDTRACK AVAILABLE ON VARESE SARABANDE RECORDS AND CASSETTES.

DOLBY STEREO™ IN SELECTED THEATRES

AN EMBASSY FILMS ASSOCIATES PRESENTATION

EMBASSY PICTURES Release

DISTRIBUTED BY RANK FILM DISTRIBUTORS

1▲

2▲

3▲

**1.,2.,3.** The lettering was first drawn freehand in various thicknesses using a Magic Marker on absorbent paper (so that it would bleed and create the jagged edge). It was then photocopied on a larger scale to give the artist a crude idea as to how it would look when reproduced. Two PMTs of different sizes were then taken.

4▲

5▲

6▲

7▲

**4.,5**. The PMTs were covered with an overlay indicating the shade of red required with a Pantone swatch. This was then sent to a typesetter with an autotype facility.

**6**. Autotype is a process whereby the PMT is transformed into dry transfer lettering. It is possible to have any color you wish.

**7**. The first lettering was rubbed onto an acetate overlay to enable the artist to experiment with positioning and the second onto a black background.

1▲

**1.** The artist decided to add an extra illustration, which was put on an overlay, since he felt there was too much space. These were taken from stills of the film. The finished posters were printed both landscape and portrait to cater for the varied formats required for the chosen sites.

2▲

3▲

**2**. A border made from black card-board was placed over the illustration to crop it down to a portrait format. The lettering on the black background was placed on another overlay.

**3**. A further alternative illustration was added, on another overlay, to give the client more choice. The final result was a combination of the two alternatives.

# PROJECT 7

## · ROYAL CARIBBEAN CRUISES ·

### THE BRIEF

In this project we take an overview of a highly successful campaign, examine the various stages and the reasoning behind each one. The campaign was created for Royal Caribbean Cruise Line with the objective of promoting them as the premier way to see the Caribbean. The brief involved establishing an identity for the company, which was carried through posters, point-of-sale material, advertisements and travel brochures.

The creative key to the campaign was to sell the Caribbean and not cruise ships. The visual material was connected with the idea of sailing from island to island, and nowhere on any of the promotional material is a cruise ship featured. This innovative concept was accepted by the client. A dramatic illustration was required to give visual impact to the campaign, and it was decided that a Rousseau-style painting was the answer. Before the original was commissioned the concept was worked through in-house.

The original artwork, created in oils, was based on Rousseau's jungle paintings and, although brighter and more vibrant than his original work, remained true to the artist's technique.

HAND LETTERING

COMMISSIONED ILLUSTRATION

LOGOTYPE

ILLUSTRATION

HEADLINE SETTING

TEXT SETTING

HAND LETTERING

Fly free

Just two words and our Caribbean holidays are even more attractive.

Starting first of January 1986 everyone taking a 12 or 16 day Royal Caribbean fly cruise will be flown absolutely *free** to their Caribbean holiday. First, if necessary, on a domestic carrier to Heathrow and then on a regularly scheduled airline to Miami.

Those taking the shorter 9 or 10 day fly cruises, including New York–Bermuda cruises will be charged only £59* for their return flights.

What other cruise line offers that? And what other cruise line offers as many tantalising Caribbean choices as Royal Caribbean.

Four quite fantastic ships (consistently voted 'the favourite' by experienced cruisers) that cruise regularly from Miami and New York.

It's the perfect way to experience the Caribbean and now you've got the perfect package to sell.

A package Royal Caribbean will be backing with a national 48 sheet poster campaign in the autumn and again early in the New Year. Big, colourful posters in your area that your clients will be seeing day and night, rain or shine, seven days a week.

Plus advertising in the leading national Sunday newspapers. Plus the most attractive point-of-sale material from a cruise line in many-a-year and the greatest brochure for agents in a month-of-Saturdays. A brochure featuring an easy-to-use, fold-out deck plan section.

Soon you'll be receiving our brochures. If you don't, simply contact Royal Caribbean Cruise Line at 35 Piccadilly, London W1V 9PB. Tel: 01-434 1991.

No doubt about it, 1986 will be ours. Do be on board!

ROYAL CARIBBEAN CRUISES

1▲

2▲

**1**. This is a studio rough done in crayon in order to test the concept and to give the illustrator some idea of the brief.

**2**. This is the illustrator's rough, which is more highly finished and will be presented to the client.

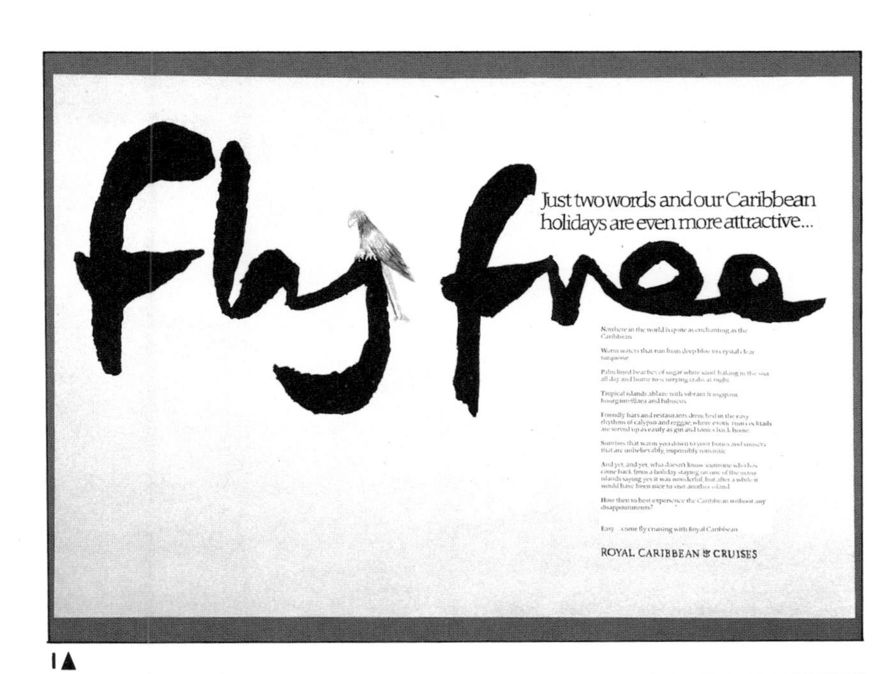


1▲

2▲

3▲



4▲

**1.,2.** The "Fly Free" concept was developed for trade press advertising, and roughs investigating two different treatments of it were prepared. This first rough gives prominence to the "Fly Free" slogan and features the parrot from the poster as a symbol of free flight. The headline is "live". The copy, which is flush left and has been set, does not relate to the headline and is intended simply to give an impression of the appearance of the advertisement.

**3.,4.** This is the second rough. The copy has been handwritten and, in this case, relates directly to the story line. The parrot is still a visual feature but "Fly Free" is considerably less prominent.

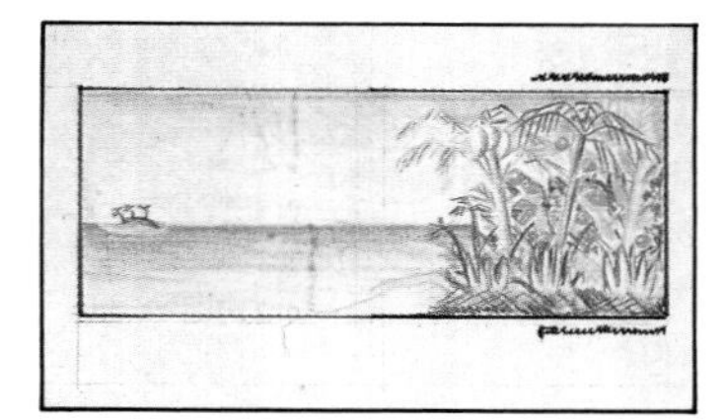

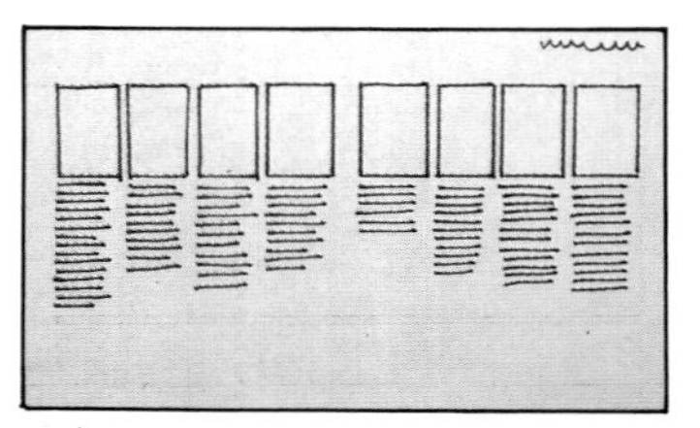

1▲

**1**. The travel brochure was a key element in the campaign, and it was decided that the poster would form the wrap-around illustration for the front and back covers. The spreads were roughly executed, with illustrations and the copy depicted by boxes and lines, and a freehand illustration was crayoned, indicating the cover.

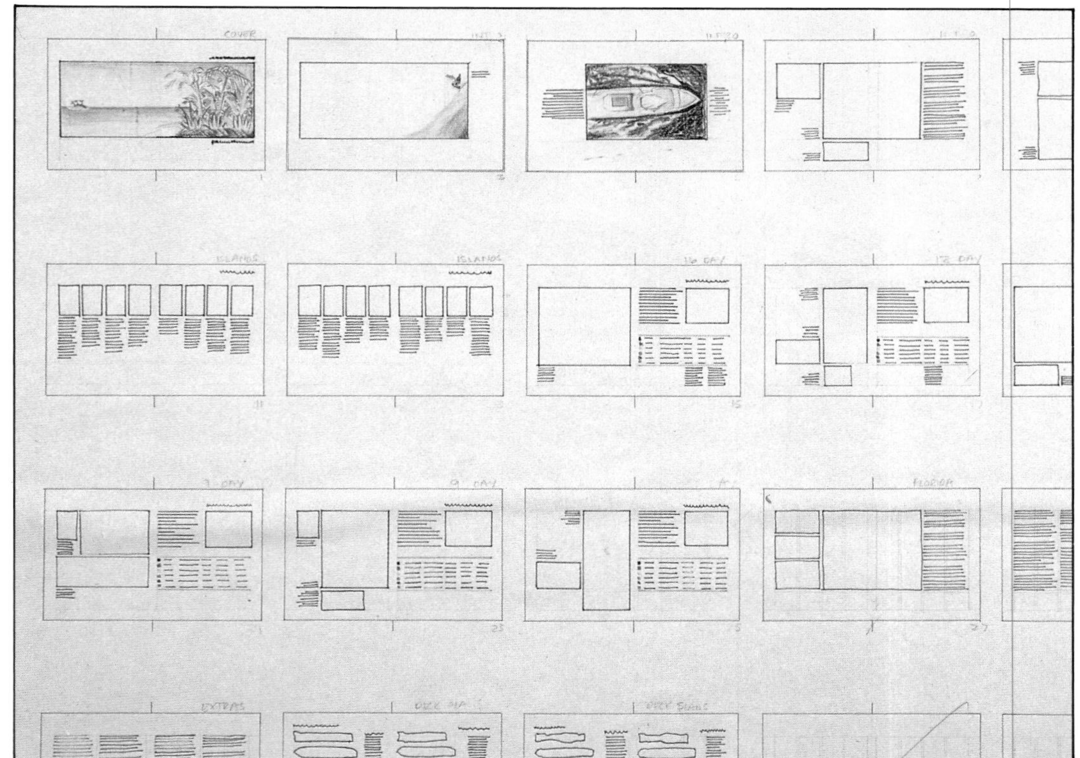

2▲

**2**. This is a more detailed flat plan of the brochure showing the versatility of the basic grid chosen. This instantly shows if the material will fit the specifications, i.e., whether it is too dense, or whether there is too much white space.

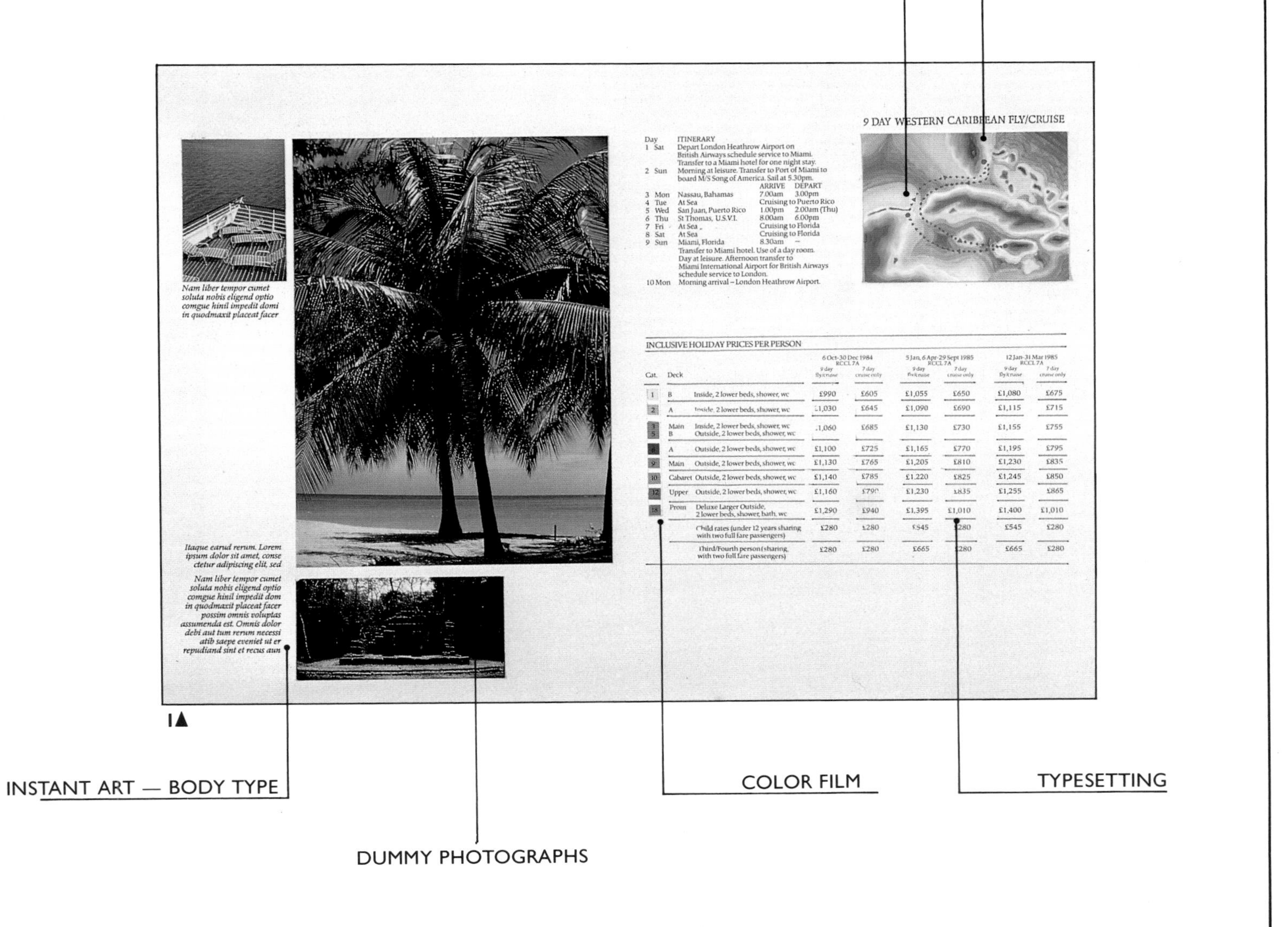


2►

**1.** A more detailed rough shows the treatment of a specific spread. This has been produced same size and features a route map drawn in crayon and a color illustration taken from a photography library. Care has been taken to show how a color coding system would be used for rates.

**2.** The captions have been indicated with dummy text.

1▲

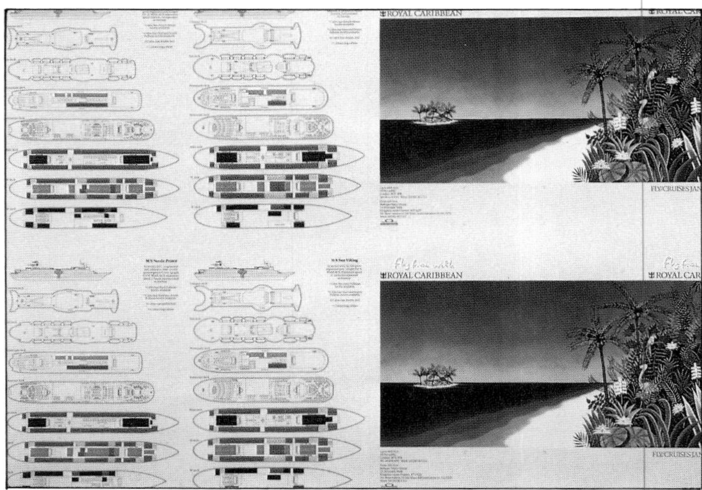

2▲

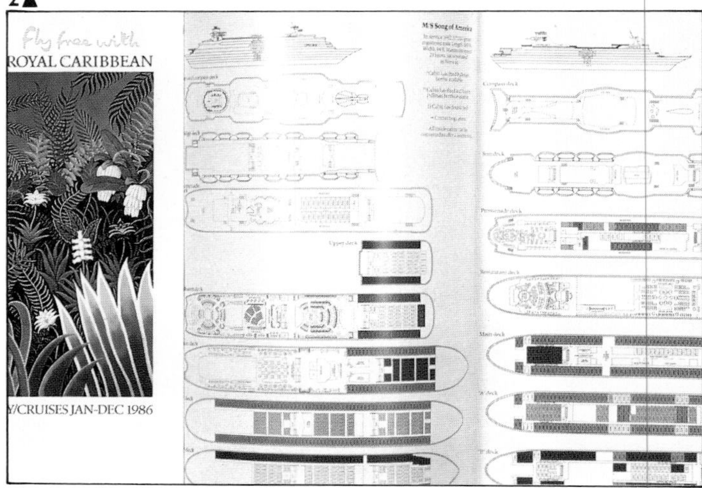


3▲

**1**. To provide a continuing link between the brochure and other promotional material, various elements from the poster, such as fruits, flowers, ferns and animals, were featured on each page. This double-page spread from the printed brochure, shown alongside a rough paste-up, utilizes the pink flamingo.

**2**. The final brochure features an innovation that made the book easy to handle and therefore popular with travel agents. The use of a pull-out spread at the back allowed them to consult cabin plans and route details in one exercise, without having to flip back and fourth through the book.
**3**. A color proof of the front and back covers with the three-page pull-out of cabin plans shows how this worked.

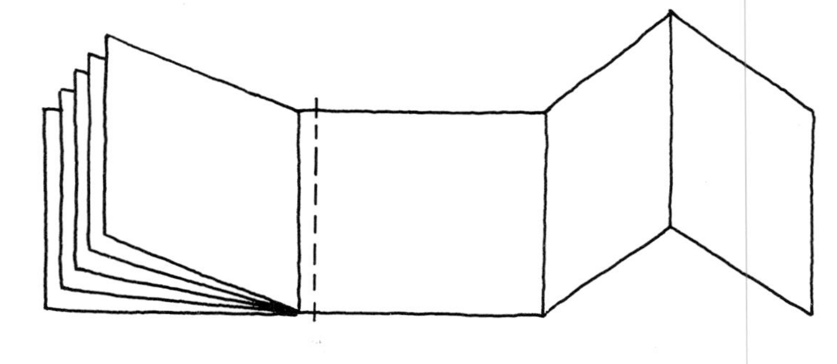

1▲

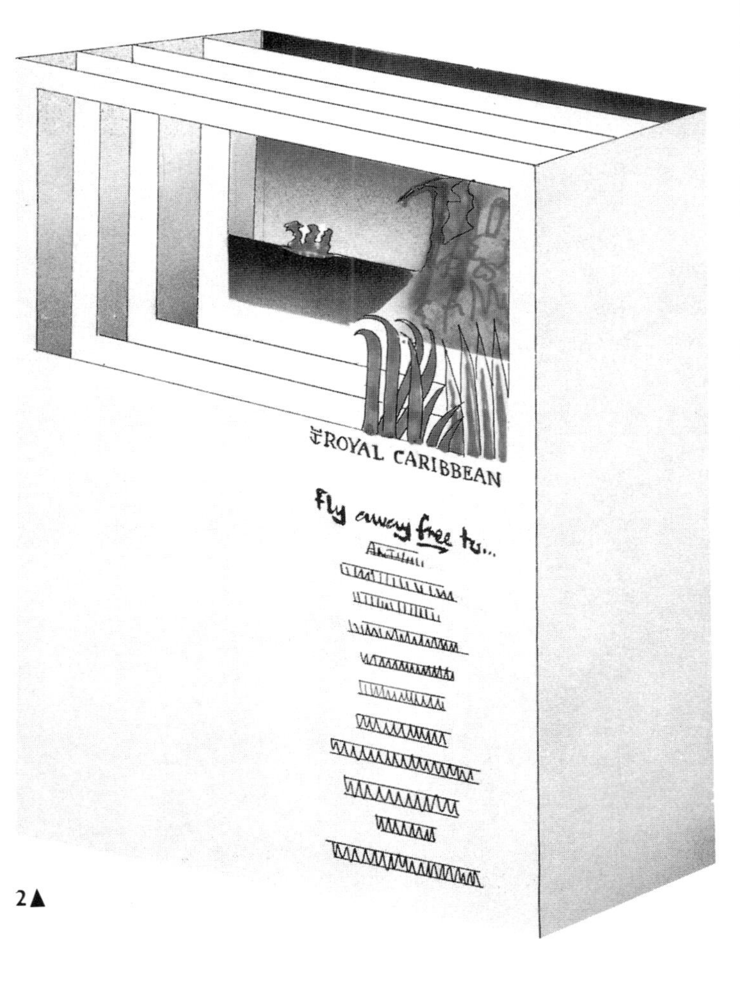


2▲

**1**. The final part of the promotion was a three-dimensional point-of-sale unit for travel agents. A very early rough sketch shows how this was to be tackled.

**2**. The final unit was so successful that, rather than following the normal practice of charging a fee for incorporating it in window displays, travel agents were specifically requesting it.

# PROJECT 8

## · POINT-OF-SALE PACKAGING ·

THE BRIEF

For this particular project the client has four products that require individual packaging and a point-of-sale counter display to contain them. While the artist must bear in mind how the packaging will translate in terms of production costs, the main priority is to create a design that consumers will always relate to that specific product.

The studio will initially supply the client with a full three-dimensional mock-up, which will be constructed from material of a type similar to that finally adopted. The point-of-sale will have to be quite sturdy to protect the individual products while in transit, yet convert easily to an eye-catching display on arrival. The obvious solution was to use the box method, in which the lid converts into a "crowner" holding the client's message. The first client presentation will not carry any graphics. When the graphics are added they will be drawn on a separate sheet which will be attached to the dummy. This makes any changes or corrections far easier and will not spoil the pack. The last pages demonstrate this by showing famous packages that are instantly recognizable, even without their brand names.

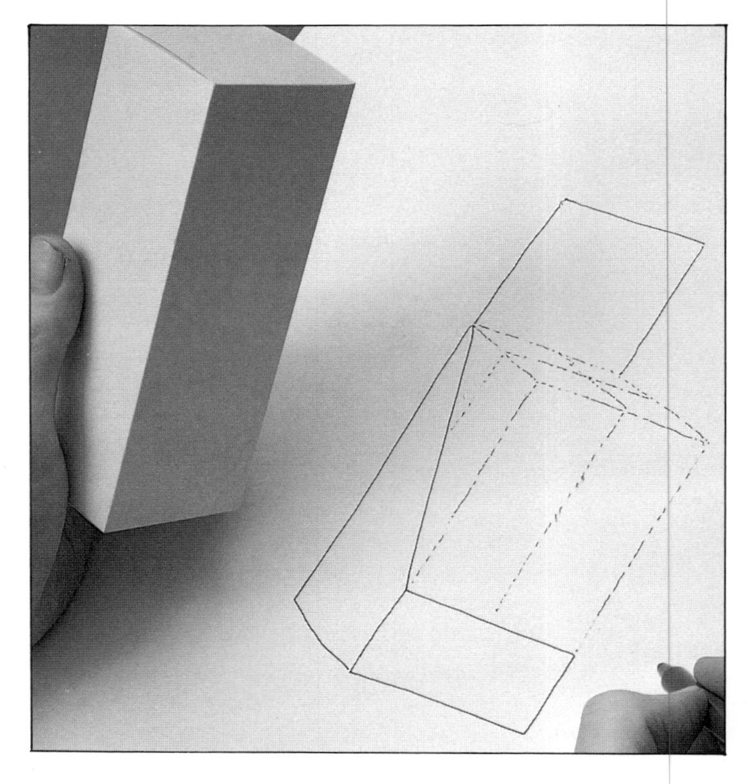

**1.** The next three photos illus-rate in a highly edited form how the method works. This is started by drawing the point-of-sale display to establish the proportions, dimensions and scale, which are based on the individually-packed products.

**2.**,**3**. Here we see the final point of display (including the products) with the crowner, which is the showcard that folds over to form a protective lid for traveling. The advantage of this method is that the display needs to be printed · only on the one side.

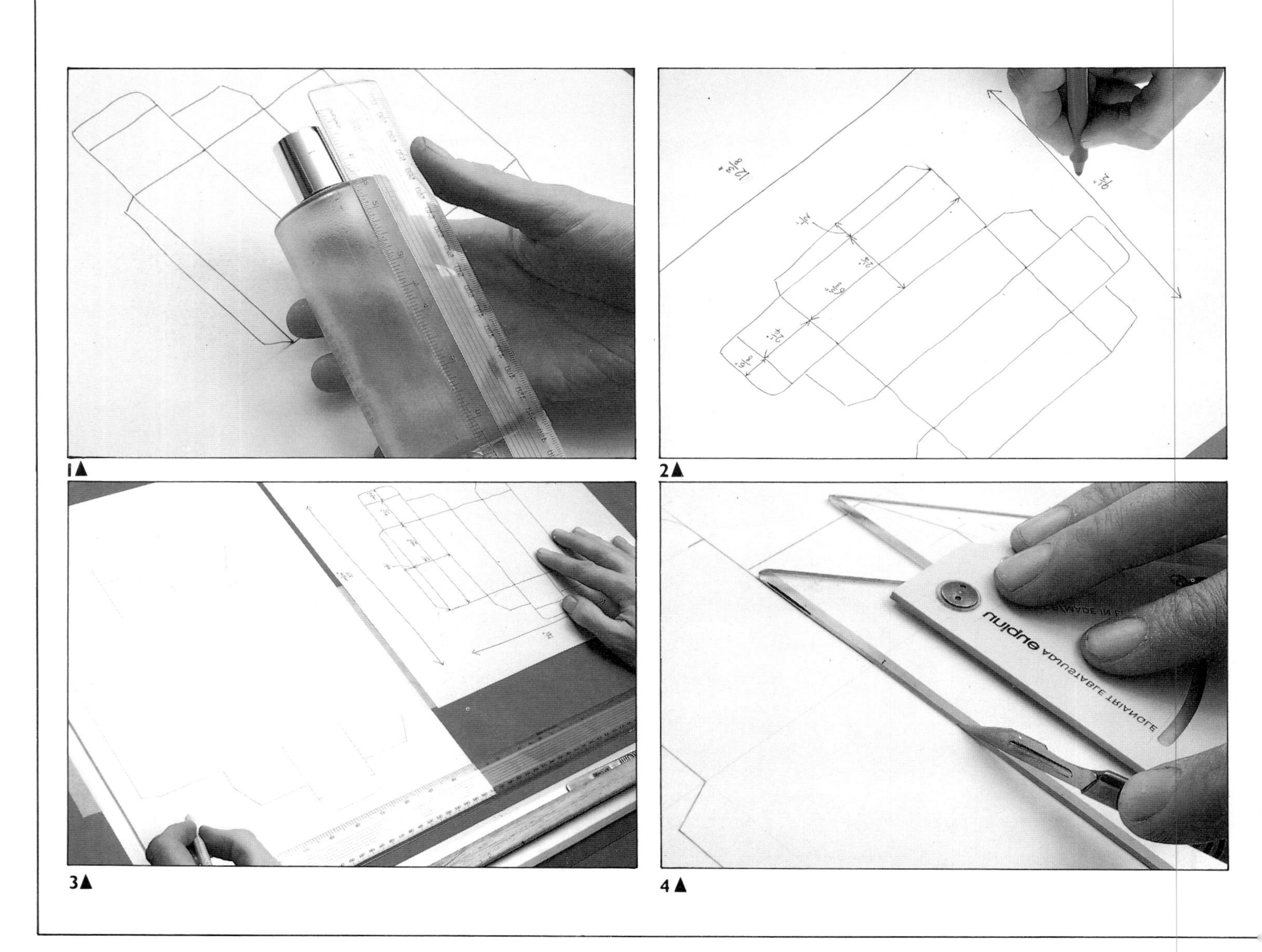


1▲ 2▲ 3▲ 4▲

**1.,2.** Before embarking on a project of this nature, to avoid spending hours on working out the mathematics involved to obtain the correct folds, etc., the artist will usually find it profitable – for a simple project like this – to purchase an already existing similar pack and dismantle it. This will show immediately how a pack is folded, and all the artist has to do is roughly sketch the flat shape and work out the dimensions by scaling up or down.

**3.** From this initial rough the layout is drawn accurately on the chosen material. Although this should be sturdy, it must be flexible enough to be folded without the surface cracking. Do not forget that the guide lines for the folds must be drawn on the side of the board that will eventually form the inside of the display.

**4.** To make possible a clean accurate fold, the vertical lines must run parallel to the grain of the board. Every artist has his or her own technique when it comes to scoring cardboard, from a used-up ballpoint pen to the blunt end of a pair of scissors, but here the blunt end of an X-acto knife is drawn along the fold line. Whatever the implement, a steel rule is always used.

5▲

7▲

6▲

▼8

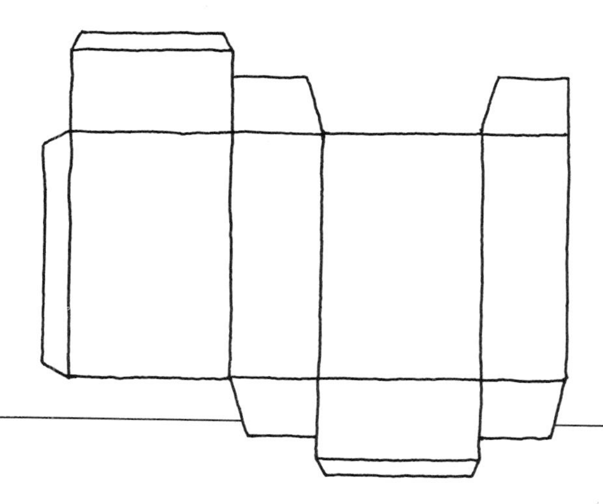

**5.,6.,7.,8.,9.** The drawing is now secured to a cutting board and the outlines carefully cut. Double-sided tape is applied to the flaps and the folds – made by placing a steel rule along the score lines and gently lifting the sides until they bend around to form the three-dimensional main body of the box. Finally the top and bottom flaps are folded in the same manner. The bottom flap is secured with double-sided tape and the securing flap for the top of the box is fitted over and slit to allow for easier folding. This final artwork will be transposed onto an overlay, which will be placed over the graphics as a cutting guide for the printer.

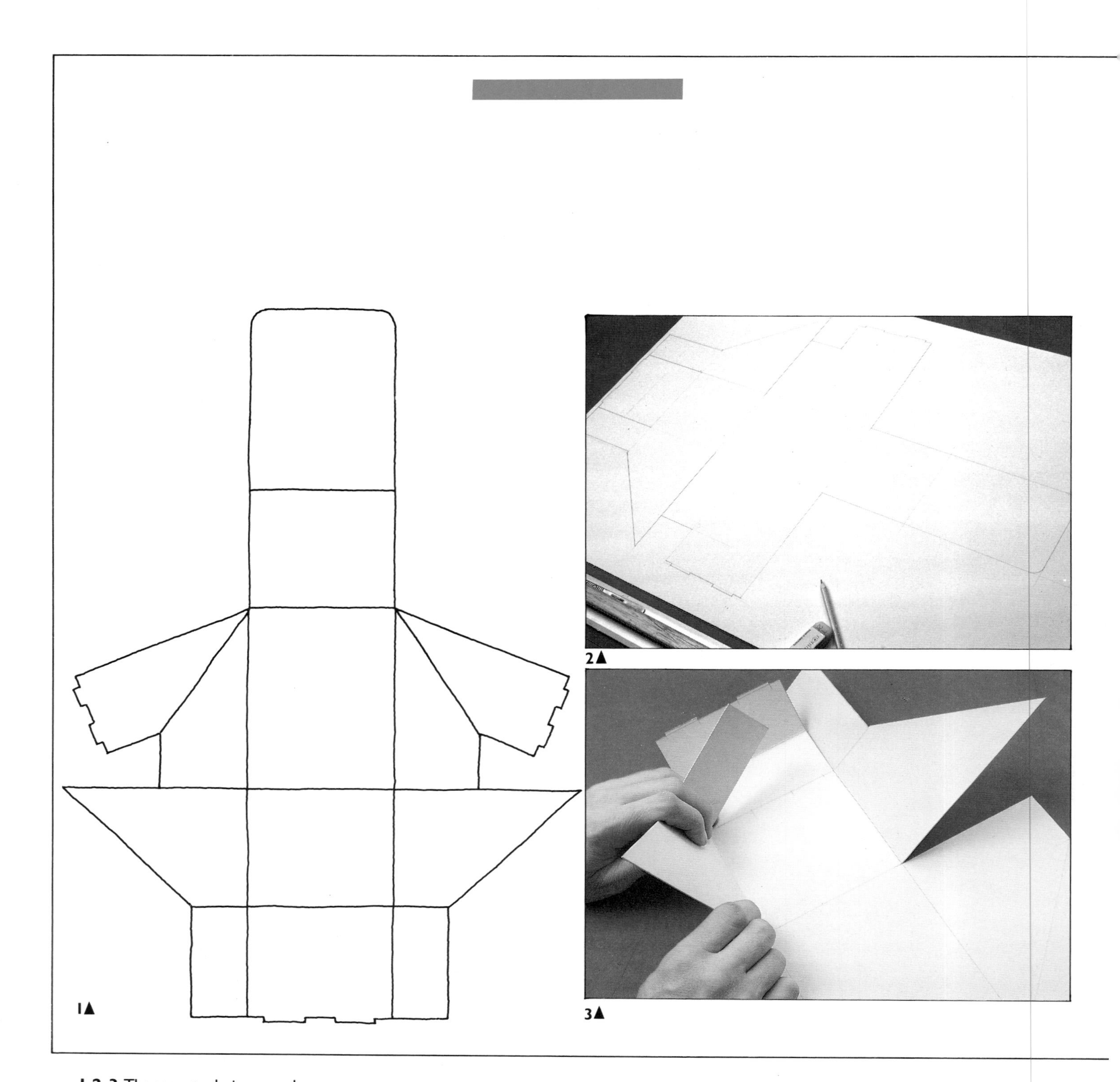

**1.,2.,3.** The same technique used to construct the individual packs was employed for the point-of-sale display. First the flat pattern was worked out; then, in this case, a small scale mock-up was made in order to make sure the design would work. Once this has been satisfactorily worked out, the artist draws the full-scale plan on the board and proceeds with the cutting out and scoring.

4▲

5▲

6▲

**4**. As already mentioned, the display pack has to be quite sturdy. Instead of using thicker cardboard, the designer gives the pack strength by engineering the construction so that the sides are folded over to give double layers, which will be secured by slots.

**5**. These have to be absolutely precise. They are drawn on the plan as parallel lines, with the use of a triangle and parallel motion. When cutting the slots out the designer cuts the short edges before the long ones.

▼7

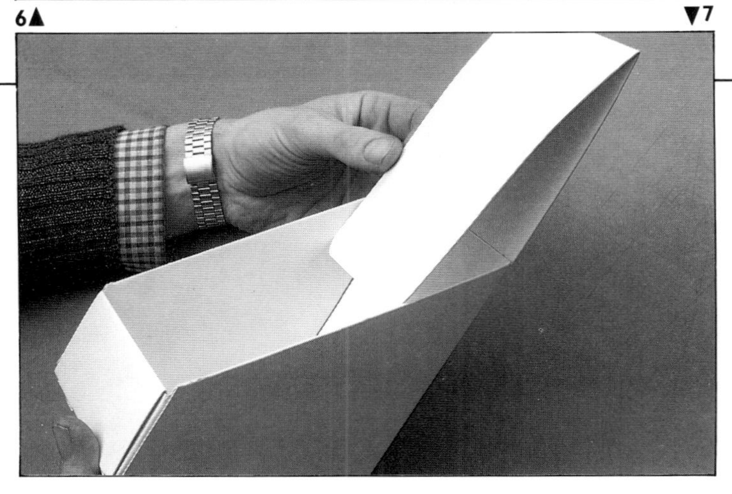

**6**. Never be tempted to pick up your X-acto knife without changing the blade first. The point of the knife is used to pick up the unwanted piece.

**7**. All the folds are then made, finishing with the lid, which folds back to create the double layer and crown at the back of the pack.

1

**1**. Here we have chosen some examples of well known package forms adopted by leading manufacturers. These designs have successfully created a unique visual identity without forgetting the practicalities of protecting the products and making them easily accessible.

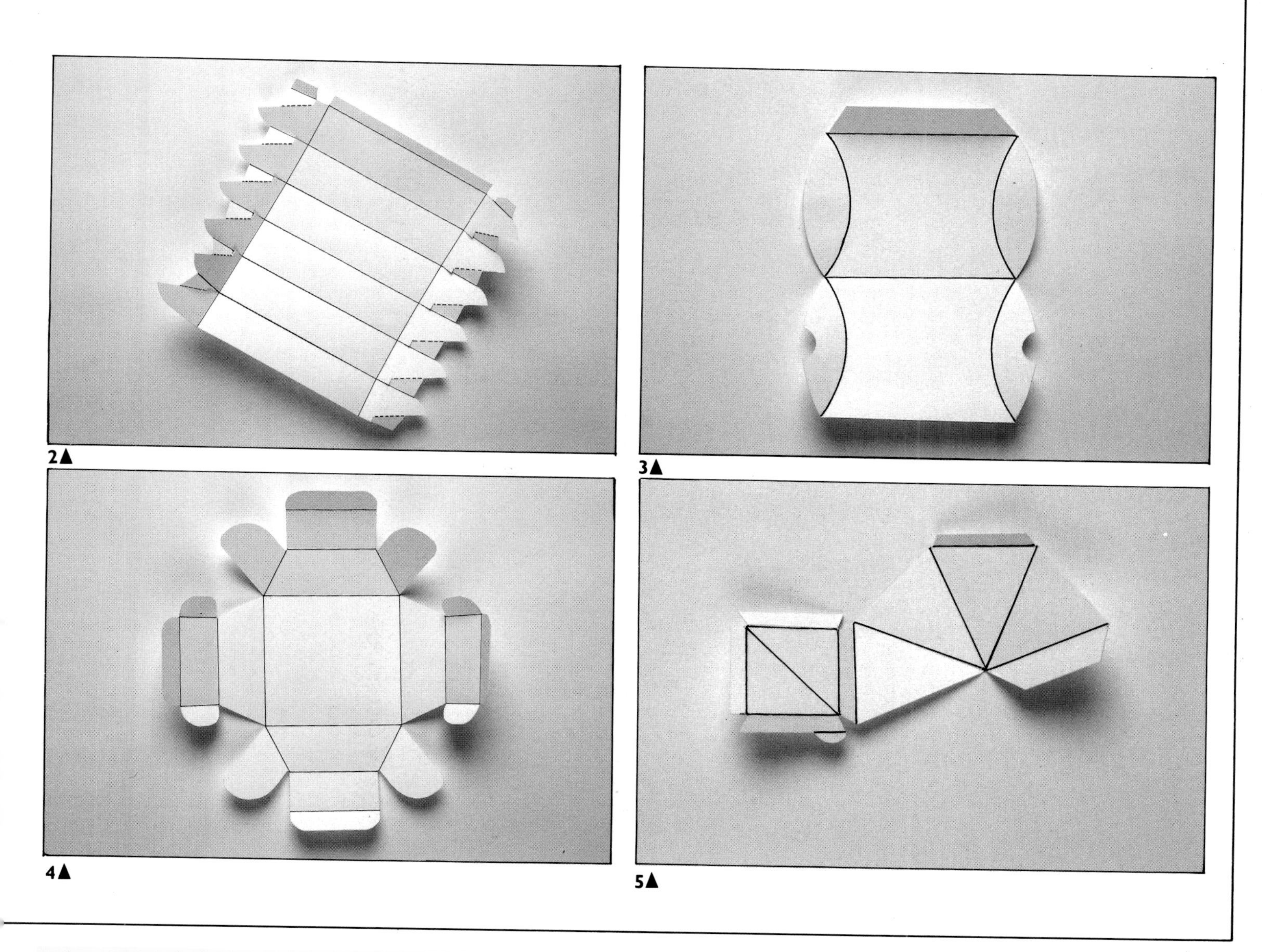


**2.,3.,4.,5.** These are the flat patterns from which the packs shown on the left were constructed. It is worthwhile noting the basic simplicity of the mechanics and how they were all created from a single sheet without any separate components, making it comparable to the ancient Japanese art of origami. Careful thought was also applied to the design, so that during make-up the maximum number of packs could be cut from a single sheet. The combination of all these criteria add up to the true definition of a successful pack.

▲1

3►

▲2

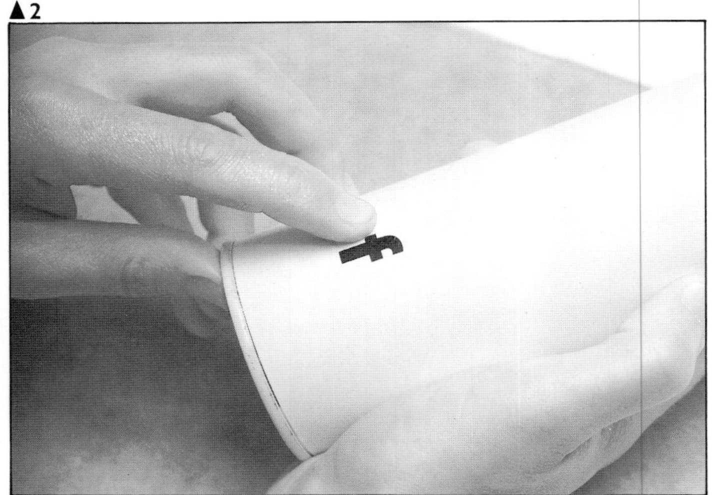

Applying Letraset onto a difficult or uneven surface can be tricky, especially if you are attempting to get it right first time. Shown above is a technique for pre-releasing Letraset. If you are working on a delicate surface such as cardboard the pre-released lettering will leave no indentation.

**1.** Hold the sheet of Letraset in the air and rub the letter with a soft pencil. The letter will go paler in colour and will be released from its backing sheet.

**2.,3.** Place the sheet onto the surface, in this instance an aerosol can, and apply slight pressure to the letter. Do not forget to burnish the letter with the backing sheet or tracing paper to secure it.

▲4

**4.** When you are designing letterforms and logos for packaging check which printing process is being used. For example, flexography can print six colors on some machines but the quality of the fine detail color work is not very high – this will effect your design. Also, the letterforms and logos must be designed within the limitations of the shape of the package. You can see above how the shapes themselves have been used to their best advantage.

# PROJECT 9

## · CORPORATE IDENTITY ·

### THE BRIEF

The creation of an identity for a company or corporation gives the graphic artist the opportunity to put all his or her skills to the test. Nowadays many major advertising campaigns are aimed at promoting not a product or a service but the company itself. This is known as 'corporate advertising'. The aim is to put forward a carefully constructed image of how a company sees itself and its concerns. This image is designed not only to attract new clients and customers, but to involve employees, inform stockholders and potential investors, and to educate the general consumer: corporation recognition as opposed to product recognition. A new corporate image may be necessary and a whole new advertising campaign will be launched if the products or services are familiar while the parent company itself remains virtually unknown; or if the current image lacks appeal and no longer coincides with what the company now represents.

Many corporations wish to move away from the facelessness associated with large business concerns and make their corporate strategy visible to the targetted audience. Once such an image has been created, of course, the company can diversify, even change the nature of its associated products, while its image remains constant.

Several different approaches to and applications of corporate advertising appear on the following pages.

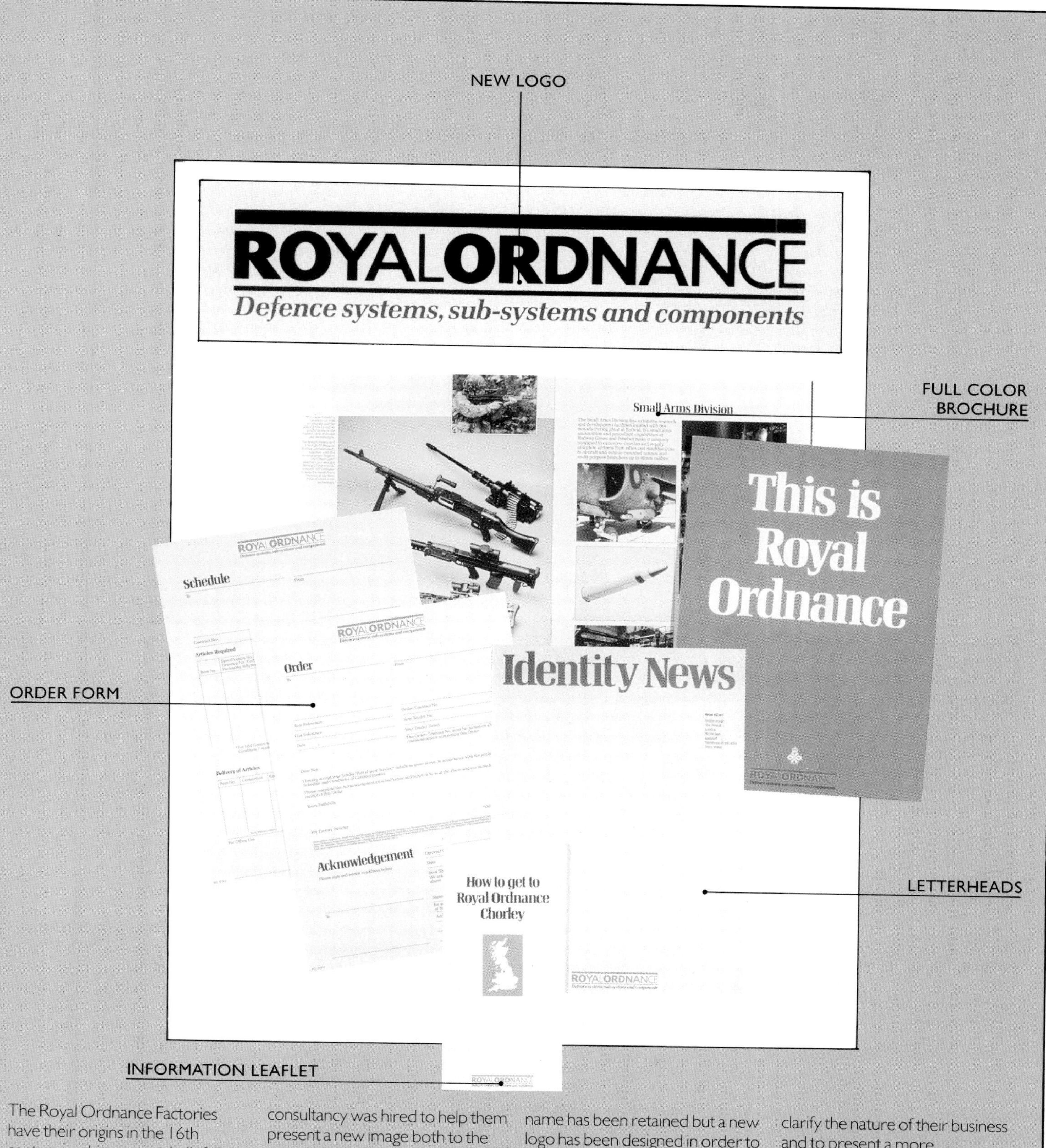


The Royal Ordnance Factories have their origins in the 16th century, making cannonballs for the Tudors. The company presented a confused identity to the outside world – part Civil Service, part military and part commercial. It was old-fashioned in its approach and it looked old-fashioned. The Wolff Olins/Smythe consultancy was hired to help them present a new image both to the outside world and to their staff.

The company now has a rationalized structure, a strong marketing thrust and a commitment to up-to-date systems – all are represented in its new visual identity *(above)*. The name has been retained but a new logo has been designed in order to present the Royal Ordnance as a state-of-the-art commercial defence company and not a government department – hence the choice of a crisp and clear typeface. The phrase 'Defence systems sub-systems and components' was adopted to clarify the nature of their business and to present a more sophisticated approach.

From this one example you can see that a new logo is only part of the process of creating a new corporate identity.

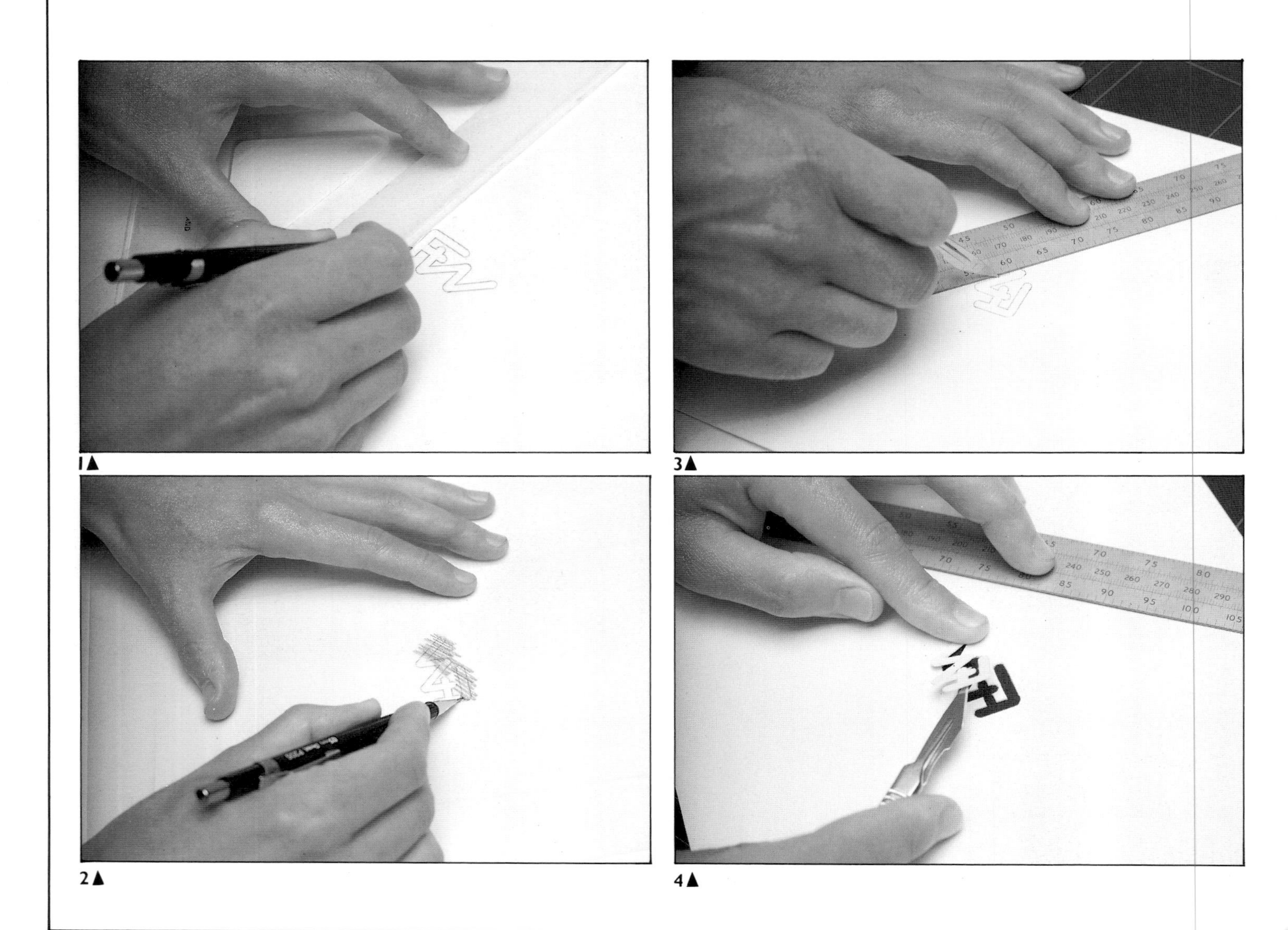
1▲
2▲
3▲
4▲

**1.,2.** The design for the letters FW is drawn accurately then traced down onto thin card, so that the image appears the wrong way round.

**3.,4.** The image is carefully cut around and the resulting template removed from the surrounding cardboard.

5▲

6▲

7▲

**5**. The template is stuck down securely, the right way round, on the board.

**6**. The chosen paper or cartridge is placed over it and rubbed gently with a burnisher or your thumbnail until the template raises an image of itself.

**7**. The type is added and the finished business card cut to size.

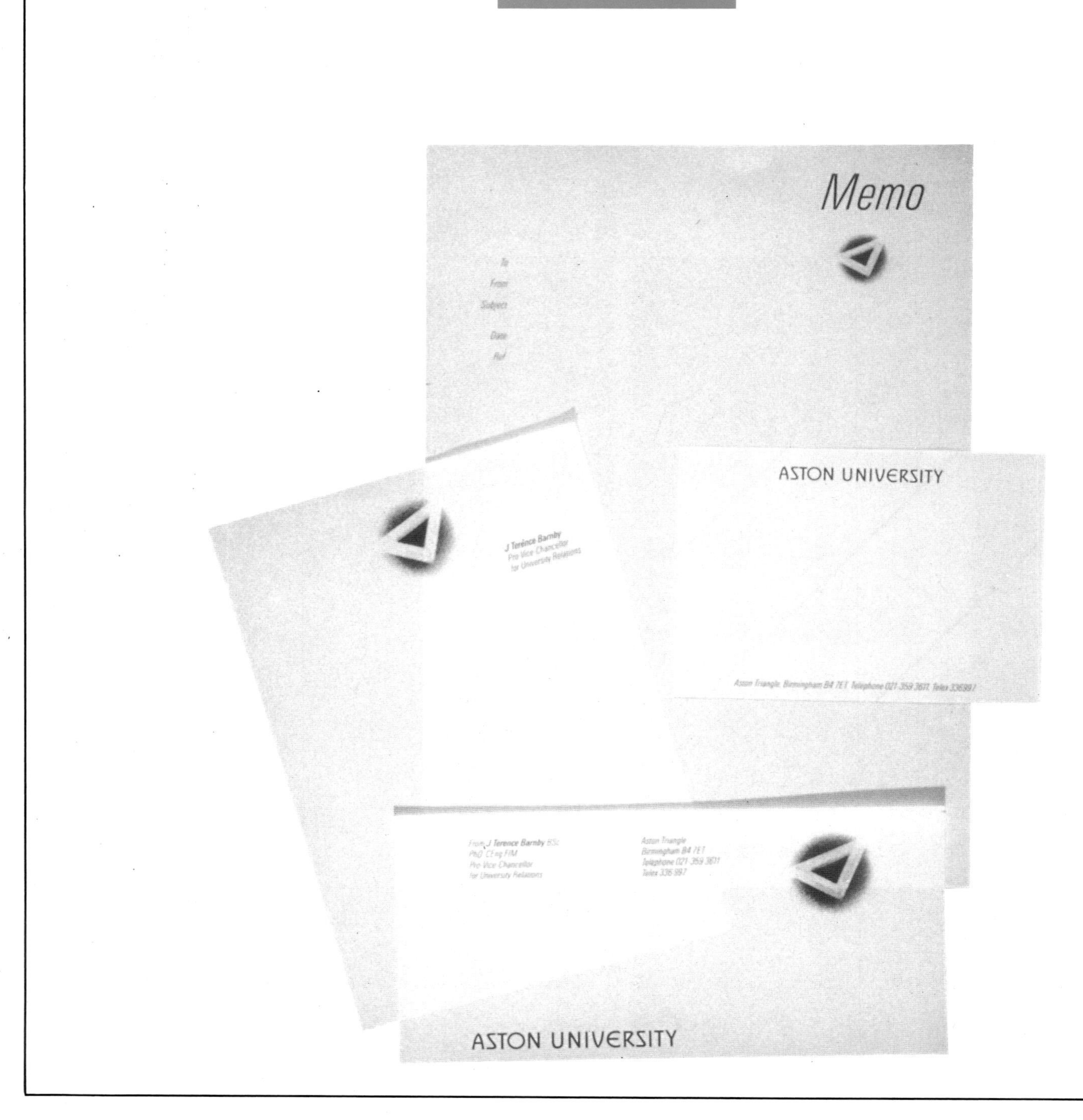


American universities are much more attuned to their environment than their British counterparts. Aston University in Birmingham, England, decided to follow their example and introduced a corporate redesign in order to counteract ailing student applications, and to improve the image and reputation of the college.

The university is bounded by three roads – called the Aston triangle – which provides the central theme for the stationery. The design decided to celebrate Aston as a campus in the middle of Birmingham; a high-tech establishment rather than an ivory tower. The graphic artist threw out the 750 years of heraldic shields which had been the university's logo and accepted the new triangular, graffiti-like mark.

This logo was ideal as the university (which does most of its own printing) could use it at any size, in any position on the page, at any angle or in any color. The triangle is blue for the university, red for the science park and split red and blue for the Aston triangle. For the letterhead it is used with a specially drawn alphabet creating the logotype. Aston University with Univers light condensed as a secondary typeface.

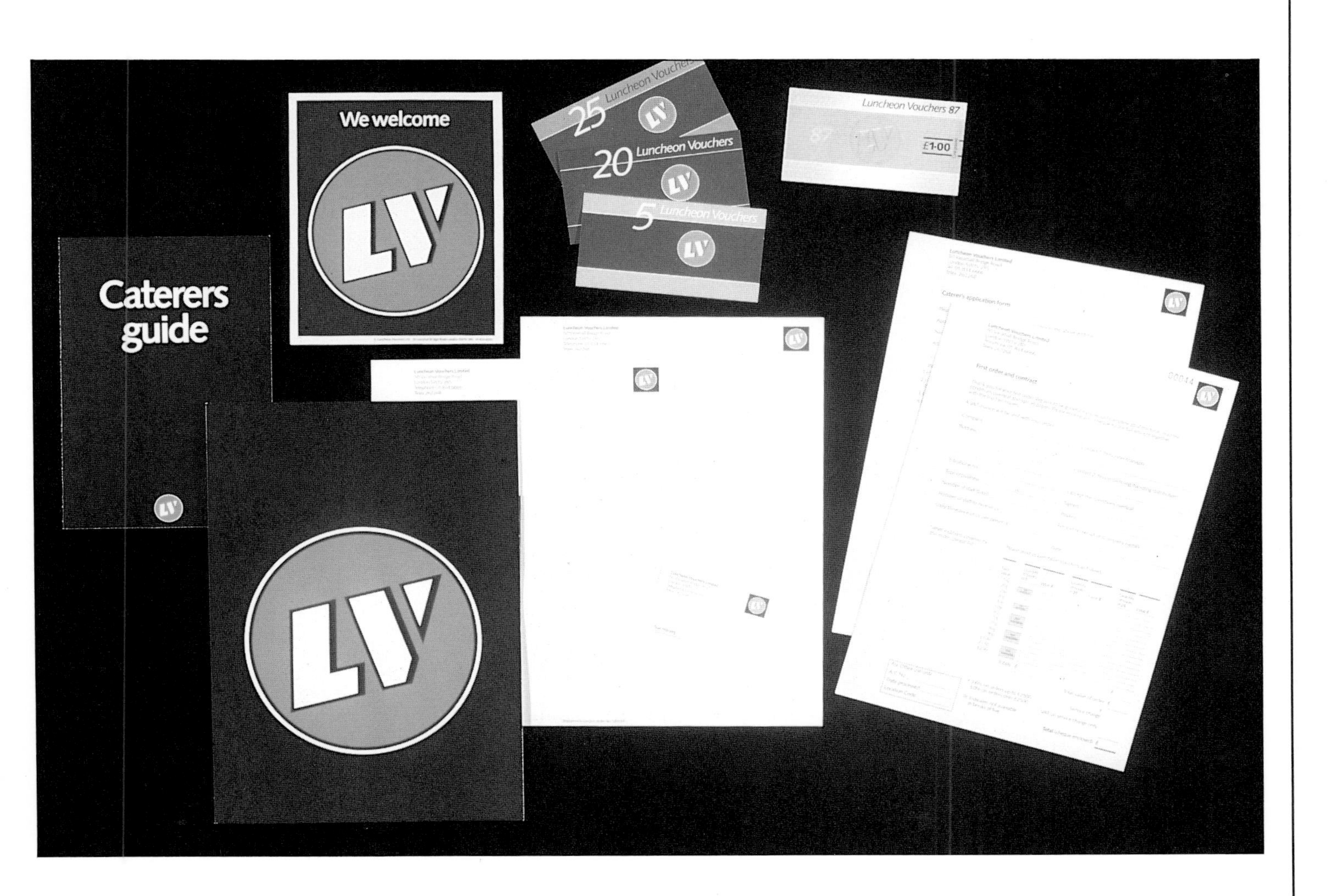


The brief was to create an eye-catching and up-to-date identity for the forty-year-old Luncheon Vouchers, as a visual representation of their move up-market, and one that would be acceptable, especially in terms of a window display sticker, to new outlets such as wine bars and bistros.

Though the new design keeps a circle as a visual link with the old one, the original green, to which research had shown that people responded badly, has been replaced by a strong red, white and blue combination.

# PROJECT 10

## · SEALINK ·

THE BRIEF

Here, Sealink not only wanted to show the attractiveness of their ferry service by showing the on-board services and destinations but also all the other advice and information they could provide on the destination itself, such as trailer and camping sites, hotels, routes, and leisure activities. In other words, not just a ferry service but a complete holiday! The client provided all the photographic material, their logo and all the copy. This project shows how the artist makes use of modern graphic materials when the client feels that the message would be more directly conveyed pictorially. The final page will be made up from twenty-six individual images, which will all have to be prepared specifically for the half-tone process. In this case the artist supplied the printer with the various tones. If the studio does not have these facilities, the tones are specified.

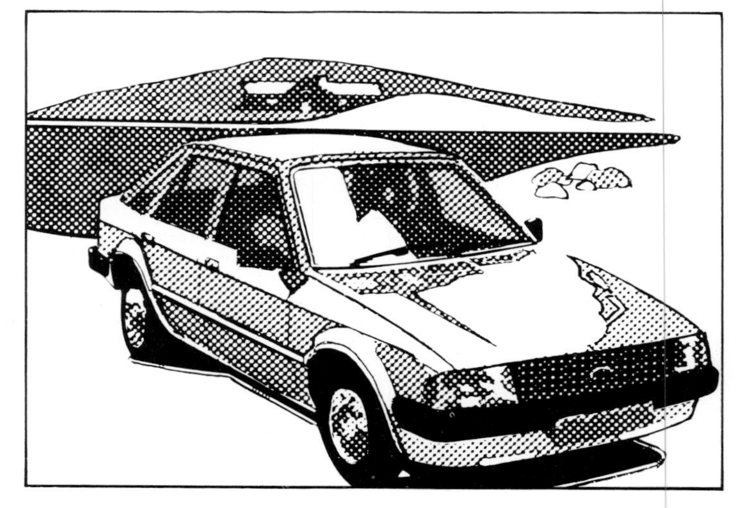

*All the photographs will have to be converted to line drawings with added tones or screened to convert them into half-tones.*

LINE AND TONE ILLUSTRATION

LINE DRAWING AND TYPE

DISTORTED LETTERING

RETOUCHED PHOTO

LINE ILLUSTRATION

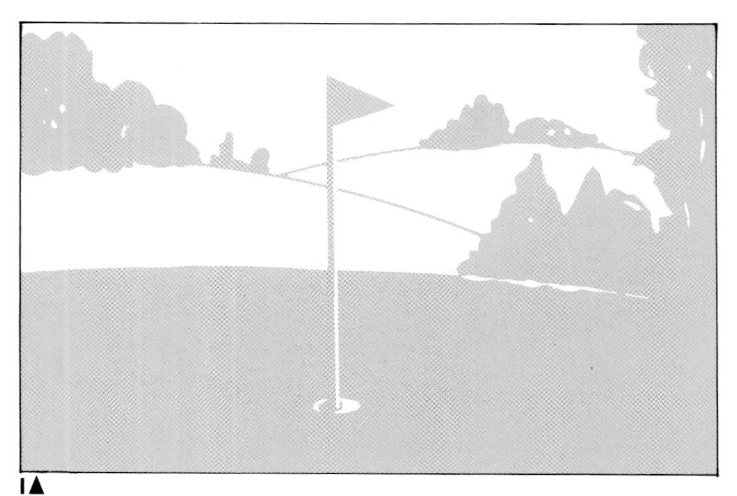

1▲

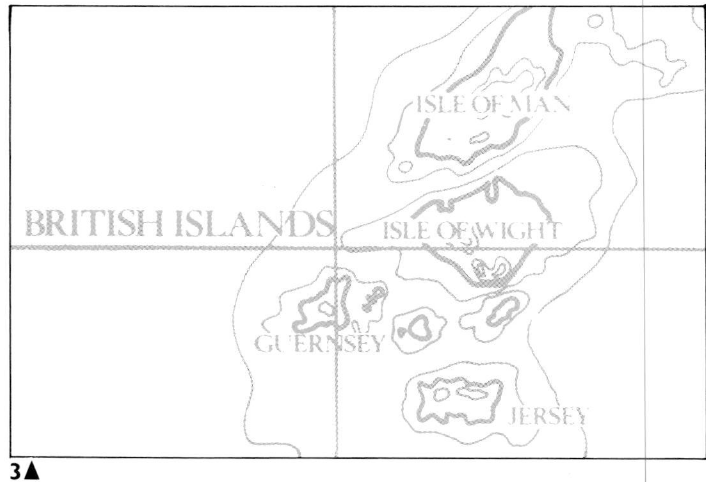


3▲

2▲

DOVER - CALAIS Sealink
DOVER - BOULOGNE Sealink
DOVER - DUNKIRK Sealink
FOLKESTONE - CALAIS Sealink
FOLKESTONE - BOULOGNE Sealink

4▲

**1**. Sealink wanted to show that even golf addicts need not suffer withdrawal symptoms while on vacation. A simple line illustration with solid areas, using the hole marker flag as the main central image, says it all. The outlines are drawn first before being blocked in, and the small white details or outlines that separate specific images out of the black are painted on afterward in white paint.

**2**. To show that the client has information on routes abroad, the same principle is adopted as in **1**., except that the lettering is laid down in Letraset. When laying down individual dry transfer letters it is always a good idea to lay a sheet of paper over the letters already rubbed down to protect them from being lifted off accidentally by the "steadying" hand.

**3**. The initial outlines are traced from a map, transferred onto the board and drawn over in black. The Letraset is laid down and cut into tight strips which are stuck directly onto the illustration. By doing this you automatically create breaks in the line. The compass lines are drawn; and, in the case of the N and D in ISLANDS, where a clean break was not wanted, the black outline was re-introduced by hand.

**4**. To produce white lettering against a black background the letters are laid down in black Letraset, and when the PMT is made the process is reversed.

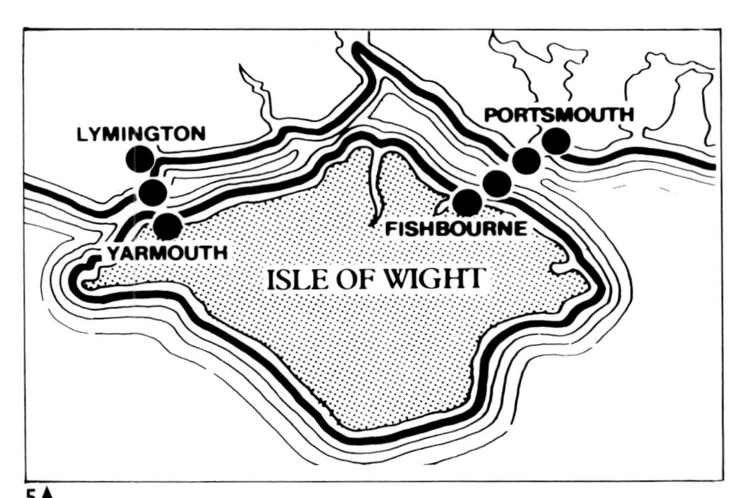

5▲

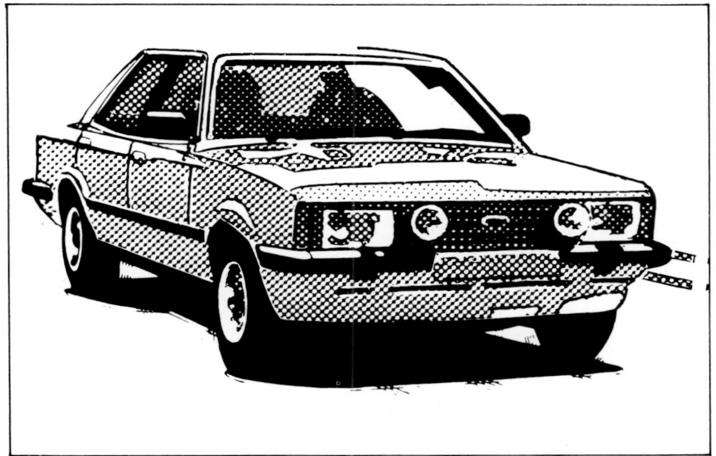
7▲

6▲

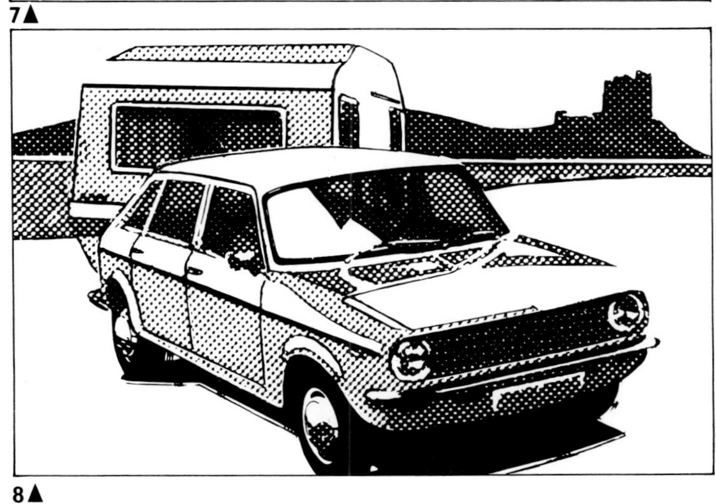
8▲

**5**. Although this map shows several ports, the idea was to define the two specific ports that Sealink sails to on the Isle of Wight. The whole island was highlighted by laying down a Letraset tint to cover the island before adding the lettering.

**6**. Here a simple line drawing needs varying tones to define the shading. These are all created by half-tone Letraset, with the highlight and shadow areas differentiated by the size of the dots.

**7.,8**. These line drawings are taken originally from photographs. The outlines are traced and transposed onto the board. This process is covered in detail over the next two pages.

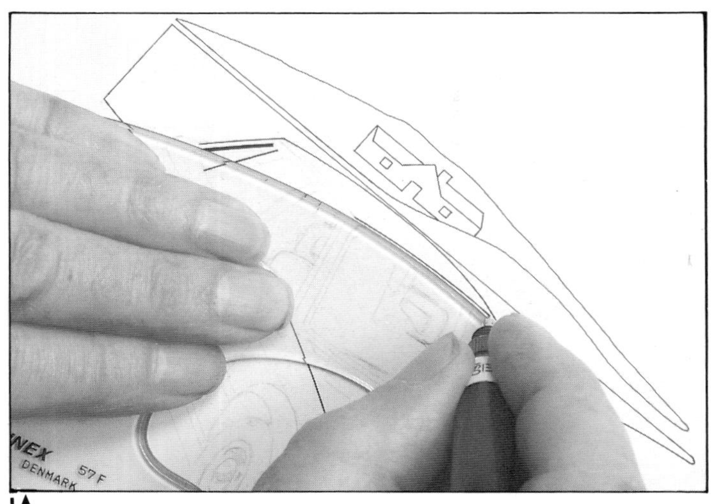

1▲

2▲

3▲

4▲

**1**. An outline tracing is made directly from the photograph supplied. This is transferred onto the board and drawn over in black with the help of French curves and rules to create clean, crisp lines. The solid areas are then filled in with black.

**2**. Remember, to prevent ink from spreading under tools, stick several layers of tape to the underside of the edge. This will lift it away from the surface and prevent the line from smudging.

**3.,4**. The artist now begins to spray the tones. This is done with an opaque body paint to make it look more like a photo again. The varied tones are achieved with the same paint, and the darker areas are achieved by spraying them several times. Rest your steadying hand on a piece of cardboard or paper to prevent handmarks on the surface.

5▲

6▲

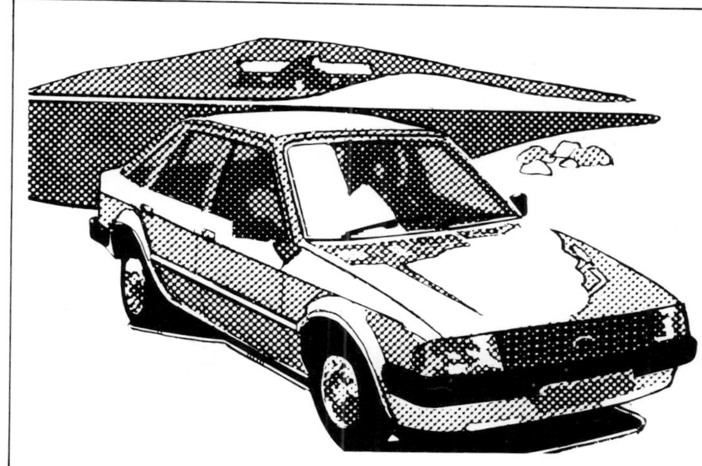
7▲

**5.,6.,7.** A screen PMT is taken, converting the tones into dots. This comes back to the artist, who will re-draw the black outlines that became uneven and broken during the screening process. At this stage any extra highlights will be added by painting out the dots with white paint.

1▲

2▲

3▲

4▲

**1**. Again, a photograph was supplied. A screen PMT was taken directly from it and the artist cleaned up the areas that looked muddy with white paint.

**2**. After this photo was PMT'd, the sky and background looked dull. To make the picture look less flat and more appealing the printer would normally be instructed, on a tracing overlay, to cut out – ie. mask – the sky. This is very time-consuming at the film stage when the same result can be achieved by painting the sky (on the PMT) with white masking paint, thus obscuring the dots.

**3**. This photo had to be commissioned, so the goods that are available in the duty-free shop on board ship were supplied by Sealink. A screen PMT was taken, but it did not show the brand names clearly enough. To save time, rather than re-touch this photo, an ordinary line PMT was taken and the necessary labels, such as the front of the cigarette pack and the clock face were cut out and stuck over the original PMT.

**4**. An illustration was required to show the brochure available for planning car trips. Only a dummy of the front cover was supplied. To create the illusion of a complete brochure, black outlines were drawn around the picture to fake the pages.

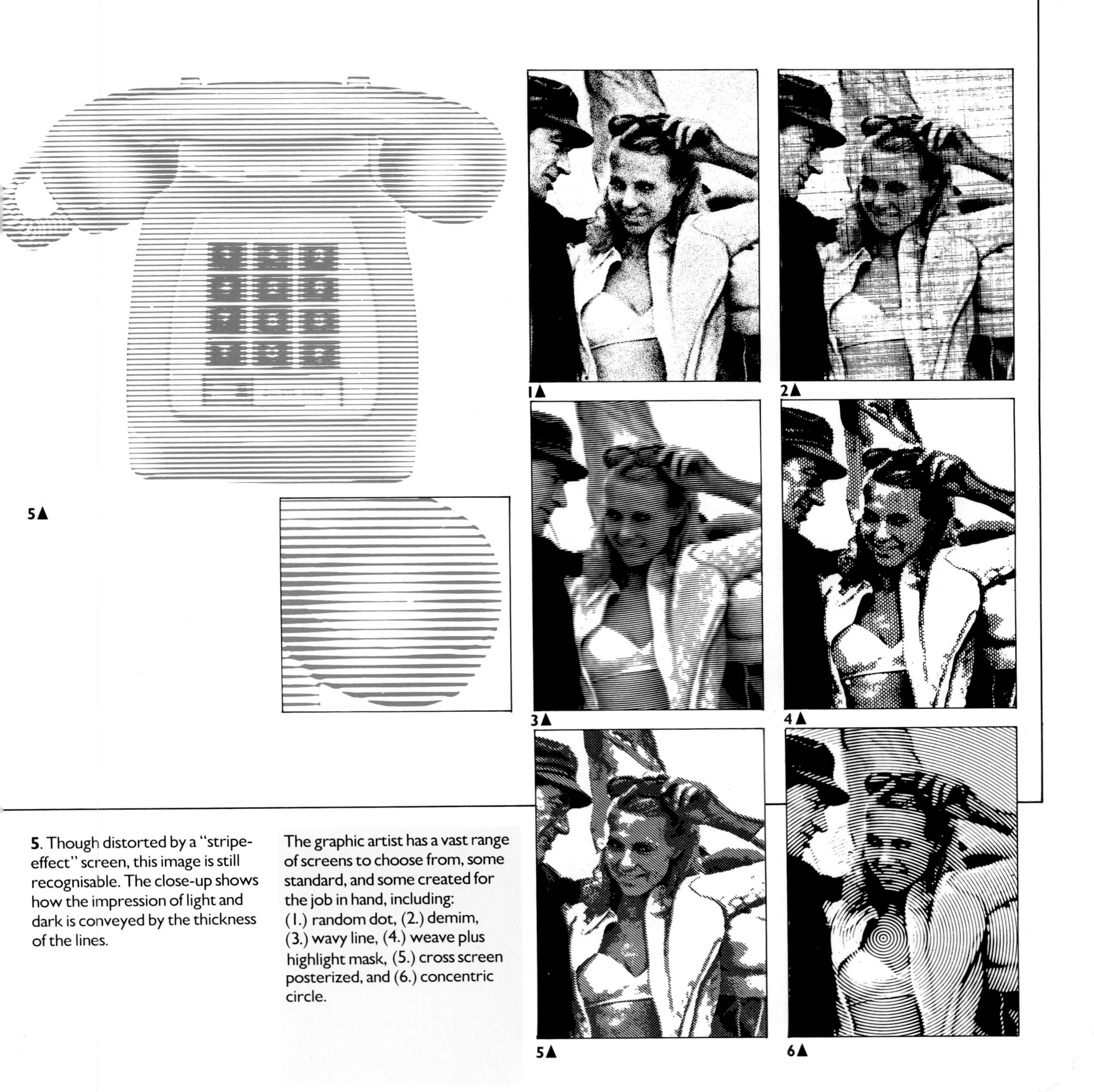


**5**. Though distorted by a "stripe-effect" screen, this image is still recognisable. The close-up shows how the impression of light and dark is conveyed by the thickness of the lines.

The graphic artist has a vast range of screens to choose from, some standard, and some created for the job in hand, including: (1.) random dot, (2.) demim, (3.) wavy line, (4.) weave plus highlight mask, (5.) cross screen posterized, and (6.) concentric circle.

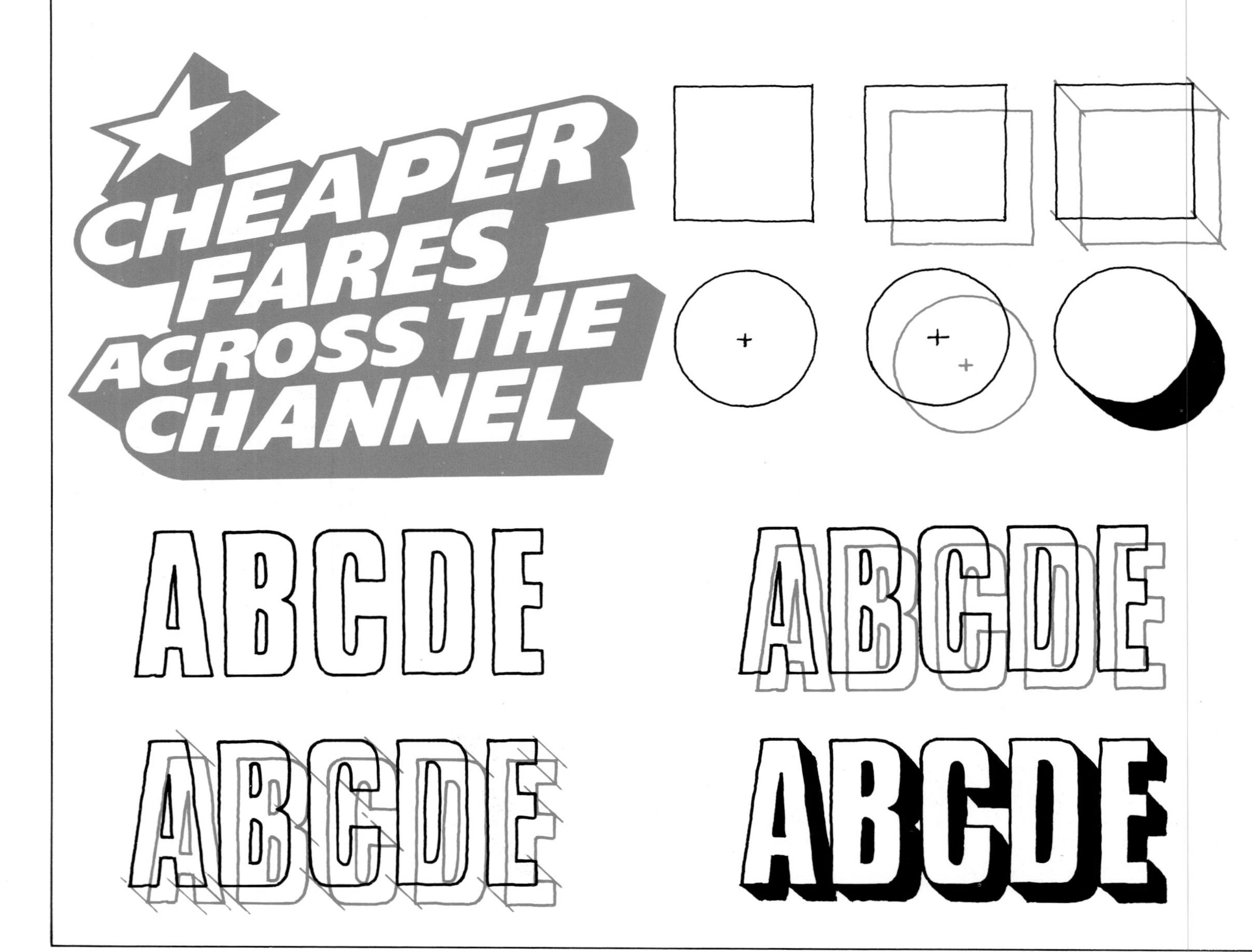


It is amazing how much impact can be added to a piece of lettering by simply introducing a drop shadow. It can take the form of various styles from solid black to a contrasting color, or it can simply be left open to create a double image. Different effects can also be produced depending on where the shadow is positioned; take a tracing of the original lettering and experiment by moving it around over the original until you achieve the desired effect.

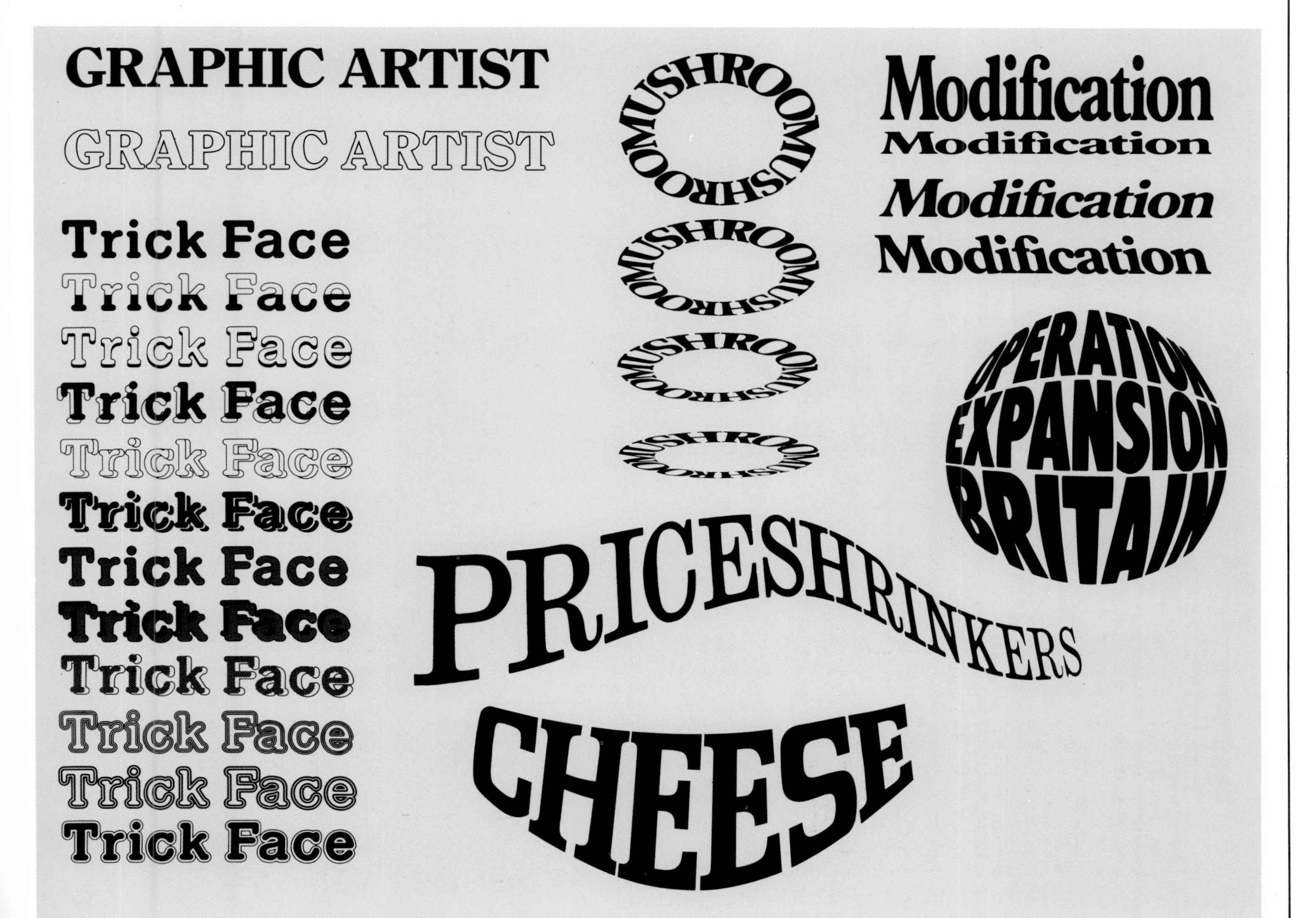


These are examples of type distortions and special effects that can be created on modern photosetting machines. This is due to the fact that the individual characters are projected as light onto a photographic film, so spacing can be varied to a fraction of a millimetre. Also by introducing prisms into the light path type can be condensed, expanded, slanted or outlined at will. The range is so vast that most typesetters now produce a catalogue showing all the individual effects with their respective names or descriptions; so before placing an order it is always best to request a copy of this, thereby avoiding confusion. The catalogues are usually free, but if there is a charge it is worth the investment as they also provide a great source of reference from which tracings can usually be taken directly.

# PROJECT 11

## · BOOK JACKET ·

**THE BRIEF**

The airbrush can be used for laying down large areas of flat or subtly gradated color, or for modeling and highlights. Though often tricky and time-consuming, it can give even the beginner's work a professional polish, while in the hands of an expert it will produce a stunning array of tones and textures.

This project, the word AIRBRUSH, to appear as the focal point of the jacket of a book on the subject, gave the artist the opportunity to use the widest possible range of effects to show the technique's versatility. To emphasize and contrast with this freedom it was decided that the letter-forms themselves should be kept as simple and hard-edged as possible and should be based on solid rectangles and semicircles. An instant lettering catalogue, such as that for Letraset, is a good source of reference for such standard shapes, since they can be traced directly from it and enlarged as necessary.

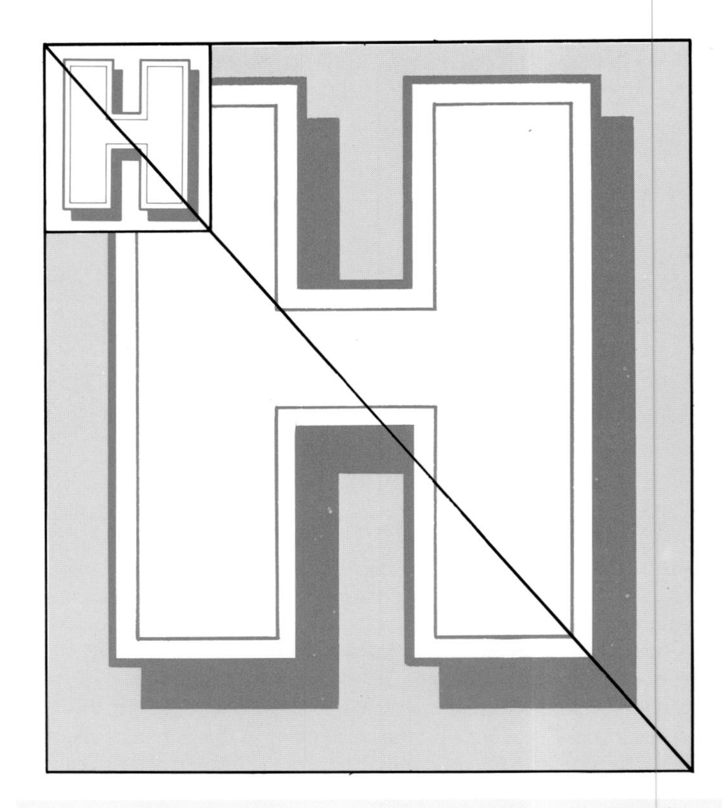

If camera lucida is not available, then once the lettering has been traced, you can enlarge it by using a grid and simply redrawing the image freehand, guided by a diagonal line. The shadow is drawn in with an outline, using a technical pen and black ink.

AIRBRUSH

OUTLINE KEYLINE
WHITE HIGHLIGHT
GRADATED BACKGROUND
DROP SHADOW
REFLECTION
CHROME EFFECT
BEVELED EDGE

1▲

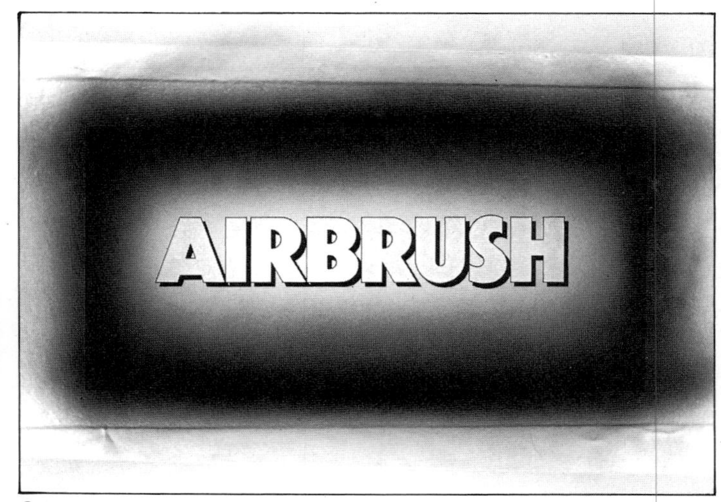


2▲

3▲

**1**. The artist has chosen to lay the background areas in first. The initial line work will have already been inked in, as well as the shadows. Masking film is laid over the whole image and the outline of the letter forms followed with an X-acto knife so that the background areas can be lifted off.

**2**. To create the background glow the artist will use ink, which is a transparent medium, in black, blue and scarlet.

**3**. Darker areas are worked up to the required depth by over-spraying and should be applied first, since lighter colors are more prone to contamination by darker colors than vice versa. They may also be smudged or fingerprinted as you lift and replace masks. The black is sprayed first, gradually changing to blue and finally scarlet.

AIRBRUSH

4▲

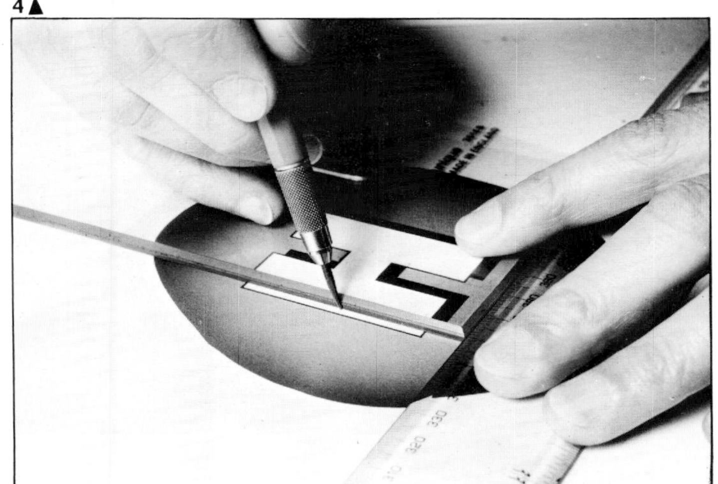

5▲

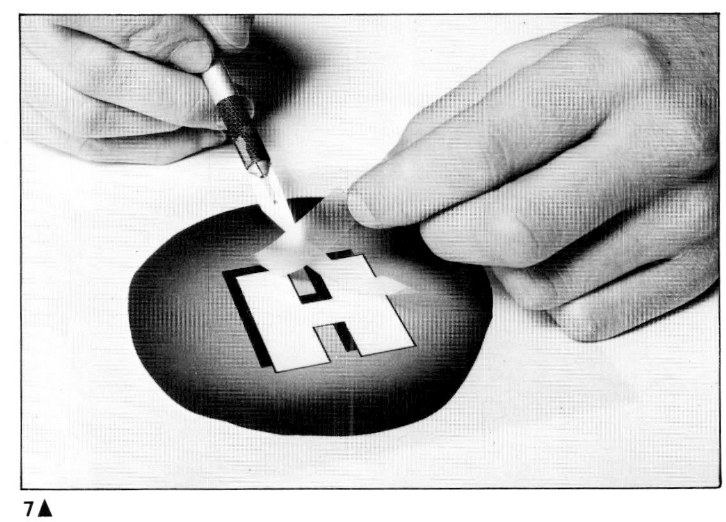

7▲

6▼

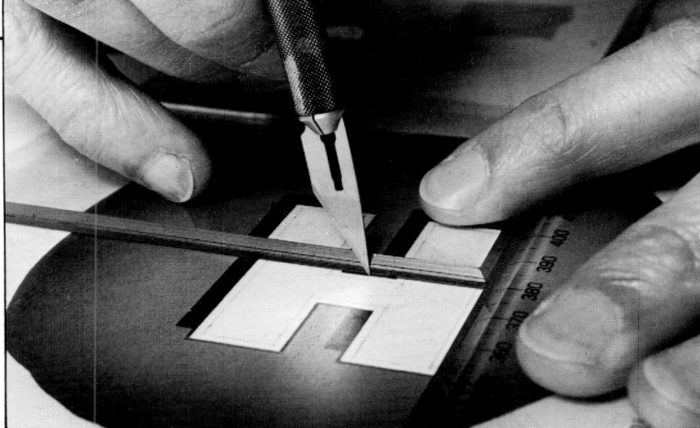

**4.,5.** The mask is lifted, and the next step is to create the beveled border. A matte masking film is used here, since this will take the pencil lines which will have to be drawn directly onto it.

**6.,7.** The pencil outlines are then followed with the X-acto knife and the inner part of the letters lifted out. Do not throw these away, because they can be stored for later use.

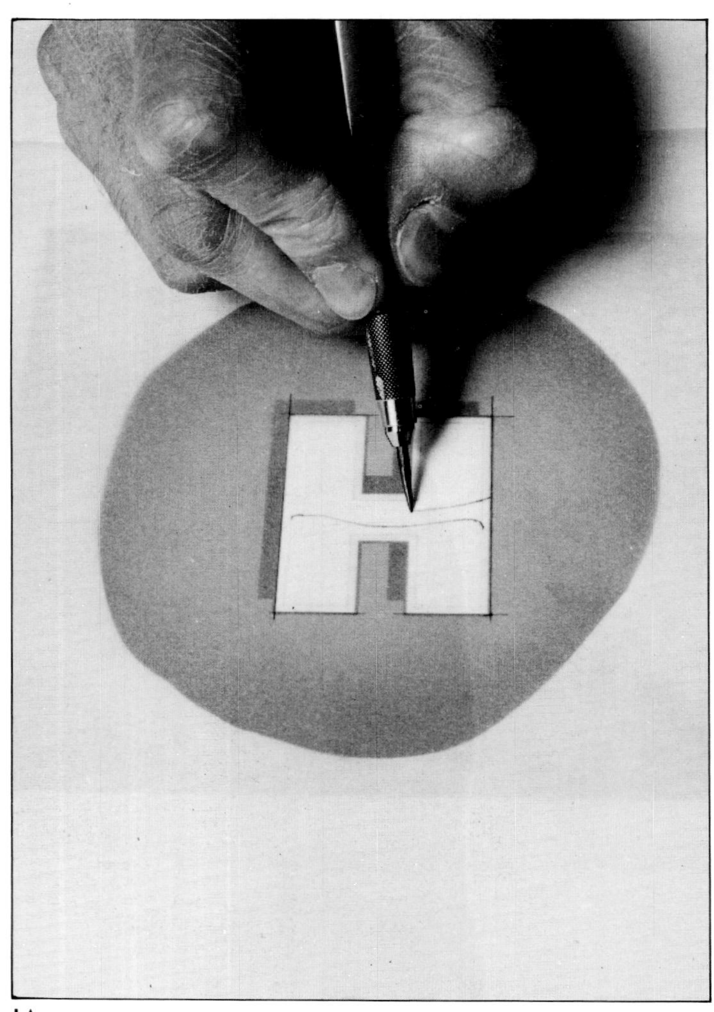

1▲

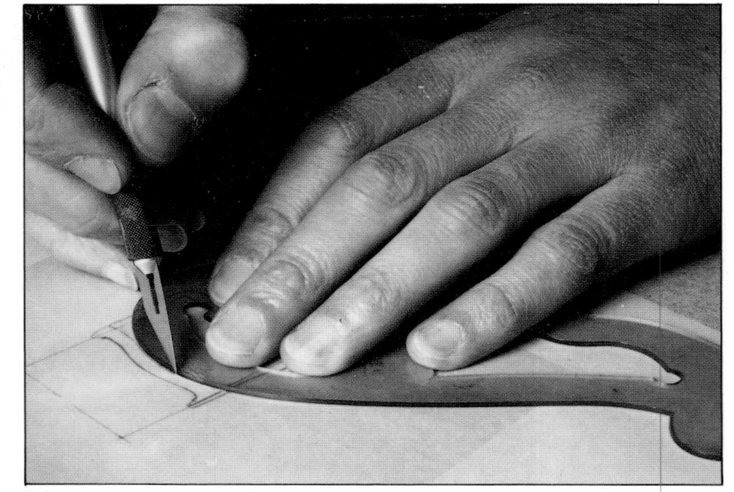

2▲

3▲

**1**. The next special effect is the creation of the wavy line across the center of the letters. Tracing paper is secured over the letters and the wave drawn freehand in pencil. The tracing is removed and reinforced with masking film before cutting to prevent it from tearing. The mask is then cut with the aid of a French curve.

**2**. Tracing paper was used to create a soft edge, since it does not adhere to the surface but "lies loose," allowing some of the spray to spread underneath. The mask is cut away below the wave and vignetted down in violet and blue. Because the ink is transparent, it will not matter if the black wave is over-sprayed.

**3**. The last step is repeated for the blue vignette in the upper part of the letters. Remember that the background mask is in position throughout this whole process.

**4**. To complete the inner letters the beveled borders have to be sprayed with shadows. Replace the previously cut inner part of the letters, fitting them exactly against the border mask.

4▲

5▲

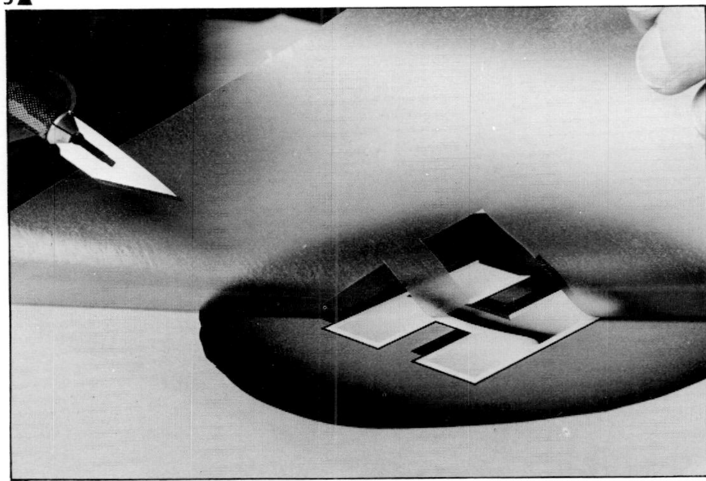

6▲

7▼

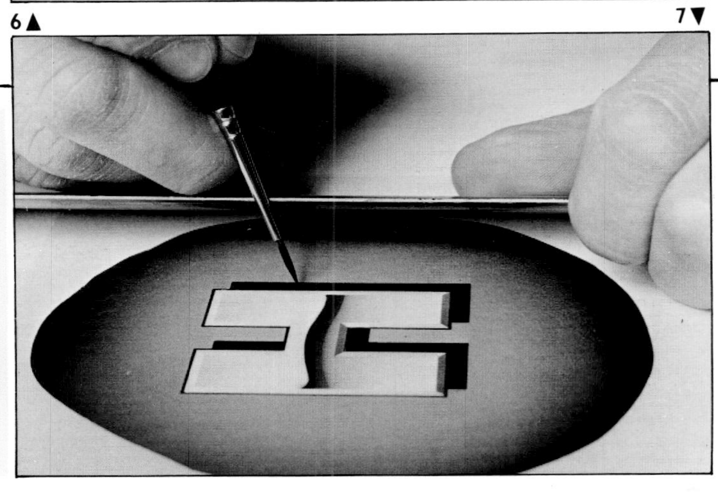

**5**. The light source for this title is from above, so the bottom edge of the letters will be the darkest. Remembering the rule of dark areas, you should cut out and spray these first, following them with the sides and finally the lightest area at the top.

**6**. Now all the remaining masks can be removed and any imperfections touched up by hand using a good quality sable brush and a ruler for the sharp edges.

**7**. Protect the artwork immediately, since moisture from the pores of the fingers will lift off the surface and leave white fingerprints which are virtually impossible to repair.

# GLOSSARY

## A

**Absorbent paper** Unsized paper with the ability to take up liquid or moisture.
**Acetate** A transparent cellulose sheet, available in matt or gloss, and in varying thicknesses. It can be used for any type of *overlay* or as a surface in animation, where individual sheets are used to record every small change in a sequence of movement.
**Agate** A size of type approximately 5½ point.
**Airbrush** A pen-shaped pressure gun, invented by Charles Burdick in 1893. Compressed air mixes with the paint to produce a fine spray. Used for photographic retouching and for creating effects of gradated tone.
**Align** To square up type or any other graphic components to a horizontal or vertical line.
**Artwork** Any form of graphics taken to a high enough standard for reproduction.
**Autotype** A process that converts a PMT of original lettering into dry transfer form, in any specified color.

## B

**Background** The area over which the main images or components are superimposed.
**Billboard** A large-scale outdoor method of advertising ranging from posters to sophisticated, electronic moving images.
**Binding** The securing of the printed pages and outer cover of a publication, transforming it into a book, magazine, brochure, etc. *See comb, perfect, spiral* and *wire-o binding, saddle* and *side wiring* and *thread sewn.*
**Bleed** 1. An image that extends to the edge of the paper or page without leaving any free space. 2. When ink or paint is applied to an unsuitable surface and the lines run and blur.
**Blurb** A term used for selling copy in an advertisement or on a book jacket.
**Box rule** A solid rule used to enclose any graphic material or copy on all four sides.
**Brief** The initial instructions for a project given to the artist, either directly from the client or through an agency.
**Brochure** Pamphlet or short publication often used for promotional purposes.
**Bullets** Large dots used to emphasize specific points on a page of copy.
**Burnish** Generally used to describe the rubbing down of dry-transfer forms.

## C

**C-type** A method, developed by Kodak, of processing color prints directly from a negative.
**Calligraphy** Derived from the Greek word *Kalligraphia* meaning beautiful handwriting, calligraphy is the art of producing fine writing.
**Camera lucida** Electrically powered piece of equipment for scaling an image up or down. The image is placed on to a lit copyboard above which are a lens and glass viewing screen. The sized image is projected through the lens up onto the screen where is can then be traced. Also known as a Grant projector.
**Camera-ready** Term applied to artwork that is ready to be photographed in preparation for reproduction.
**Carbon paper** A thin sheet of paper coated on one side with carbon. When the coated side is placed over a sheet of paper and another sheet is placed on top, an image drawn, typed or written on the top sheet will be duplicated through the carbon onto the underlying sheet.
**Client rough** See *Presentation visual.*
**Coated paper** Paper that has had a mineral coating applied to the surface to improve the finish.
**Cockle** The wrinkle or pucker in paper.
**Collage** The art of using cut-out shapes to create an image, sometimes utilizing mixed media.
**Color bar** A set of standardized bars carried on all color proofs in the four-color process, enabling the printer to check at a glance the density of color and the amount of ink used.
**Color proofs** Printed sheets that are run off to enable the artist, client and printer to check color accuracy and register prior to final printing.
**Color separation** The division of an artwork into the four processing colors by photographic filtration or electronic scanners.
**Comb binding** Mechanical binding method in which slots are drilled through the cover and pages, then secured with plastic ringed fingers.
**Compass** Instrument used for drawing circles and arcs. It consists of two legs connected by an adjustable joint, one carrying a metal point and the other a lead.
**Continuous tone** An original in which the image contains a complete range of shades from the lightest to the darkest, without being broken up by dots.
**Copy** Any written material that has to be typeset.
**Copyright** See *Universal Copyright Convention.*
**Correction overlay** A translucent sheet secured over a visual or artwork, on which changes and corrections are made.
**Crop marks** The lines that indicate to the printer where the image must be trimmed.
**Cropping aid** Two L-shaped pieces of cardboard which can be moved over an image until the most complimentary position for cropping is found.
**Crowner** The lid of a point-of-sale display that folds back to make a show card.
**Cut-out** An image that is cut from its original background, leaving an outline shape.
**Cyan** Shade of blue ink in four-color printing.

## D

**Dashes** Punctuation marks used to denote a pause in a sentence before expanding on a previous statement.
**Decorative devices** An ornamental way of separating blocks of copy or images.

**Density** The measure of tone or color value in a printed image.
**Divider** An instrument similar to a compass except that there are metal points on both legs. It is used mainly for transferring dimensions from one sheet or object onto another.
**Doctored photograph** Original photographic image which has been altered or added to.
**Documentary** A factual film based on real events.
**Double-sided tape** A tape coated with adhesive on both sides enabling two surfaces to be stuck together.
**Drop shadow** Shadow added around an image or letters to create a three-dimensional effect.
**Dry-transfer sheets** Sheets holding letters, images, tones, etc. that can be transferred onto a surface by applying pressure to the reverse side of the sheet.
**Dummy** Prototype made to represent a book, magazine, package, etc., using the proposed materials but not necessarily showing all the graphics or page layouts.
**Duotone** A two-color halftone that involves making two negatives from a monochrome image; one holds the black for the shadow and darker tone, whereas the other picks up the middle tones.

## E

**Ellipse** A regular oval shape that corresponds to an oblique view of a circular plane.
**Engraver** The person responsible for making the color separated films from which the printing plates derive, even if this is done electronically.

## F

**Finished art** See *Artwork.*
**Finished rough** See *Presentation visual.*
**Flat color** This refers to solid areas of color without any tonal values.
**Flush left/right** Used to describe lines of type aligned vertically to the left or right margin.
**Focal point** The emphasized part of an image on which the eye is forced to focus.
**Format** The general term for the size, shape and appearance of a page or illustration. For example, a horizontal or landscape format means that the width will be greater than the height.
**Four-color process** Printing process used to reproduced full color by separating the image into the three primary colors — cyan, magenta and yellow — plus black. A plate is made for each of the four colors; when printed over each other the plates reproduce the effect of all the colors in the original.
**Freehand** A way of working without any artificial aids. Can be applied to drawing, airbrushing or using a scalpel.
**French curves** A set of clear plastic line-guides designed to provide as many different degrees of curve as possible.

## G

**Gags** Short lines of copy, usually provided by an agency to accompany the illustrations in a storyboard. They are chiefly designed to give the client an even clearer idea of the proposed sequence of events for a filmed advertisement.
**Gradation** The transition, by almost imperceptible degrees, from one color or tone into another.
**Grain** 1. Main direction of the fibers that run through a sheet of paper — important to follow when scoring and folding. 2. In photography, it is the various densities in a developed print caused by the distribution of tiny silver crystals.
**Grid** Transparent sheet representing a double-page spread of a publication designed to insure consistency. It is printed with ruled lines and shows the exact page size, margins and trim marks over which all the components of the spread can be positioned accurately. Alternatively, it can be used to scale an image up or down. The image is traced and divided into equally ruled boxes. The key points are plotted and transferred onto a correspondingly larger, or smaller, boxed grid.
**Gripper edge** The edge of the sheet clamped by the grippers as it is fed through the printing process.

## H

**Halftone** A continuous tone image which is broken down into a series of dots by a cross-line screen. The gradated tones are obtained by the size and density of the dots.
**Hand lettering** The process of constructing letter forms with the aid of parallel lines and accurate measurements.
**Hard edge** Used to describe the outline of an image that is sharp and well defined.
**Headline** Prominent line of type that draws the eye to a piece of copy, often summarizing the content.
**Highlights** The lightest tones of an image which are used to pick out specific features or details.
**Hyphen** A punctuation mark used in line or word breaks.

## I

**Illustration** 1. The term used to describe any type of drawing, diagram or color image that enhances a text. 2. An image that is drawn as opposed to photographed.
**Image** 1. The visual contents as whole. 2. An illustration or photograph for reproduction.
**Imposition** The organization of the pages on each side of a printed sheet so that they run in the correct order when the sheet is cut, folded and trimmed.
**In-house** Used to describe a process carried out within a company rather than commissioned out to an individual or service.
**Instant art** Images or letters created by the use of dry-transfer forms.

## J

**Justified** Lines of type that are set and aligned to both left and right margins.

## K

**Kerning** Deliberate reduction of spacing between specified characters to improve the letter fit, legibility and evenness of a line of typesetting.
**Key lines** Drawn outlines that are used as a guide for positioning specific areas and components either on a layout or in the printing of flat colors.

## L

**Lay down** A general term used to describe the placing of material.

**Layout** A sheet representing how a printed page will look showing all the components in their correct positions.
**Layout paper** Translucent, tough paper used for paste-up or illustration at the rough stage.
**Letraset** Brand of dry-transfer sheets.
**Line illustration** An illustration simply using lines without incorporation any tone or color.
**Logo** A word or letter cast as one unit, usually for a trademark or company signature.
**Loose mask** Any type of mask that does not adhere to the surface.

**Magenta** Shade of red ink used in four-color printing.
**Magic Marker** Brand of felt-tip marker.
**Marked proof** The proof holding all the instructions and corrections that will act as the printer's guide.
**Markers** Although a general term for colored felt- or fiber-tipped pens, it usually refers more specifically to the broad felt-tip pens used widely for presentation visuals.
**Mask** Anything that is used to block out certain areas of an image.
**Masking film** A transparent film with a low-tack adhesive backing widely used in airbrushing. The mask can be cut in position on the surface, allowing greater accuracy.
**Masking tape** Tape coated with a low-tack adhesive. It can be used as a mask and is ideal for attaching transparencies to layouts because it can be peeled off without damaging the surface.
**Mechanical** Camera-ready copy or artwork.
**Medium** Any kind of paint, dye, or coloring agent used to cover a surface.
**Mock-up** Rough visualization of a publication or packaging design showing size, color and design.
**Mono adoption** A single-colored image taken from a full-color original.
**Monochrome** An image of only one color but of varying tones.
**Montage** The combination of several different images to create a new single original.

**Origami** Ancient Japanese art of folding paper into intricate shapes.
**Original** Copy and artwork prepared for reproduction.
**Outline letters** Letters formed from outlines and not solid strokes.
**Overlay** 1. Translucent sheet placed over an image on which instructions or corrections are written. 2. Some pieces of multi-colored artwork consist of four overlays, each holding a separate color for reproduction.

**Packaging** The construction of individual product packs for points-of-display.
**Pantone** The trade name of the company that produces an extensive color matching system which is standardized throughout their complete range of designers' materials.
**Parallel motion** A drawing board that holds counterweights and has a straight edge to insure accurate measurement and positioning.
**Paste-up** Layout showing all the components of a page or advertisement in their correct positions.
**Perfect binding** The method of binding in which the pages are trimmed and glued, but not sewn.
**Photocopy** An instant method of copying by a variety of photographic techniques.
**Photomechanical transfer** An extremely versatile process camera with functions that include changing black to white and vice versa, converting color to black and white, and producing screened halftones. The standard is high enough for use in artwork. Commonly known as PMT.
**Photomontage** The combination of images from various photographs or transparencies to produce a new composite image.
**Photo-restoration** The careful repair of an irreplaceable old or damaged photographic print.
**Plate** Sheet, usually made of metal, that carries the image for reproduction.
**PMT** See *Photomechanical transfer.*
**Point-of-sale display** Type of packaging used to display and unify a range of products for promotional purposes.
**Presentation visual** Illustrations or any graphic material taken to a high standard, for the purpose of showing the client the proposed appearance of the artwork.

**Rapidograph** Brand of technical pens.
**Register marks** A set of marks (usually in the form of a cross in a circle) which are carried on overlays, artwork, film and plates to insure that images are in register when superimposed during reproduction.
**Retouching** To alter a photographic image or artwork by hand, usually to remove imperfections, make corrections or modify tonal values prior to reproduction.
**Reverse out** Term applied to an image that appears white out of a solid background, usually reproduced by photomechanical techniques.
**Rotring** Brand of technical pens.
**Rough** An initial sketch representing a proposed design or idea.
**Ruling pen** A pen used to draw lines of constant width. The ink or paint is held between two metal fingers.
**Run-around text** Type which is laid out to follow the outline shape of an illustration.

**Saddle stitching** Method of binding brochures or magazines by opening them over a saddle support and firing staples through the fold of the spine.
**Scaling** Calculating the amount of enlargement or reduction necessary to fit an image into a given space.
**Score** To crease board so that it folds more easily along a clean line.
**Screen** Finely cross-ruled glass plate that is used to break down a continuous tone image into dots for halftone reproduction.
**Script** Hand-written lettering, or a typeface that imitates it.
**Sheet** A single piece of paper or board.
**Shoot** A term used in photography referring to a photographic session.
**Side wiring** Method of binding. The cover and pages are secured by inserting staples from the front through to the back.

**Soft edge** Outlines of an image that are not clearly defined.
**Solid** Letters or areas that are completely covered in flat color.
**Spine** The "backbone" of a publication that encloses and secures the back edges of the pages in binding.
**Spiral binding** A form of mechanical binding in which a spiral wire is threaded through pre-punched holes.
**Spray** The fine mist of air and paint expelled from an airbrush.
**Spread** Two facing pages of a publication.
**Stipple** An irregular series of dots applied by hand to create tone and texture.
**Storyboard** A series of illustrations, rather like a comic strip, that represent a sequence of events that will eventually be filmed.
**Stripping** Two or more photographic images assembled to produce a composite or multiple image.
**Sub-head** Minor headlines that are used to divide copy into separate items on a printed page.
**Swatch** A color specimen supplied to the printer to which the ink can be matched.

# T

**Technical illustration** A highly-finished illustration designed to show mechanical objects or systems in a totally accurate and realistic manner.
**Technical pen** A pen with a tubular nib designed to draw lines of an even width.
**Template** Drawing aid, usually in the form of a plastic sheet, used as a guide for cutting out shapes.
**Text** The main body of written matter.
**Thread sewn** Method of binding in which a sewing machine inserts threads through each folded back section and sews them together.
**Three-dimensional (3-D)** 1. In illustration, an image creating the illusion of physically standing out from the page. 2. An object, such as a package, which has depth as well as height and width.
**Thumbnail sketches** Small, rough sketches used to work out an idea.
**Tone** The variations of shade in one color.
**Tracing** Transferring an image from one surface to another by placing a transparent sheet over the original and copying the outlines by hand.
**Transparency** A positive color image produced photographically on transparent film.
**Triangle** Drawing aid in the form of a flat plastic or metal right-angled triangle.
**Typeface** The general term used to describe the various styles of lettering in typesetting.
**Typesetting** The assembling of typographic material suitable for printing by hand or mechanical methods.
**Typography** The art and process of arranging type.

# U

**Universal Copyright Convention** An international assembly that in 1952 agreed to protect the originator of a design or illustration against their material being reproduced without permission being granted. The work must carry the copyright mark.

**Vignette** In airbrushing, any area with gradated tone.
**Visualize** To translate an initial idea into graphic terms by way of illustration.

**Wire-o binding** Method of mechnical binding in which slots are drilled through the cover and pages, then secured with ringed wire fingers.
**Widows** A single word standing as the last line of a paragraph — to be avoided.
**Work and tumble** In printing, a term used when sheets are turned over so that the opposite edge becomes the gripper edge.
**Work and turn** In printing, when sheets are turned over left to right so that the same gripper edge is used.
**Work up** To keep developing an initial sketch until the desired effect is achieved.

**X-height** The height of a letter without an ascender or descender.

# INDEX

# ACKNOWLEDGEMENTS


**DESK EQUIPMENT** (p.12)

Langford & Hill Ltd. (Graphic Art Suppliers)

**STUDIO EQUIPMENT** (p.30)

Drawing Boards — Essex Drawing Equipment Co. Ltd.
PMT material — Agfa-Gevaert Ltd.
Photocopiers/Overhead Projectors —
The 3M Visual Products Group
Marketing Team and Harris/3M
Copying Products

Grant Projectors Ltd. — Grant Equipment Supplies

**BASIC SKILLS** (p.42)

Eric Church; Collet Dickenson Pearce & Partners Ltd; Steve Legatt, The Bull Pen; Johnathan Elliot, Zomba Music; Vic Fair, Downtown Advertising; David Evans Studio; Elan Litho; John Fowles; Grandfield Rork Collins Ltd; Geoff Halpin; Jigsaw Studio; Perception; Quay & Grey; Roughouse; Rabbit Repro; Rabbit Studio; Mike Wren.

Special thanks to Jacqui Graham, Roger Hicks and P.L. Frankson

**PROJECTS** (p.76)

Stuart Jane, Steve Howell and André Klarenberg from the Wolff Olins/Smythe Consultancy in Communications for the Corporate Identity project. Wolff Olins is one of the UK's foremost corporate identity consultancies.

Samples of letter distortions and modifications — (pp178-179)
Conway Group Graphics Ltd.
Face Ronchetti Ltd.
Headliners (London) Ltd.

•

**Special thanks to Presentation Design — Martin Angel, Les Dearsley, Colin Houliston, Kevin Johnson, Stephen Mold, Rob McCaig, Ken Walters — for providing all other projects and for the use of their studio.**

•